D1570269

A beautiful guide to recovery, which we all need now.

—MARK HYMAN, MD
senior advisor at Cleveland Clinic Center for
Functional Medicine, host of *The Doctor's Farmacy*,
and #1 *New York Times* bestselling author

Neha not only knows the symptoms, she also has risen to the challenge of dealing with one of burnout's most intimate causes: the inability of so many of us to recognize what is happening to us and to take charge of ourselves. Step by step, she helps us to become aware of the hallmarks of burnout—physical and emotional exhaustion, depression and anger, cynicism and indifference—and she shows us how to regard these challenges as opportunities to recognize, embrace, and grow through and beyond.

—JAMES S. GORDON, MD
founder and CEO of The Center for Mind-Body Medicine and
author of *Transforming Trauma: The Path to Hope and Healing*

Dr. Sangwan combines the science of medicine, the practicality of an engineer, and the heart of a healer to simplify the global epidemic of burnout. She provides a comprehensive tool kit to heal our mental health epidemic. That said, this book is way more than a tool kit. It is a way of being more alive. *Powered by Me* is a potent prescription for what ails us in our chaotic world of corporate burnout. It's a must-read for both leaders of today and tomorrow.

—ROBERT J. ANDERSON
creator of The Leadership Circle,
cofounder of Leadership Circle, and coauthor
of *Mastering Leadership* and *Scaling Leadership*

Brimming with actionable guidance, this is an important read for all of us in today's busy world. Neha shares her story with honesty and thoughtfulness, inviting us to learn and grow alongside her. Whether you are struggling with burnout at work or at home, or just looking to lead a happier, healthier life, this book will help you heal yourself from the inside out.

—KIP TINDELL
cofounder of Container Store

Neha has written a beautiful guide to help us remove the internal road-blocks keeping us from experiencing the true joy and beauty in life and knowing that we matter. This book is essential reading for us all, especially for those who accept the responsibility of leadership and want to bring their full selves to be present to those within their span of care.

—BOB CHAPMAN
CEO of Barry-Wehmiller and coauthor of *Everybody Matters:*
The Extraordinary Power of Caring for Your People Like Family

In a rapidly evolving world, Dr. Neha's understanding of medical, human, and societal drivers of burnout in our world is spot on. She offers her own experience with burnout with authenticity and vulnerability that is seldom displayed. As entertaining as it is informative, *Powered by Me* provides practical tools to empower us to take charge of our own physical, mental, emotional, social, and spiritual health. This is a truly amazing book.

—GERVASE WARNER
President and Group CEO of Massy Holdings and
Chairman of CARICOM Private Sector Organisation

In *Powered by Me*, Dr. Neha Sangwan offers transformative insights and practical tools to manage stress, prevent burnout, and foster resilience. Her unique blend of medical expertise, storytelling, and practical wisdom makes her teachings impactful for people from all walks of life. Join me and the thousands who have benefited from her guidance to unlock a healthier, happier, and more fulfilling life.

—JO RILEY
cofounder and CEO of Censia

As with everything Dr. Neha tackles, she combines the structured thinking of an engineer with the insights and intelligence of a medical doctor to provide a uniquely holistic and actionable prescription for identifying and healing burnout. Her stories make it relatable and interesting. Every person can benefit from her work.

—CHRISTINE HECKART
founder and CEO of XAPA World, Inc.

In the battle against burnout, *Powered by Me* is the practical tool leaders, organizations, and communities have been searching for. Given Dr. Neha's diverse background as an engineer, medical doctor, and executive coach, she is able to uniquely diagnose what's draining your energy and getting in the way of your living a productive and meaningful life.

—CHRISTA QUARLES
CEO of Alludo

Neha's unique methodology combines physical science, universal healing, and practical tools to transform behavior and heal burnout. Her personal guidance has been invaluable to me, my executive team, and my company. Through powerful mindset shifts, profound self-care techniques, and personal accountability, she catalyzes women to thrive in our twenty-first-century world. Dr. Neha will awaken you to your personal power—and then empower you to live it!

—JAYNE MILLARD
executive chairman of Turtle & Hughes

Unlike traditional cookie-cutter solutions to burnout, Dr. Neha Sangwan offers practical and measurable tools to increase self-awareness, solidify critical listening, improve communication skills, and inspire individuals to build unity and respect.

—KEN YANAGISAWA, MD, FACS
president of the American Academy of
Otolaryngology–Head and Neck Surgery

With her background as an engineer, a physician and an executive coach, Dr. Neha Sangwan possesses strong expertise in understanding systems, processes, and people. Her intimate knowledge of healthcare barriers and stressors that lead to physician burnout uniquely position her to offer sage advice to current and emerging leaders. Her impressive workshops and keynote speeches inspire people to make changes that lead to wellness and resilience in the workplace. I fully endorse her outstanding work in this space.

—CAROL R. BRADFORD, MD, MS, FACS
dean of The Ohio State University College of
Medicine and VP for Health Sciences at The Ohio
State University Wexner Medical Center

We accept burnout as the natural byproduct of our sense of responsibility, work ethic, and our commitment to others. Dr. Sangwan teaches us to question the inevitability of burnout and shares a powerful plan for both prevention and recovery. Neha provides insight, relatable examples, and practical advice to elevate our commitment to ourselves, feel more joy, and increase our impact.

—SUSAN SOBBOTT
former president of Global Commercial
Services at American Express

Neha combines a laser-like focus on hearing what you are saying with her wide knowledge and deep experience to produce actionable insights and results.

—THERESA GATTUNG
chair of Global Women and
former CEO of Telecom New Zealand

Powered by Me is exactly the book we need at this time. The burnout epidemic is at an all-time high and in this step-by-step guide, Neha teaches us to recognize burnout symptoms and create sustained recovery to build a healthier, happier *you*. Dr. Sangwan's insights and case studies make the material accessible and actionable. If you want to experience more joy and less exhaustion, this is the book for you!

—TERRI COLE
bestselling author of *Boundary Boss: The Essential Guide to Talk True, Be Seen, and (Finally) Live Free*

Powered by Me is a remarkable and timely guide to awareness, prevention, and healing of burnout by strengthening your energy across physical, mental, emotional, social, and spiritual levels. This approach reflects Neha's unique combined experience as an engineer, medical doctor, and communication expert, as well as her authenticity and passion to unite, heal, and elevate the world. The insights and actionable practices have helped me in my own self-care journey.

—TUSHARA DILANIE
founder and CEO of Nadastra, Inc.,
and cofounder and EVP of Virtusa, Corp.

Powered by
Me

Powered by
Me

From
Burned Out to Fully Charged
at Work and in Life

Neha Sangwan, MD

NEW YORK   CHICAGO   SAN FRANCISCO   ATHENS   LONDON
MADRID   MEXICO CITY   MILAN   NEW DELHI
SINGAPORE   SYDNEY   TORONTO

1 2 3 4 5 6 7 8 9   LCR   28 27 26 25 24 23

ISBN   978- 1-265-44338-2
MHID   1-265-44338-6

e-ISBN   978-1-265-44345-0
e-MHID   1-265-44345-9

Library of Congress Cataloging-in-Publication Data

Names: Sangwan, Neha.
Title: Powered by me : from burned out to fully charged at work and in life / Neha
    Sangwan.
Description: New York : McGraw Hill, [2024] I Includes bibliographical references and
    index.
Identifiers: LCCN 2023018120 (print) I LCCN 2023018121 (ebook) I ISBN 9781265443382
    (hardback) I ISBN 9781265443450 (ebook)
Subjects: LCSH: Burn out (Psychology) I Work environment. I Bullying in the workplace.
Classification: LCC BF481 .S226 2024 (print) I LCC BF481 (ebook) I DDC 158.7/23—dc23/
    eng/20230705
LC record available at https://lccn.loc.gov/2023018120
LC ebook record available at https://lccn.loc.gov/2023018121

McGraw Hill books are available at special quantity discounts to use as premiums and sales promotions or for use in corporate training programs. To contact a representative, please visit the Contact Us pages at *www.mhprofessional.com*.

McGraw Hill is committed to making our products accessible to all learners. To learn more about the available support and accommodations we offer, please contact us at *accessibility@mheducation.com*. We also participate in the Access Text Network (*www .accesstext.org*), and ATN members may submit requests through ATN.

TO RAJ SISODIA
Thank you for being a man as ambitious as you are generous and kind. Your beautiful soul and unconditional love have restored my faith in what is possible for the future of our world.

TO OUR ANCESTORS
You innately knew the wisdom of living in connection and harmony with Mother Nature.

AND TO THE NEXT GENERATION
Your passion, curiosity, and conviction will guide us back to what matters most.

CONTENTS

CONTENTS

FOREWORD
by Mark Hyman, MD

It is easy to lose ourselves in our overstuffed lives, which are fraught with the endless pressures of work and family, with the relentless barrage of tasks, to-dos, and requests, all while we are trying to manage our health, sleep, and nutrition in a world under siege from existential threats—climate change, never-ending gun violence, and the constant presence of war. It is easy to get overwhelmed, exhausted, and anxious. Easy to neglect the simple practices of self-care that keep us grounded and resilient.

As a young physician with two children, a wife struggling with alcoholism and mental illness, and a rural family practice in Idaho, who was putting in 80 hours a week, doing 24-hour shifts in the emergency room alone, working all the next day, and delivering babies in the middle of the night, I hit a wall. When I got home, I had to shop, cook, and take care of my young children. I prided myself on my ability to push through the pain and exhaustion. I was powered by caffeine and sugar. After four years of overdoing, overgiving, and running myself into the ground, I had to stop. I had intended to take a little break before my next job. We had bought a VW camper van and planned a tour of the West, but as soon as I stopped working, I couldn't move. I literally couldn't get out of bed or I spent most of my time on the floor, feeling completely drained, as if all the gas in my tank was gone. As a medical student, I was told that "real doctors" don't need sleep or lunch. I wanted to take my family on a trip, but my body, my nervous system, and my brain all said no. It took four months of doing nothing, being at home, walking, sleeping, and renewing myself to finally feel a little better.

But I didn't learn my lesson very well. After leaving Idaho, I worked in Beijing, setting up medical clinics for expatriates, before I came back to the United States and got a job in the emergency room—not just one but *three* emergency rooms with different schedules. Sometimes I would do 24-hour shifts, sometimes morning or afternoon shifts, sometimes overnight shifts.

My schedule was erratic. My circadian rhythms were completely disrupted. I also had to accept the truth that I was married to someone who couldn't face their own demons and who refused treatment and sobriety. I had to fight for sole custody of my two young children. Ignoring the signals of my body and jacked up on a quadruple espresso, a pint of ice cream, and a giant chocolate chip cookie, I would head to my night shifts. Then I would come home and get my children ready for school and hope to get a few hours' sleep before I had to pick them up. Despite being a trained physician, I had no idea how to create health.

One day, everything changed. I went from managing my life (sort of) to total physical and mental collapse. My incessant pushing through whatever life sent my way led to full-blown chronic fatigue syndrome. It was then that I finally had to deal with the choices I had made, the underlying beliefs and habits that no longer served me. Slowly, piece by piece, over a long period of time, I learned how to address the root causes of why I fell apart. First, I quit the emergency room. Then I started slowing down, eliminating extraneous inputs, eating whole foods, doing meditation and yoga, waking and sleeping at regular times, and taking vitamins, minerals, and herbs to support my adrenal glands and build back my stress resilience. For the last 30 years, I have drawn from my own suffering and the lessons I've learned about how the body works and the science of creating health and applied them to thousands of patients, helping millions more through my books, my podcast *The Doctor's Farmacy*, and social media, empowering them to learn the foundational skills of self-healing and self-care.

It is still surprising to me how little we know about how our bodies function or how to properly operate them. In *Powered by Me*, Dr. Sangwan provides a hard-won road map for recovery from any stage of burnout and for building a life founded on a healthy body, mind, and spirit. Learning the operating manual for our bodies is not rocket science. In a step-by-step process of self-inquiry and simple self-care practices, Dr. Sangwan teaches us how to heal. This book is the medicine we need to build a healthy, happy life, healthier relationships, and a healthier world.

—MARK HYMAN, MD
senior advisor at Cleveland Clinic Center for Functional Medicine and host of *The Doctor's Farmacy*

FOREWORD

by James S. Gordon, MD

At the beginning of this energizing, inspiring, happily practical book, Neha Sangwan, MD, gives us a picture of herself 22 years ago, an "overworked, undernourished, stressed-out internal medicine physician." Every day, she tells us—in the clean, clear language that makes *Powered by Me* so accessible—she "pushed harder and faster, running headlong in the direction others wanted me to." She came to realize she was burned out.

The picture Neha paints is painfully familiar to physicians and other healthcare professionals, especially since Covid-19's tide of death and loss overwhelmed just about everyone working in healthcare. However, so many others easily recognize the phrase "pushing harder and running faster." I hear the refrain from people I work with everywhere: unhappy high school students anxious about the future, frustrated police, fearful elected officials, rich people who have what appears to be too much, as well as poor people struggling to survive.

Neha not only knows the symptoms, she has also risen to the challenge of dealing with one of burnout's most intimate causes: the inability of so many to recognize what is happening to us and to take charge of ourselves. Step by step, she helps us become aware of the hallmarks of burnout—physical and emotional exhaustion, depression and anger, cynicism and indifference—and she shows us how to regard these challenges as opportunities to recognize, embrace, and grow through and beyond.

Neha reminds us that all aspects of our lives—physical, mental, emotional, social, and spiritual—are interconnected and that her program for attending to and learning from each of these enhances our functioning and satisfaction in all of them. She guides us in enhancing the self-awareness that tells us which change is appropriate and sustainable. And she gives us tools for dealing with the self-defeating beliefs and fruitless anger we may discover and a program of meditation, movement, nutrition, and self-expression that reduces stress and enhances well-being. She continually reminds us that we can, indeed, be *powered by me*.

Neha credits me as a mentor, someone who helped her shape her own approach and realize her possibilities and power. I am honored to be her teacher, and now also to be her student and to share with you this deeply healing, passionately helpful book.

—JAMES S. GORDON, MD
founder and CEO of The Center for Mind-Body Medicine and author of *Transforming Trauma: The Path to Hope and Healing*

CHAPTER 1

HOW WE
GOT HERE

It was early 2001, when I officially became an overworked, undernourished, stressed-out internal medicine physician caring for 18 hospitalized patients a day. By definition, anyone admitted to the hospital was *enough of an emergency* that they couldn't be handled as an outpatient. I didn't walk—I ran from task to task, patient to patient, crisis to crisis. Pulled in multiple directions by my pager beeping, lab techs calling, and new medical complications arising, I desperately tried setting priorities to guide my actions—only to have them dismantled by the next emerging catastrophe.

My day started by getting sign-out from my coworkers on the night shift. "Neha, same as usual—we were slammed last night *and* understaffed. I've only done cursory workups and am still waiting for lab results and scans. Sorry about that. And rumor has it that the ER and cardiac nurses are short-staffed today and considering another union strike next week. Good luck."

Message received: *do more with less.*

As I glanced at my new patient list, I saw two intensive care patients, a liver transplant patient, three more waiting in the ER, and someone who had been in the hospital for six months with multiple comorbidities. I felt drained, and the day hadn't even begun. Just before my colleague walked out, he added, "Oh yeah, don't forget there's a mandatory department meeting at noon today. I'll be passed out in the call room. If you don't see me at the meeting, please wake me up—I'm beat."

Our department chief began the meeting with, "So team, the theme for this month is efficiency. Leadership has unanimously agreed that the best way to improve hospital flow is to prioritize all patients that are ready to leave and discharge them before 11 a.m. This way, we'll know exactly how many beds are available for the day. The 11 a.m. discharges are effective immediately, so please get tomorrow morning's discharges ready today. We'll be tracking your progress, and for those of you that lead the charge, you can expect a bonus at the end of the year."

Message received: *faster is better.*

After the meeting, I approached the department chief and expressed my concern about repeated bullying behavior by a colleague on our team. He looked at me emotionless and responded, "Tyler's a physician partner and one of the most efficient docs we've got. If you hope to become a partner someday, you'll need his vote—and mine. Just keep your head down and focus on patient care, OK?" I nodded in disbelief.

Message received: *success requires struggle.*

Every day I pushed harder and faster, running headlong in the direction *others wanted me to go* . . . until one day, I hit the brick wall of burnout and was put on a three-month compulsory medical leave to recover.

After taking time to heal and reflect, I realized I had been listening to and following everyone else's guidance rather than my own. Burnout forced me to look inward and figure out how I'd gotten so far off track that my body, mind, and heart had shut down on me.

OUR DRIVING BELIEFS

We find ourselves in a world moving faster than most of us can keep up with. A global tsunami of overwhelm, energy depletion, and burnout is upon us. At the root of this epidemic are three simple phrases:

Do more with less.

Faster is better.

Success requires struggle.

These beliefs have been the engine driving how we think, behave, and live. In fact, our collective brain power, time, and resources have been laser-focused on accelerating our *external* world. Each year, we ask ourselves some version of:

How can we . . .

- Be more efficient?

- Move at a quicker pace?

- Make more than last year?

Despite all we've accomplished with these efficiency-driving, money-making measures, why do we feel so depleted and behind? It's no wonder many of us are completely overwhelmed. I've been there.

You don't have to be a doctor pulling all-nighters and saving lives to burn out. As a human, you naturally multitask, care for others, and work to exceed expectations—at work and at home. After all, hard work, ambition, and dedication have gotten you to where you are. You know how to push through nearly anything. Yet those very characteristics that have helped you accomplish so much may also become your Achilles' heel. It's no wonder so many of us are on the fast track to burnout.

How did we get *here*?

For 90 percent of human history, we were hunter-gatherers, whose focus was finding our next meal while outsmarting predators and keeping our tribe safe. In this more precarious, but less complicated existence, we had to be present. The ability to use our body's physical signals as important internal data to guide us was the difference between life and death: a rustling in the trees or a sinking feeling in our gut were signs that alerted us to lurking danger. As we foraged, feasted, and communed, we did so with safety in numbers and an innate understanding that we were more powerful *together.*

The evolution from a hunter-gatherer society to an agricultural one created many benefits. We no longer had to travel in search of food, so life became more predictable and convenient. We began to own land, cultivate crops, and domesticate animals, which led to better health, longer lives, and larger families. The next challenge emerged: how to feed a growing population.

Beginning in the eighteenth century, with the rise of farming machinery and mass food production, we entered the Industrial Revolution. Securing and developing *external energy sources* powered the quest to advance the pace and quality of our lives. Coal-powered railroads and steam engines sped up our ability to transport food and products over long distances. Socially separated communities could now travel to see one another with greater ease and speed. The nineteenth century saw electricity illuminating our homes and factories. Manufacturing assembly lines could now mass-produce products 24/7 with day, evening, and night shifts. The disruption in our biological circadian rhythms was a new way of life. The twentieth century saw the ubiquity of gasoline-powered automobiles, which provided independence and freedom. Thanks to programmable computers, manufacturing processes became more automated. In the twenty-first century, the intersection of computers with the internet, smart phones, and online identities became an intrinsic part of our lives. Since the 2000s, we've had instant access to the world's information—and to nearly every human being on Earth. The flip side was that we were also able to *be accessed* by anyone at any time.

As a result of this last phase, the "conversations" happening between algorithms, devices, and us as users have dramatically shaped not only the speed of communication but nearly every facet of our lives by blurring the boundaries between our biological, digital, and social realms. As we've become accustomed to using apps, programs, and artificial intelligence, we have become deaf to our own internal human software.

Here are a few everyday examples:

- Don't know where your company laptop is? Why tax your memory? It's embedded with a tracking device. Just ask the cloud.

- Wondering what your bulldog Olive is up to? No need to walk downstairs—just view your backyard from the live feed on your home security app.

- Want to know how you slept last night? No need to check in with your body—just glance at your readiness score on your wearable technology to see if you're well rested enough to take on the day.

Several millennia ago, our hunter-gatherer ancestors could never have imagined the internet, let alone how it's become such an integral part of our daily lives:

- Alerting us of upcoming weather patterns or surrounding danger

- Delivering food and groceries with the click of a button

- Connecting us with our tribe or helping us find a mate

If the hunter-gatherers who came before us were *one with nature*, we've become *one with technology*. It's almost as if we've become machine-like ourselves. But even machines must rely on feedback mechanisms to function properly.

And we humans are more than machines. Mother Nature has built the most sophisticated, evolved life form on the planet. When we operate merely mechanically—and ignore internal feedback—we miss the most important data telling us how we're doing and where we really are in life. That data is invisible but essential. In fact, if we only pay attention to what we can see, then we've already missed a huge opportunity to change course before we hit a wall. We must learn to pay attention to what we cannot see—what's going on inside us. Let me explain.

FROM BURNED OUT TO FULLY CHARGED

Burnout is not merely a case of working too hard or feeling physically exhausted for an extended period of time. And most certainly, burnout is not a personal failure. Burnout is due to prolonged stress on multiple levels—not only physical but also mental, emotional, social, and spiritual—resulting in a net drain of energy on one or more levels. And over 75 percent of professionals experience burnout at some point in their careers.[1]

Burnout is a misalignment of our inner and outer worlds. It occurs when we ignore the invisible data such as our body's physical cues, our mind's conflicting thoughts, our heart's painful emotions, and our spirit's longing for purpose and meaning. Why would we ignore such important information coming from within us? There are many possibilities, but near the top of the list is our desire for love and belonging from others. Our quest to feel a sense of connection began as children in our families of origin. Then as teenagers, that need was transferred to our peer groups and expanded into our romantic relationships. And sometimes, without our consciously realizing it, the drive to meet societal definitions of success resulted in us overriding these important internal signals and wondering *how we got here*.

If you're burned out, your work, health, and relationships suffer. Your capacity to navigate challenging emotions, address conflict, or draw healthy boundaries diminishes. Naturally, it becomes easier to lose your cool in any situation. It's like driving a car from Calgary to Río de Janeiro and not paying attention to whether the tires have good pressure, the gas tank is full, and the oil has been changed. To make it on the cross-continental adventure of your life, you need to keep your vehicle in tip-top shape and use a navigation system. Otherwise, at some point, you'll wind up out of gas in the wrong place, all alone with no idea how you got there.

To reverse burnout, we need a different kind of map—one that identifies and addresses burnout on the level(s) where it's happening and replenishes our energy with simple, powerful steps toward healing. When you're in alignment, you generate a powerful *internal energy source* rather than seeking your energy externally.

Each of us has a unique *internal dashboard* that integrates data from five main parts—the body, mind, heart, relationships, and spirit. When we're in sync with ourselves, and our relationships are aligned, we can navigate a complex world with ease, clarity, and speed. When the incoming data from any part of this high-performance vehicle is not received, is misinterpreted, or is even dismissed, we shift out of alignment and can find ourselves struggling, confused, or stuck. This is one of the primary ways we lose precious energy, leading us down the road toward burnout.

For example, our minds are clever and have gone into overdrive to make sure we measure up to society's definition of success. Fueled by sugar and caffeine, we sacrifice sleep in the name of to-do lists. And we don't dare consider the exhaustion of our body, the pain in our heart, or our spirit's true definition of what would make us happy. We do all of this to belong and not get booted from the pack.

Only now can I see how easy it was to fall into this trap myself. I happened to be good at math and science. I loved Mr. Russo, my accounting teacher, and thought that a career in accounting might be a good option. But after witnessing the disappointment on my father's face, I chose to become an engineer, and then, at the urging of my mother and grandparents, I went on to become a physician. Subconsciously, I believed those accomplishments would garner the love and approval of my family and our Indian community. I ignored my inner signals, rather than tuning in to them. My mind overrode my body's needs, ignored my emotions, and traded my spirit's passion and purpose for external approval. So at the tender age of 33, I burned out.

After three months of medical leave (and a significant amount of reflection, stress management, therapy, and coaching), I returned to work with fewer blind spots and a new approach—one that included paying attention to the invisible internal data that had been trying to guide me all along. I had to listen more deeply to my own needs and shift from being motivated by the outside world to becoming *powered by me*. When I realized that my physical health was connected to my mental, emotional, social, and spiritual well-being, I expanded my understanding of self-care. I began using my body's wisdom to guide me and communicate honestly in order to take care of myself *while* I cared for others. Not only did I become healthier and happier, I also felt physically repleted. I was able to be present for my patients in a new way, which resulted in greater healing for everyone.

It took this dramatic life event and two decades of studying the causes and effects of burnout to realize that in order to thrive in a world that believes *faster is better*, we must also embrace the idea that *together is faster*. By *together*, I'm suggesting—on an individual level—each of us integrates our physical, mental, emotional, social, and spiritual data to regain energy, know what we value, and make effective decisions to get back on track. The next level of *together*—on a community level—includes powerful relationships that provide connection and synergistic collaboration. Think of how inspired, innovative, and fulfilled we would be if we were well fueled, had a clear destination, followed the best guidance, and paid attention to all the signals coming our way. That kind of journey leads to a new level of self-confidence, collective synergy, and dare I say . . . vibrance, connection, and joy!

Having learned this the hard way, I am inspired to simplify and personalize how to identify, heal, and prevent burnout for you and those you love and lead. This book provides a powerful guide to assess where you are on the spectrum from burned out to fully charged. To do this, you must be able to recognize and decipher important visible and invisible data to pinpoint where you're losing precious energy. Last, you must have simple, powerful, and practical steps to replenish yourself and get back on the road to health and happiness.

In your life, as new challenges arise, your energy will fluctuate. The skills I share in this book will guide you back to being fully charged, again and again. It will serve as a road map to:

- Identify where you are experiencing a net gain or drain of energy

- Decipher the early signals coming from your body so that you can change course

- Overcome mind traps that drain you of energy (i.e., perfectionism, control, judgment, blame, and comparison)

- Learn to navigate challenging emotions by responding rather than reacting

- Draw healthy boundaries and prioritize your own self-care

- Reconnect to meaning and purpose in your professional and personal lives

When you heal burnout in a comprehensive and balanced way, you decrease your stress, build a foundation of self-care, strengthen your relationships, and most of all, save precious time and energy!

Over the past 20 years, I have paved a path forward where burnout is not an experience of guilt, shame, devastation, or failure, but instead a great awakening to self-compassion, self-trust, and deeper fulfillment—so that you can achieve a life with vibrant health, fueled by connection, meaning, and purpose. I'm excited to be on this journey with you!

CHAPTER 2

THE BASICS OF BURNOUT

"Dr. Sangwan—are you OK?"

That question was my first clue that I might *not* be.

As a hospitalist with 18 critically-ill patients under my care, it was the fourth time *in less than five minutes* that I had asked the cardiac nurse the same question, "Nina, could you please replete 40 *mEq* of IV potassium for the patient in Room 636?" And I had no recollection that she had answered yes each time.

I walked into the sterile white bathroom, took out my phone, and called a psychiatric colleague: "Roger, my name is Neha. A colleague and friend, Jacqueline, mentioned that six months ago you helped her through a tough time. I'm hoping you might be able to help me too. When is the earliest I can see you?"

"Happy to help, Neha. How about the end of the day—say 5 o'clock?"

The mirror reflection of my pale, weary face willed my mouth to say, "How about now?"

Sensing my desperation, Roger replied, "Of course, come on over. I'm in my office."

An hour later, he declared, "Neha, you're burned out. I'm writing you two prescriptions: one for time off for stress leave and the second one for Prozac. I'd like to see you weekly. It sounds like there are some dysfunctional team dynamics draining your energy. My suspicion is you also have a classic case of people-pleasing. Just because the hospital is understaffed doesn't mean you're single-handedly responsible to fill all the vacancies. It will be much safer for you, your patients, and the hospital if you learn how to draw healthy boundaries and invest energy in your own self-care."

Naturally, I resisted. "But Roger, I still have 16 more patients to see, and my colleagues are totally overwhelmed."

Roger calmly leaned forward, "Neha, I assure you, those patients will be seen . . . just not by you."

I was shocked. Naively, I thought I was making a quick pit stop to get some words of wisdom from Roger so I could go back to work. Instead, in an hour, I had become a patient myself, standing in line at the pharmacy to pick up my own medication.

As a physician, I had written multiple prescriptions for antidepressants for patients and found them to be useful for the right person, with the right ailment, at the right time. But now as a patient myself, the lessons from my pharmacology class on the side effects of antidepressants began flashing before me:

- Agitation

- Anxiety

- Sweating

- Dry mouth

- Nausea

- Vomiting

- Weight gain

- Abnormal dreams

- Sexual dysfunction

- Tremors

And they scared me more than my current experience. On the drive home, I glanced at the passenger's seat, looking at my newly filled prescription, thinking, "I don't know what's wrong with me, but I'm pretty sure it's not a Prozac deficiency."

I don't remember much more from the drive home, except the relief of having the weight of my remaining 16 patients lifted off me. I stuffed the bottle of pills in my top dresser drawer—just in case I needed them.

The next several weeks were painful and eye-opening. I was someone who unconsciously used busyness and saving the world as a noble excuse to avoid my own emotions. Now, all my suppressed self-judgments came rushing to the surface. So much shame and feelings of utter failure washed over me as I ran worst-case scenarios in my mind:

Would I ever be able to walk into the hospital again?

What if I had made a catastrophic mistake that hurt a patient?

What were my colleagues saying about me?

Would I be able to regain my own or anyone else's trust?

How might this epic failure change the trajectory of my career?

I needed to know what this overwhelming, amorphous experience was and how to fix it—*now.* I found myself up at night, asking questions you might be asking yourself.

WHAT IS BURNOUT, ANYWAY?

The engineer in me began by exploring the work of researchers Christina Maslach and Michael P. Leiter, who laid the foundation for our current scientific understanding of the epidemic of burnout.

I was shocked to learn that burnout *was not an actual medical diagnosis*, and the International Classification of Diseases (ICD) described burnout as "a psychological syndrome that involves a prolonged response to chronic interpersonal stressors on the job."[1] I needed more clarity about what that meant. According to Maslach, the three dimensions of burnout were exhaustion, cynicism, and ineffectiveness.

1. Exhaustion

When people feel physically and emotionally exhausted, they often describe it as feeling overextended. They feel drained, used up, and unable to unwind and recover. When they awaken in the morning, they often complain of being as tired as when they went to bed. Exhaustion is the first reaction to the stress of job demands or major change.[2]

Reading that, I wondered, *what's the big deal?* That sounded like my everyday life. I had severe throat constriction. I wasn't sleeping well. I lived on hospital cafeteria food . . . and it was a bonus when the vending machines supplied Flamin' Hot Cheetos. I was a doctor, for crying out loud. Somewhere along the way, I had been conditioned to believe that exhaustion, sleep deprivation, and ignoring my own needs so I could take care of others were *badges of honor.*

And emotional exhaustion? Hilarious. Weren't we in the business of life and death? This came across as absurd. Using that definition, wouldn't the entire hospital staff be burned out? If so, why was I the only one on stress leave? Maybe something was uniquely wrong with me.

2. Cynicism

When people feel cynical, they take a cold, distant attitude toward work and the people on the job. They minimize their involvement and even give up on their ideals. In a way, cynicism is an attempt to protect oneself from exhaustion and disappointment. People may feel it is safer to be indifferent, especially when the future is uncertain, or to assume things won't work out, rather than get their hopes up. But being so negative can seriously impact a person's well-being and capacity to work effectively.[3]

Along with cynicism also comes "depersonalization." This second criteria of burnout stumped me too. I certainly would never do something like that. I loved my colleagues. They were my lifeline. I mean, without them, who would I complain to about how ridiculous our stress was? I couldn't imagine distancing myself from them or my patients—until the following week's session with Roger, where it all became clear.

"Since hindsight is 20/20, we might get some clues as to how you got here by reflecting on the past few months. Over the past year, do you remember not quite feeling like yourself? Or any behaviors that surprised you?" Roger asked.

"Sure," I responded. "A couple of months ago, I do remember being on call when a colleague called out sick, and there was no backup coverage, so I needed to cover all floors of the hospital. I was particularly exhausted after several late admissions. And at 4 a.m., I had just laid my head on the pillow when a nurse paged, "Dr. Sangwan, Mr. Becker in #303 just spiked a fever. Would you like me to give him anything?"

Realizing that the IV teams wouldn't be back in the hospital for three more hours, it meant I would need to get out of bed to draw the blood cultures myself. I snapped, "Dan, what do you mean he spiked a fever? That's ridiculous."

Unsure how to respond to me arguing with the patient's vital signs, he replied, "Should I not have notified you, Dr. Sangwan? I'm one of the new nursing graduates. I thought we had to report any changes in our patient's status to the doctor on call."

The moment I heard his words, I realized what had happened. I had just scolded a nurse for doing his job. What was wrong with me? I loved taking care of patients and had dedicated my life to being able to serve them. On top of that, I had consistently been praised as an empathetic physician who built strong relationships with the patients and staff.

Roger's simple but profound question allowed me to connect the dots between what was happening that, until then, seemed unrelated. Suddenly, I understood exactly how cynicism and distancing myself from others had slowly crept in and accompanied my exhaustion, edging me further down the path toward burnout.

3. Ineffectiveness

When people feel ineffective, they feel a growing sense of inadequacy. Every new project seems overwhelming. The world seems to conspire against each of their attempts to make progress, and what little they do accomplish may seem trivial. They lose confidence in their ability to make a difference. And as they lose confidence in themselves, others lose confidence in them.[4]

Now this one was unmistakable. I didn't even realize what was happening. My inability to function was exactly what prompted Dan to respond in a gentle, clear, and inquisitive way. My asking Nina the same question multiple times had her question if I was able to function, and then my conversation with Roger solidified the need to put me on stress leave. Thank goodness, Dan, Nina and Roger had the courage to redirect me.

HOW DID I GET HERE?

"Roger, I've been trying to figure out why this hospital rotation ended up so different from all the others. I swear I started my five days on service feeling the same as I always did . . . but then I suddenly hit rock bottom. How is that even possible?"

Roger smiled, and began, "Neha, I know it can feel that way, but burnout doesn't happen overnight. It's a gradual process, like the proverbial frog in hot water that doesn't even notice that the temperature is rising degree by degree until it has literally boiled to death." He went on to describe the three phases of burnout I had moved through without even realizing it.

Phase 1: Alarm

Roger began, "The first phase of burnout feels like jumping on a treadmill that's going a little too fast. Your body feels like it's in danger, so your heart rate and blood pressure can be elevated, your stomach might be upset, and if it goes on for some time, you might even experience insomnia, headaches, heartburn, or intestinal issues. You'll probably feel irritable, anxious, and impatient. You might miss deadlines, have difficulty concentrating, or just be generally more forgetful than usual."

"OK," I said. "I definitely felt that way at the beginning of each stage of my education and career. I remember feeling panicked when I had to do three-hour thermodynamics labs in engineering school, thinking I was way out of my depth. And the summer I spent dissecting a cadaver in medical school brought up that same rush of panic. The first code blue I had in residency jolted me into a similar state. So I definitely get what you're saying. It's the moment you feel like the stakes are getting higher."

Roger said, "We're not done yet."

. . . .

Symptoms of the Alarm Phase Can Include Intermittent:

- Elevated heart rate

- Stomach or intestinal issues

- Heartburn

- Lack of appetite or binge eating

- Elevated blood pressure

- Insomnia

- Headaches

- Irritability, anxiety, or impatience

Phase 2: Adaptation

Roger explained the second phase of burnout. "Neha, I bet those times you remember being on that treadmill are blazed in your memory, right? They were startling. But tell me—how much time did you take off during your 12 years of schooling and before starting work at the hospital?"

I blinked a few times. "Um. None. OK, that's not totally true. I did work full-time at Motorola as a manufacturing engineer for a year in between undergrad and graduate school. But it was pretty intense and lonely. I longed for more human interaction. So I went back to med school."

Roger chuckled. "Neha, you never got off the treadmill. In fact, it sounds like you kept turning up the speed. You went from the stress of school to the stress of a challenging job to the even greater stress of medical training. I can't think of a more challenging path. Were you experiencing any of the same symptoms I described in the alarm phase?"

"Well, for me, it showed up more as intermittent throat constriction, shortness of breath, and occasionally an upset stomach. Over time, my throat constriction became more severe and was continuous. I was certain I had a tumor in my throat. I even convinced two separate GI docs to administer anesthesia and scope me. But after both procedures revealed nothing, they told me it was likely a stress response. While I was relieved that I didn't have cancer, I was even more confused. I didn't know what to do with the information that stress was causing it all. I still had to do my job and make a living."

"How did you cope with the discomfort in your throat and stomach?"

"The short answer is I didn't. I just kept powering through. At one point, I was drinking three lattes a day, and I knew the perfect equation to get me through my 36-hour shifts: two ice-cold 16-ounce Mountain Dews and a king-sized Snickers bar. The carbonation seemed to help with my throat, and now that I think about it, three lattes and a Snickers bar every third night on call were probably the cause of my upset stomach."

"Did you ever procrastinate or call in sick?" he asked. "Those are also signs of the adaptation phase kicking in."

"Oh no! I would *never* call in sick. This is crazy, but I went to work *even when I was sick*, just to avoid anyone thinking I was a slacker. Come to think of it, about a year ago, I began procrastinating on completing my patient dictations and insurance paperwork. I even got threats from the medical records department of the hospital that they were going to suspend me—and the strangest part was, I didn't even care," I admitted.

"It sounds like you were under a lot of stress," Roger said.

"But it didn't always *feel* that stressful. It felt more like I was just chronically depleted of energy," I said.

"Well," Roger replied, "that's because humans continue to adapt to their environments. When you spend consistent time in the alarm phase, you move into what is called the adaptation phase. This is when the alarm phase has now become your new normal. Does that make sense?"

"Kind of. On a practical level, other than calling in sick or procrastinating, how would I know I was in the adaptation phase?" I asked.

"Well, did you ever notice yourself making adjustments in the weeks and months prior to burning out—coming up with strategies just to survive? I know we've talked about how much you strived to be a high performer by repeatedly volunteering to cover your colleagues' night shifts—sometimes even after you'd already worked a full day. And since quitting was never an option, my guess is that you got creative around how you continued to carry such a heavy load—long after your body was begging you to stop."

"Wow, Roger. This is embarrassing to admit, but you're right. I went into conservation mode. Each member of our team had been carrying 16–18 hospitalized patients per day. We were chronically understaffed, and it didn't seem like anyone was in a hurry to get us more help. And then, you know how last year, the hospital mandated that we discharge patients before 11 a.m. and then tied those numbers to whether we got our year-end bonuses or not?"

"Yeah, I've heard about those new cost-saving initiatives," he nodded.

"Well, if I missed that discharge deadline and a patient was ready later in the afternoon, there was no way I was going to let myself be penalized by a stupid rule. So I just came up with a reason why they needed to be discharged the next day. Yes, I wanted to make my numbers, but the bigger reason was I knew that my reward for discharging a patient in the afternoon would be *yet another new admission* that evening. And that was the last thing I needed. I was spent. I didn't have the energy to take on a new sick patient and their concerned family at 6 p.m."

"Thanks for being so open, Neha. I know it's not easy to own how you got here. But your personal accountability is the reason I know you're going to get better," he replied.

"Is it possible to be in the adaptation phase for longer than a year, Roger?"

"Absolutely," he nodded. "As our world keeps moving faster and faster, it's becoming more common for people to live in the adaptation phase for a majority of their careers and lives. You're only in your early thirties. That makes you one of the lucky ones who's pausing to learn from this early. Trust me, the effort you're making right now and your curiosity to learn is already changing the trajectory of your future."

"But I still don't understand what made me crash? Why was this time on service different from all the others?" I pleaded.

Symptoms of the Adaptation Phase Can Include Chronic:

- Sleep issues, feeling tired and wired

- Anxiety, pain, or bodily discomfort

- Recurring infections

- Strategies to avoid taking on more work

- Distancing oneself from others in order to avoid social engagement

- Procrastination or calling in sick

- Increasing reliance on coping mechanisms such as food, caffeine, medication, alcohol, and so on

Phase 3: Exhaustion

"Adaptation phase comes in once the alarm phase has been going on for an extended period," Roger explained. "Then all it takes is one more stressor to tip you down the slippery slope of the exhaustion phase. Whereas the earlier phases have intermittent symptoms, this phase comes with more intense and unrelenting symptoms such as extreme fatigue that doesn't improve with time off, a compromised immune system with more frequent and severe illnesses, debilitating headaches, depression, or in extreme cases, even suicidal thoughts.

"Neha, you've been running on empty for a long time—I'm guessing more than a decade. Pushing your biology beyond its limits has become an unsustainable way of life. It was just a matter of time before something tipped you into the exhaustion phase."

Symptoms of the Exhaustion Phase Can Include:

- Extreme fatigue (not improved by rest)

- Consistent heaviness and bodily discomfort

- Debilitating headaches

- Depression

- Inability to function

- And in the most severe cases, suicidal thoughts

"You know, Roger," I said. "The day I had my emergency session with you was the last day of my hospital rotation with 18 sick patients. Our colleague had a death in the family, so we were down a team member—on an already overstressed team. We all had to cover his patients. I was given his 'alpha' pager, responsible for air-traffic control—meaning I was the one in charge of screening all incoming patient transfer requests from nearby hospitals. The constant interruptions made an already stressful day so much worse. I was so inundated that before I asked Nina, the nurse, the same question four times in a row—I had seen only 2 of my 18 patients. And I'd been working for five hours already! So when I got a call to coordinate a liver transplant patient, it was the last straw. I think my mind actually short-circuited."

"Yes, your physiology literally stopped you," Roger said. "You had slid down the slippery slope of exhaustion all the way to ineffectiveness. I'm so glad you knew to call for help. Neha, your disproportionate sense of duty to your job responsibilities blinded you from honoring your primary duty to your own self-care. By the look on your face, I saw how unhappy you were when I prescribed Prozac and extended time off. Remember, this didn't happen overnight. And it won't heal overnight either.

"Think about how a stressful day can lead to a sleepless night . . . and worse, a stressful period at work leads to several sleepless nights in a row, leaving you depleted and just barely hanging on. That's when the weekend can't come soon enough. Eventually, the body gets so tired and wired that sleep becomes elusive altogether. Chronic insomnia perpetuates a vicious cycle of stress and no sleep, eventually leading to a compromised immune system and illness. Many people make the mistake of transferring their work busyness into home projects. Please think of this time off as a gift for your body, mind, and heart to rest."

Important Note

Prior to embarking on the self-diagnosis of burnout, please get a clean bill of health from your medical provider. Physical symptoms including but not limited to fatigue, elevated heart rate, chest discomfort, insomnia, headaches, and intestinal issues may require immediate medical attention. That said, the approaches in this book are complementary to any medical treatment, as they will facilitate stress reduction. Lowering your stress is beneficial to a wide range of conditions, as research has shown that stress causes or exacerbates more than 80 percent of all illnesses. Getting to the root of what is causing your stress is critical to healing on every level.

. . . .

Emergency Toolkit

If you identify with either the chronic adaptation phase or the exhaustion phase and need immediate relief, please contact a medical professional and visit the Emergency Toolkit resources at *intuitiveintelligenceinc.com/pbmresources*, which includes relaxation strategies to provide temporary relief until you can get back on the healing path.

. . . .

HOW DID I NOT SEE BURNOUT COMING?

"Hey, Roger, why isn't burnout taught in medical school? Or even in our residency programs?"

"Neha, do you really think we would have made it through our medical training if anyone had taught us about this? Most of us were burned out the entire time. So don't take it so hard," he added. "I didn't learn about burnout until well into my psychiatry residency when a colleague of mine burned out."

. . . .

Measuring Burnout

The Maslach Burnout Inventory (MBI)[5] is useful for determining whether you are burned out—meaning how *physically and emotionally exhausted* you are and whether you have progressed to also experiencing *depersonalization* (the need to protect your social energy). Or if you're feeling what Maslach speaks about as *diminished personal accomplishment*—like what you do doesn't really make a difference. The challenge with the MBI inventory is that even if you do figure out that you're burned out, you may not know exactly why.

Other tools, such as the Stanford Physician Wellness Survey,[6] not only assess whether healthcare teams are burned out but also provide insight as to the underlying causes.

The American Medical Association (AMA) also has a simple, quick (and free) assessment for individuals called the Mini-Z. If you're a physician, use the Mini-Z. If you're in a different profession, use the Mini-Z General. Both can be found at *www.professionalworklife.com/mini-z-survey*. I've found these surveys to be useful but limited to a work setting.

. . . .

WAS BURNOUT MY FAULT?

As my world slowed down, self-doubt kicked in. I wished that I had noticed my energy depletion sooner and avoided needing to take months off. Months (plural) seemed excessive. But how was I supposed to figure out something that came on so gradually? I hadn't even known what burnout was. There was no way I could have self-diagnosed it earlier.

I had never spent more time alone with my thoughts than I did while I was on stress leave. And the question that kept me awake night after night was: *Was this my fault?*

In our next session Roger began, "Sometimes you're overly responsible for situations that aren't your doing. We talked about you ignoring your own self-care in the name of serving your patients. It's true that your growth edge is learning to balance your own needs alongside the needs of others."

"I know, I know, I'm a people-pleaser," I said with a sigh. "That's a big factor in how I got here. I'm working on it, Roger, but it's not easy."

"It's also not the whole story," he added. "The day I met you, I remember you casually mentioned being bullied by a colleague and complaining to your chief, but he told you to 'put your head down if you want to be a physician partner someday.' I want you to know that you've also been enduring a toxic work culture. It's not just about the amount of work you do—you're happy to work hard. It's about you not having the resources and support to meet the challenges of your job. A big contributor to your burnout is that you have been adapting to a dysfunctional work environment."

"Oh my gosh, Roger! When I interviewed for my first job as a hospitalist, I was solely focused on impressing my interviewers. I paid no attention to whether the environment was a good fit for me. I guess I had to figure it out the hard way."

Roger sighed, "Neha, it's bigger than this hospital. I've worked at a few different places and don't know that it would necessarily be significantly different somewhere else. The healthcare industry is a world of its own—and it can be a pressure cooker. When you're in a broken system that meets its budget by chronically understaffing and overworking its people, your job is to learn to draw healthy boundaries and take care of yourself in order to be able to care for others.

"Here's the bottom line I've learned after decades as a psychiatrist: no matter what environment you're in, or even what uncertainties the world brings to your doorstep, how you *choose to respond* will determine what happens next."

On the ride home, my head was spinning. I was starting to realize how much power I actually had. I was the one who chose this profession, this hospital, and this practice. It was the first time I could see it clearly. If I was honest with myself, I had made this choice, not only because I loved my patients (I did), but because I also wanted to meet the expectations of my family and the Indian community. I kept powering through because I thought this was the only path. In truth, I had much more agency than I realized.

WHERE DO I GO FROM HERE?

Over that month, my weekly sessions with Roger helped me sort through my confusion and damaging self-talk until, at last, I began to open my heart and transform my perspective. I began to wonder, *Do I really need more time off? Maybe it's time I get back to work?*

As soon as I walked in the door for our fifth session, Roger exclaimed, "Neha, you look so much better! That Prozac is really kicking in."

Realizing why doctors make challenging patients, I confessed, "Roger, I filled the prescription the day you gave it to me, but I haven't taken any yet. I wanted to see how our sessions went before starting Prozac. I'm feeling so much better now. I don't think I need it."

He raised his eyebrows. "Neha, then I can't be the one seeing you. As a psychiatrist, I can't bill for someone who isn't on medication. So if you aren't taking Prozac, you'll have to find another provider."

"Whaaat? Are you serious? I was going to tell you how I started sleeping through the night. And for the first time in a long time, I didn't have throat constriction last week. What we're doing is working! Please don't leave me now. I'm just starting to heal."

"Neha, I am glad that this experience has been so helpful. We work in a healthcare system that has rules about who I can and can't treat.

Unfortunately, insurance doesn't cover sessions with a psychiatrist for a patient who isn't taking medication. You still need time off to recover, so I will extend your time for two more months and refer you to some highly recommended behavioral therapists."

Something was very wrong with what was happening. I had listened to my intuition when I decided to hold off on taking the medication. I thought not needing to be on medication was a good thing—but right now, it wasn't.

Fortunately, I had learned so much from Roger and made good progress in a short period of time—by understanding my own patterns, the work environment I was in, and how all of that fit into the bigger context of what led to burnout. My time off combined with Roger's sessions provided the roadside assistance I desperately needed to get out of a ditch. These five weeks had provided key awarenesses of what went wrong, but had not yet healed the underlying patterns that burned me out.

In my heart, I knew Roger had gone above and beyond for me. His knowledge, guidance, and care had empowered a new way of thinking. Now I found myself in uncharted territory, but I was determined to keep moving forward, using my inner GPS to guide me.

I was devastated, but also grateful.

CHAPTER 3

A DIFFERENT KIND OF PRESCRIPTION

You know that saying, "When the student is ready, the teacher appears"? After Roger, I was lucky enough to find a new mentor, James S. Gordon, MD. As the founder of Center for Mind-Body Medicine, he offered a highly recommended weeklong stress management training for healthcare providers, and I eagerly signed up. It wasn't long before I knew how to interpret the early stress signals my body was sending me. Jim also taught me about the gap in the medical world's understanding of how to identify, recognize, and effectively treat burnout. I was surprised to learn that this discrepancy dated back decades.

In 1974, psychologist Herbert Freudenberger[1] coined the term "burnout" in a medical journal, after researching the impact of excess stress in the workplace resulting in mental health concerns, such as depression.

When I burned out in 2004, it wasn't even recognized as an official medical diagnosis. After all, there was no way to measure it. It was invisible. In fact, just one year earlier, burnout had been recognized as a *symptom*—a state of exhaustion. Fast-forward to 2019: it was a big step forward when the World Health Organization (WHO) designated burnout as an occupational phenomenon, and it was acknowledged as a full-blown *syndrome*—a group of symptoms that, together, are characteristic of a specific disease or disorder. But it's only been associated with chronic stress *in the workplace*. In my opinion, that is a narrow viewpoint.

While work stress is an obvious contributing factor to burnout, it's only one part of the equation. Isolating it from personal life stressors didn't match my decade of clinical experience with patients. Once I returned from stress leave, I began to recognize burnout in patients of all ages and walks of life. Single parents caring for sick or special needs children. Students at college getting recurrent infections. Teenagers who buckled under the stress of social, parental, or cultural expectations and had overdosed on drugs or alcohol. Nearly anyone who was enduring chronic stress in the form of illness, toxic relationships, or life transitions could end up in one of the phases of burnout. Simply attempting to face life's challenges with all the resilience they could muster was enough to catapult a wide variety of my patients into various phases of burnout. These examples and countless others provided the evidence I needed to recognize that chronic life stressors—whether professional or personal—can cause burnout. Yet only some of these stressors are visible to us. So we tend to focus on what we can see and ignore what we can't (inner stressors). That's why burnout can be so tricky and often goes unhealed.

It's now clear how both of these types of stressors contributed to my own burnout. My people-pleasing nature combined with poor choices around sleep and nourishment steadily depleted my energy. My desire to be "a good Indian daughter" drove my eternal pursuit of perfection. Joining a toxic work environment with a conflict-avoidant culture added even more stress. And on top of it all, I worked in a healthcare system that was chronically understaffed and primarily focused on crisis-care.

So here's the deal. I couldn't single-handedly solve our broken healthcare system (although I tried). I also couldn't force my chief to hold my colleague accountable for his behavior (tried that too). And I couldn't change the cultural and familial expectations I was born into.

Here's what I *could* do: I could change how I responded to all of the above.

This begs the question: Where should we put our focus when tackling such an overwhelming, pervasive experience of stress that can span our personal life, work culture, community, and the world?

This shows up in thoughts or comments muttered under our breath, such as:

I can't be in three places at once.

What more does my boss expect of me?

Does management seriously think we're giving up working remotely?

Will there ever be equality or justice for women and girls?

How has half of my family gone politically crazy?

We all struggle with dynamics in our external environment, which at times can feel out of our control. In this century alone, there was the uncertainty of the 2000 dotcom bust, 9/11, the economic meltdown of 2008, the 2020 global pandemic, the Black Lives Matter movement, the January 6th insurrection, the war in Ukraine, and climate change, to name a few.

During the pandemic, almost overnight the world shifted from being in air-conditioned cubicles in corporate attire from nine-to-five to beaming in virtually, half-dressed from bedrooms, couches, and home offices. Some people longed for the structure, teamwork, and camaraderie an office provided, while others awakened to the dysfunction and toxicity of their work environments, and discovered the flexibility and freedom of working from home.

Research published in MIT Sloan Management Review reported that in Culture 500 companies during the Great Resignation (April–September 2021), "toxic corporate culture" was the number one reason people left their jobs. And toxic culture was 10.4 times more likely to contribute to attrition than financial compensation.

If you find yourself casting blame on your employer, the government, capitalism, technology, or even the world, over time it naturally leads to feeling trapped and resentful. It's funny how easy it is to identify what your boss, your colleague, or your company could do differently that would make your world less stressful. This *outside-in* approach has us disproportionately blaming our environments, and all that does is *drain our energy.*

The reality is that you may not be able to control a meltdown of global markets, but you *can* choose how you react or respond to it—and any event in your life. It may feel counterintuitive at first, but I promise you, the secret is focusing on how *you* can change, rather than on what's happening in the world around you. The moment you do this, you become part of the solution to reversing the symptoms of burnout.

When you use an *inside-out* approach, you take into account all factors, visible and invisible, to create more spaciousness, creativity, and personal power. This will expand your inner resourcefulness, allowing you to *do more with less* and knowing when to *do less.* Don't be mistaken: resilience is *NOT about enduring the adverse circumstances that you may find yourself in.* Rather, it is about becoming empowered to take care of yourself, understanding how the situation you are currently in has served you, recognizing how your needs have shifted, while also becoming a catalyst for necessary change. You may not be able to imagine it now, but you're going to learn how to source your energy from *inside yourself*, to meet the ever-increasing demands of the fast-paced world around you and improve the way you work and live.

MY PRESCRIPTION FOR BURNOUT

When you understand a few key underlying principles, healing burnout becomes much easier.

- Research shows that stress causes or exacerbates more than 80 percent of all illnesses.[2] So it's really important for you to know yourself well and get to the root of what's causing your stress.

- Burnout can happen in *any* aspect of your life where chronic stress is present.

Loss of energy in your personal life will affect how much energy you have for your professional life, and vice versa. A study published in the *International Journal of Environmental Research and Public Health* revealed that individuals experiencing burnout were more likely to report personal conflicts and difficulties in maintaining a healthy work-life balance.

- Younger generations, such as millennials, are particularly vulnerable to burnout. A survey by the American Psychological Association found that Gen-Z and millennials experience the highest levels of stress compared to other age groups.[3]

- There is great power in personal accountability. There are many people, organizations, and institutions you can blame, but it will leave you feeling stuck. The moment you shift toward personal accountability, you become your own power source, generating your energy from within. I call this becoming *me-powered*.

- Once you identify where you're losing energy, if you focus on improving that area, it will positively impact the other levels as well. Bonus!

Although burnout can seem insurmountable, I assure you that's not true—if you start with *yourself*. Don't worry; I'm not going to simply suggest you take a few weeks of paid leave and learn yoga (although, that's a good start). After healing myself and helping thousands of others, I've developed a simple, practical, and personalized approach for you to figure out where you are and how to get where you want to be.

It all comes down to energy. Are you using up your energy faster than you are refueling it?

Here's the bottom line:

Revealing where you are on the spectrum from burned out to fully charged can be determined by identifying where you're experiencing a net gain (+) or net drain (–) of energy on one or more of these five levels—physical, mental, emotional, social, and spiritual.

Each level offers important *internal* data. Without tuning in to this data, you're at the mercy of everyone and everything outside of you. But that's not why you're reading this book—you're someone ready to become your own internal power source. You want to be *me-powered*.

YOUR NAVIGATION SYSTEM

Each of us has a unique *internal navigation system*—similar to the main console of a car—that integrates data from five main inputs: body, mind, heart, relationships, and spirit. When the incoming data from any part of the system is not received, or is misinterpreted, or is even dismissed, we shift out of alignment and can find ourselves struggling, confused, or stuck. This is one of the primary ways we lose precious energy, leading us down the path toward burnout. To regain that energy and get back on track, we must identify what we missed and use it to recalculate the best path on our journey.

You might be wondering how to identify these five components that are providing this valuable data for your journey. Let's start with your body.

Physical Energy

Your body is talking—just like the recorded prompts in your navigation system that tell you, "Make a right turn in half a mile." Similarly, when your body needs to communicate that something is changing, it uses a unique set of *physical signals* (heart racing, stomach turning, sweating, etc.) to get your attention—similar to the check engine light turning on in a car. Your physical energy is governed by biological rhythms and has built-in feedback loops to alert you when your fuel is running low. If you listen and catch the signals early, you can often refuel or repair what's needed before it becomes a major problem. When you ignore your low fuel gauge and instead tell yourself, "I've easily got another 40 miles," you're setting yourself up to run out of gas and be stranded on the side of the road. When the intensity of these physical signals from our bodies is low, most of us don't pay attention. Instead, because we're so busy, we override them with a variety of coping strategies such as consuming caffeine or sugar or scrolling endlessly through social media. Unfortunately, this strategy doesn't make the signals go away, they actually get louder. And by missing this early invisible data, we veer even farther off course.

Your body's energy comes from consistency and routine. Balancing hormones, nourishing yourself with whole foods at regular intervals, staying well hydrated, getting 7 to 8 hours of quality sleep per night, and exercising regularly while maintaining consistent energy levels may seem like a tall order. But over time, if you take care of your body, it will provide the vitality you need to keep your life running smoothly.

Mental Energy

Your mind serves as the micro processing unit of your internal system, using logic to transform all incoming data—internal and external—into thoughts. This is how you decide how to react (or not), whether to speak up (or not), or what action to take next. Your mind is a meaning-making machine. Anytime it doesn't have all the information, it works hard to fill in the gaps.

The mind plays an important role in guiding us, but it can easily override the other aspects of the navigation system. This is common because we value analytical thought, speed, and productivity so much that we often revere the mind above all else. Ironically, pushing ourselves too far in this direction can significantly hamper productivity. A study by Gallup found that burned-out employees are 63 percent more likely to take a sick day and 2.6 times more likely to actively seek a new job.[4]

We've glorified the mind's rational abilities while dismissing the body's cries for rest, the heart's desire to express itself, and the soul's longing for purpose and meaning. Unfortunately, when we receive physical signals (heart racing, stomach turning, jaw clenching, body aches, etc.), many of us:

1. Do not realize they are important messages.

2. Are unsure how to interpret them.

3. Override them, justifying our actions by repeating common clichés such as:

    - *Act professional.*

    - *Keep home at home and work at work.*

    - *If you can't measure it, it doesn't exist.*

    - *Keep calm and carry on.*

    - *Gotta power through.*

We have 70,000 thoughts per day and 90 to 95 percent of those thoughts are the same ones we had yesterday.[5] With this level of repetition, it's no wonder changing our minds is such a challenge.

Many of us go through life on autopilot, letting the mind direct the entire journey. *It's critical to identify when the mind is in sync with the rest of your system and when it is out of alignment.* If you become aware of the many thoughts occupying your mental real estate, you can get curious about which ones have you running in circles and are draining you, and instead consciously choose the ones that energize you.

Emotional Energy

Your heart reveals your current coordinates—exactly where you are emotionally at the present moment, like the blue dot on a map showing "You are here." People often gravitate toward emotions that feel good and avoid the awkward or uncomfortable ones. The truth is that all emotions are important invisible data from your heart, telling you how you're experiencing your life at this moment. If an event, topic, or conversation moves you, that's a signal that it's important to you. When you ignore challenging emotions, they don't go away. In fact, they grow more intense and become a consistent energy drain. But when you understand how to navigate them, they quickly transform into your trusted ally and help you conserve energy.

It's true that emotions sometimes force us to slow down. They can be confusing and uncomfortable—and the mind has little patience for that. Conditioned by society to believe that *faster is better*, the mind often prioritizes safety and speed over listening to and integrating the wisdom of the heart.

You'll notice the mind's protective behavior when you hear yourself silently repeating phrases like:

- *I'm making too big a deal out of this.*

- *I need to have a positive attitude if I'm going to succeed.*

- *I better not rock the boat.*

When your mind overrides the heart's emotional data, you can suppress key information about how you feel and what you need in a given situation. This causes confusion and a feeling of being stuck that drains precious energy. On the flip side, if you pay attention to the coordinates of your heart, you will always know where you are, allowing you to navigate easily to where you want to go next.

Social Energy

Your relationships have an enormous influence on your journey—because you're not the only vehicle on the road.

We are communal beings who require connection and belonging to thrive. We don't drive this road alone (thankfully). Some vehicles travel with you, provide support, and offer assistance along the way. Some cut you off. Others crash into you. Some get off at an exit, and you don't know why they left. Each has a different level of engagement with you at different times along the journey—and that can sometimes feel confusing or hard.

Developing strong relationships requires asking for help, valuing others' work styles, drawing healthy boundaries, and being able to navigate conflict with clear, compassionate communication. When we encounter people with an inner GPS that resonates with our own (but doesn't have to be identical), we experience an instant closeness and camaraderie. Mutual support and respect are among life's greatest energy boosts.

Navigating relationships requires us to know ourselves well. When we aren't tuned into our own internal GPS, it's easy to pick up interference from another's GPS—potentially guiding us to the wrong exit or destination.

Paying attention to your relationships determines whether you feel lonely and move deeper into burnout or experience a sense of connection and support that moves you toward healing.

Spiritual Energy

Your highest values are the core of your internal GPS, guiding you on a spiritual level to what matters most. They direct your body, mind, heart, and relationships toward what gives your life meaning. Your highest values reveal your underlying intentions—*why* you do what you do. This is how you're able to effectively navigate uncertainty, stand up for what you believe in; transition into a new job, relationship, or location; or even become an entrepreneur who forges a new path. When you step into the unknown, trusting that you can handle what comes next will allow you to take risks. This is where innovation is born.

Spiritual energy can serve as a source of faith and hope. It provides the strength to endure inexplicable, sometimes devastating experiences, such as financial loss, being fired, being passed over for a promotion, an adverse health event, or even a breakup or loss of a loved one. Spiritual energy can help you navigate a chaotic world with grace and ease. During times of chaos, knowing what you value most allows you to recalibrate in order to make smart and effective decisions.

If you're someone who says, "I'm not spiritual" or "I don't believe in spirituality," that's perfectly fine. *What matters most is that you can clearly identify your highest values.* When you follow your own higher guidance, you're able to navigate the unknown with confidence, and create a life filled with purpose and meaning.

Even if you aren't consciously aware of it, your spiritual GPS is actively communicating with you on a regular basis. Here are a few examples:

- When you accomplish a meaningful goal and feel a deep sense of pride or satisfaction

- When your creative genius shines through to solve a complex problem

- When you're inspired by an experience or new idea and suddenly get goosebumps

- When you feel deeply seen and heard by another, and you experience a warmth in your chest

- When you witness progress in those you love or lead and feel energized and elated

Experiencing the synergy of incoming data from your body, mind, and heart that are aligned with what you value most ignites your spirit. This is where *motivation*, *engagement*, and *inspiration* are born.

The flip side is true as well. When those messages are *not* aligned, you feel confused, lost, or depleted. We've all had moments where we've felt a burst of inspiration . . . only to hear our logical mind chime in with:

- *That idea sounds more like a hobby. Better keep your day job.*

- *When this doesn't work out, what's your backup plan?*

- *Following your bliss won't pay the bills.*

This is why spiritual energy is so important to know and use in your everyday life. It may seem elusive or invisible, but it's driving what you prioritize, how you make decisions, and what matters most to you.

. . . .

How Does Financial Stress Contribute to Burnout?

The American Institute of Stress estimates that workplace stress and burnout cost US businesses around $300 billion annually due to absenteeism, reduced productivity, and healthcare costs.[6] Entire books have been written about our relationship to money—and rightfully so. It's a complex topic and has been cited as the greatest source of stress by 70 percent of people in the United States, regardless of socioeconomic status. Our relationship to money impacts all five energy levels.

Financial stress can often manifest as physical ailments, such as high blood pressure, headaches, back pain, or insomnia.

Mental stress about money ranges from thoughts of *not having enough* and worrying about making ends meet or *having too much* and living in fear of losing it all. Those with large sums of money often face the dilemma of feeling valued for their wealth, rather than who they are.

Emotionally, equating one's net worth with one's self-worth is a common way that people agonize about how much money they have. Chronic financial worries of any kind can result in disappointment, anger, anxiety, or depression.

On a relational level, money often determines our social status by the neighborhood we live in, the car we drive, the schools we attend or send our children to, who we socialize with, and whether we fly business or economy.

Spiritually, how we make our money, what we spend it on, and to whom we donate it—reveals what we value.

So as you can see, money impacts all of the five energy levels— physical, mental, emotional, social, and spiritual. Once you understand these foundational principles, you'll be able to apply them to your relationship with money. Also, for resources that will teach you how to have a healthy relationship to money, visit *intuitiveintelligenceinc.com /pbmresources*.

IT'S ALL CONNECTED

Please know that just like your personal and professional stressors are deeply intertwined, so too are these five energy levels continuously influencing one another. When your body is tired, you may be more emotionally sensitive. When you have lost your sense of purpose, your mind may start blaming you for getting off track. When you face an intensely emotional situation, your body may take you down with a headache or a cold. The level of energy depletion you have on each of these five levels will determine your ability to recover from stressful situations—and when stress is ongoing, one or more of these areas will be undermined.

When you're burned out, your health declines, your productivity suffers, and you're more reactive in relationships. Not having the resources to address conflict, handle challenging emotions, or engage in healthy boundaries further worsens stress and destroys relationships.

Pulse Check Exercise

It's time to take a quick inventory of where you think you are on the spectrum from burned out to fully charged. As we move through the book, we'll go into each level in more detail. If you aren't sure, just take your best guess. And if necessary, feel free to come back and adjust your answer.

Now that you have a general idea of the five different energy levels, ask yourself: Where you are experiencing a net gain (+) or net drain (−)? Please indicate your answers below with a checkmark on each level (in pencil if you think you might want to revisit it later):

Physical	☐ net gain (+)	☐ net drain (−)
Mental	☐ net gain (+)	☐ net drain (−)
Emotional	☐ net gain (+)	☐ net drain (−)
Social	☐ net gain (+)	☐ net drain (−)
Spiritual	☐ net gain (+)	☐ net drain (−)

Skeptical?

Let's be real: you might experience resistance during this process. If you were raised in a family that valued rational logic, empirical evidence, and societal norms above all, *looking inward* may seem foreign at first. That's because you, like countless others, may have been taught to discount and even devalue this incredibly powerful internal data and wisdom that comes from your body, mind, heart, and spirit. Step by step, we'll transform ambiguous concepts into practical information that will boost your confidence and clarity.

As you open your mind to new ideas, my request is that you be willing to explore any resistance that arises with curiosity and self-compassion. Self-protection is natural when you step into the unknown. If you lean in with a sense of wonder, many new possibilities await you. Are you ready to experience what's on the other side?

Burnout happens so gradually that few of us recognize the early signs. That's because we have time-tested solutions that have helped us adapt to the growing stress in our lives. We buy our favorite comfort foods in bulk to help us power through deadlines. Our weekends are no longer enough to catch up on lost sleep because we're busy meeting family or social obligations, rather than resting. If you're finding the coping mechanisms that once kept you afloat are now less useful—or maybe even ineffective—you are not alone. We rarely include our own self-care needs in the equation of our best lives. But you will find that every time you make a choice that aligns with your inner truth, you will gain more precious energy for the life you are meant to live.

I'm excited to show you what 12 years of higher education didn't teach me.

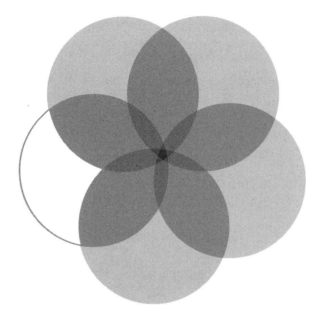

PART I

PHYSICAL ENERGY

CHAPTER 4

DECIPHERING YOUR BODY'S LANGUAGE

On a flight from San Francisco, I happened to be sitting next to a 33-year-old passenger named Alex who caught my attention as he downed three gin and tonics before takeoff. I had planned a working flight, but when he noticed the file on my laptop labeled "Healing Burnout," he sarcastically inquired, "What do *you* do for a living?"

"I'm a physician—writing a book on how to identify, prevent, and heal burnout," I responded.

"Well, I really could have used your help a few years ago. I'm the CEO of a startup and just walked out of a meeting after getting voted out by my own board," he said with a tone of devastation and surrender.

"Oh my goodness! I'm sorry to hear that," I said. "How long has this been going on?"

"Well, I don't really know—maybe my whole life. I've always been an adrenaline junkie, so I can't tell when the anxiety actually started. I've been on Xanax for ages. A year ago, after we didn't raise enough funding, my symptoms got worse. I began having headaches and couldn't sleep, so my doctor prescribed *Tylenol with Codeine* and *Ambien*. I was moving apartments and pulled a muscle in my back, so I went to a different physician who gave me muscle relaxants, but it hasn't gotten any better," he said with disgust.

As a side note, the doctor in me was alarmed about how the alcohol he just drank could be interacting with his medication regimen—but I kept those thoughts to myself.

He continued, "A couple of docs advised me to take time off. One of them even said I was burned out and wrote me an official medical leave, so I've been off for two months, traveling the world with my friends and partying. I thought time off would help me feel better, but it's only resulted in more anxiety, horrible hangovers, and me not giving a shit. So that's it, Doc. Got any solutions?"

My heart went out to him. It was clear that whatever his underlying issues were, they weren't being addressed. He was numbing his physical symptoms, and by ignoring the signals his body was sending, he was veering farther and farther off track. It sounded like he had traded his adrenaline-rush work-addiction for drugs and alcohol—and the end result was an enormous amount of stress on his body, mind, heart, and soul.

As the plane took off, he drifted into a deep slumber. I had many more questions for him, which would never be answered. When we landed, he woke up a bit groggy, and we went our separate ways.

I know Alex was just making chitchat and venting out loud in frustration and pain, but I wonder if he actually wanted my advice. I would have told him it wasn't his fault and that he lives in a world that values extremes and speed, while his body craves routine and rest. I would have told him that the traditional medical system can alleviate his symptoms, but only *he* can get to the root of why he burned out. I would have told him that I wish our education system would have taught him how to process his disappointment and grief. I would have told him that numbing his symptoms got him here, but that if he learned to listen to his body, mind, heart, and soul, they had the answers. And I would've told him that having accomplished so much in 33 short years, with the right tools to support himself, he was destined for greatness. As I have done many times before with a seatmate on a flight, I would have been happy to have a deep and meaningful exchange with him. But maybe, just maybe, Alex's purpose in my life was a different one—to remind me of how important it was to muster the courage to complete this book, so it could be in your hands right now.

THE BODY SPEAKS

Your body is talking. The question is, *are you listening?* I don't know about you, but for most of my life, I ignored the messages my body was sending me. As a healthcare provider, I made a living repairing the breakdown of other people's bodies and, in the process, somehow believed it was okay to override my own.

In retrospect, I should have picked this up in my training. Physiology class taught me how important feedback loops were to keep the body running in top condition. I learned about *both* the sympathetic and parasympathetic nervous systems required to regulate and prioritize the body's resources. The sympathetic nervous system (fight, flight, or freeze) is analogous to the accelerator of a car that allows us to act quickly and avert danger, while the parasympathetic system (rest and digest) functions more like the brakes to slow us down so we can relax, digest food, and recharge.

Just like I would never advise someone to drive a car using only the accelerator, I would never have told my patients to skip rest and nourishment and expect that their bodies could heal. Yet that's exactly how I had treated my body, like a high-performance vehicle racing faster and faster, while giving it suboptimal fuel (junk food and soda)—and not allowing it to rest. To achieve excellence in an area of expertise or just to get momentary relief, many of us have spent decades overriding our body's signals. Even if we've noticed the signals, we may have no idea what is causing them or what our bodies are trying to tell us. If we focus on accomplishing our external to-do list at the expense of our health, eventually, the energy depletion will stop us in our tracks. Too much stress for too long will ultimately undermine our physical health. That's not my opinion—it's fact. Burnout can have long-term consequences. The National Institute for Occupational Safety and Health (NIOSH) found that burnout is associated with an increased risk of cardiovascular disease, musculoskeletal pain, and even premature death.[1] It's a biological fact, one that took me a long time to surrender to.

When it comes to healing burnout, an obvious place to begin is by exploring the most basic relationship with your body—how you nourish yourself, if you get adequate rest and rejuvenation, whether you move regularly, and if you experience consistent energy throughout the day.

The first step of this exploration is to tune in to the language your body uses to communicate with you. These signals won't just alert you to a potential health condition or burnout, they will, in fact, provide critical feedback that will support you in refueling and revitalizing your physical energy.

Investing in feeling physically well and creating biological homeostasis has a ripple effect on every other aspect of your life. You'll learn how to interpret your body's signals. Your internal physiology is key to knowing what kind of self-care you need. Learning to *pause and tune in* rather than *push through and numb* is crucial. If you're interested in feeling better and reversing the course of burnout, you must start on a physical level—from the inside out.

THE BODY MAP

When we're acutely focused on everyone and everything around us (external data), it's easy to miss what's happening inside us (internal data). Recognizing and healing burnout depends on how attuned you are to interpreting your own physiology and responding to the data your body is sending.

Each person's body has a unique communication style. For some people, it's their heart racing, stomach turning, or muscles tensing. For others, it's sweating or shallow, rapid breathing. All day long, your body communicates with you, and it's critical that you're able to decipher those signals. These physical sensations are the gateway of awareness to valuable information that will guide you on this journey.

Take a look at the Body Map illustration in Figure 4.1 below to get a few ideas of how your body might be trying to communicate with you. By no means is this an exhaustive list. Feel free to add your own physical sensations to the diagram.

One of the fastest ways to tune in to your physiology is by becoming aware of your physical body in space and where it meets the external world. By this, I mean literally shifting your attention to where your body meets the chair or wherever you are sitting. If you're standing, notice where your feet meet the floor. As you take your next deep breath, focus on the expansion and contraction of your rib cage. Next, become aware of the sensations of clothing on your body, such as the tightness or looseness of your waistband.

FIGURE 4.1 **Body Map**

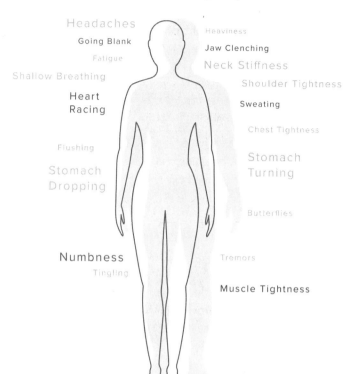

Don't worry if this doesn't come naturally. If you've experienced high stress over long periods of time, you may have adapted to *tuning out* your body's sensations. It's a common coping mechanism. For example, Alex, my seatmate on the airplane, was adept at silencing his body's signals (headaches, insomnia and back pain). He went searching for clues to heal himself, but in the interim, prescriptions and cocktails brought the only relief he could find.

If you've been relying on your own coping mechanisms, whatever they may be, and are out of practice at listening to your body, try expanding your awareness in everyday activities:

1. While you're on a call or in a meeting, hold a smooth stone or weight that fits comfortably in your hand.

2. Each time you notice the weight in your hand, use it as a reminder to check in with your body (meaning, is your body trying to get your attention? Do your wrists hurt from too much typing? Is your rear end numb from sitting for too long? Do you need to stand up, stretch, or get some water?).

3. If you don't feel anything, don't be discouraged. Instead, take a deep breath and refocus your attention back on the weight in your hand.

4. Anytime you notice an emotion arise in another person or a shift in intensity in the conversation, that's a good time to bring your awareness back to the weight in your hand.

5. Be patient. You will begin to tune in to your body's signals.

THE SIGNALS ARE ALREADY THERE

You probably feel more than you realize. What about that pesky neck or shoulder pain? A 3 o'clock energy dip? Any intermittent headaches? What about joint stiffness? These are all signals from your body.

Throat constriction was the signal that I had overridden more times than any other. I was very aware of it. I just had no idea what it meant or how to stop it. Years later, I realized my throat constriction wasn't just an annoyance to be ignored, but in fact, a powerful *early indicator* that something was misaligned in my inner or outer world.

Once I tuned in, I discovered patterns of when my throat would constrict. When I was worried that *saying no* might create conflict. When I was losing a tennis match and felt like a failure. When I was unprepared for a test. When I was perplexed by a patient's diagnosis. When I made a mistake. By the time I finally burned out, I realized that my throat constriction had been my trusted companion, diligently trying to warn me of potential danger—that I might face public humiliation, or let myself or someone else down. My throat constriction was a glaring signal that I needed to include myself in the equation of my life, which for years had been disproportionately oriented toward serving others.

Your body is in constant communication with you. Once you identify and understand its unique language, you will be able to decipher the physical clues even earlier (at lower intensity). And once you pick up these signals, get curious and ask yourself, *What happens before that? And just before that?*

When I asked myself these questions about my throat constriction, I discovered that what came just before my throat tightening was discomfort in the right side of my jaw. What came before that was tension at the base of my tongue. What came before that was shallow breathing with chest stiffness. What if I paid attention to my earliest signal, without waiting until my throat was so constricted that it left me gasping for air? What if right away, I befriended that shallow breath and chest stiffness as an important clue to get curious about what was out of alignment? *Did I need to speak up for myself? Had I just said yes when I really meant no? Did I need to express pain or disappointment? Was I afraid of potential conflict? Did I need to draw a boundary?* If I had known how to tune in to my body's intelligence earlier, I would have saved myself years of frustration and energy depletion.

Now that you are equipped with your new best friend—the body map—I invite you to notice when physical signals occur and get curious about them. What is your body trying to tell you? As you get curious, you may notice patterns. Those patterns are clues about your greatest stressors that have contributed to symptoms of burnout.

INTERPRETING YOUR BODY

Understanding your body's unique language can seem confusing at first. That's only until you learn how to interpret the *intensity* and *duration* of the signals as well as the *context of the situation*. The data from your body typically falls into one of three main categories:

1. **Everyday guidance** (low intensity, short duration) helping you navigate daily situations and changing environments while recalibrating your internal GPS in new experiences. These signals can show up in many ways: muscle, throat or jaw constriction (or relaxation), knots (or butterflies) in your stomach, chills (the good kind), to name a few.

2. **Chronic depletion** (medium intensity, medium duration) alerting you to a drain of energy and lack of alignment in your internal GPS. These physical signals can show up as individual symptoms, such as fatigue, heart palpitations, insomnia, headaches, imbalance, pain, brain fog, forgetfulness, diarrhea, constipation, or a collection of symptoms known as a syndrome.

3. **Emergency breakdown** (high intensity, longer duration) letting you know that something is seriously wrong and needs your immediate attention and / or medical support. In extreme situations, this would show up as a sudden onset of crushing chest pain, perhaps a slurring of words, or loss of function in a limb. In this case, you would call 911 for emergency healthcare.

. . . .

Medical Warning

Begin by ruling out any medical problems. Any new and unusual signals from your body need to be checked out by a medical professional. Once you've gotten a clean bill of health, *then* you can explore how the collection of symptoms may potentially be caused by burnout.

. . . .

How do you tell the difference between when your body is casually communicating with you and when it is trying to alert you to signs of burnout? Well, that depends on how closely you're listening and whether you're numbing the early signals. Your body has manners. It knows you're busy, so it starts with a whisper, at a low intensity (say 1 or 2 out of 10), but if you don't pay attention, it continues to get louder, until it eventually stops you in your tracks. If you've gotten in the habit of hitting snooze on your body's signals with various coping mechanisms, you can reach a 10—a heart attack, pneumonia, or other crisis—without even realizing it. That's scary. You, my friend, are reading this book, so that will not be you!

It's important to note that your body is more than just an alarm system. It wants to be your friend, and it talks to you about *everything*. Yes, it's also informing you in your everyday communication with others when something is:

- Important to you

- Out of balance

- Different from what you expected

- Not quite right

- Exactly right

Your body's signals will not only give you a heads-up when something is wrong and it's time to see the doctor, but also day-to-day updates on what resonates with you and what *just feels off.* Once you learn how to interpret these powerful signals, you'll have a distinct advantage in every conversation, interaction, and experience in your life.

COPING STRATEGIES

Since your body's signals can be confusing, uncomfortable, and inconvenient, a common reflexive response is to figure out how to temporarily manage them, rather than explore what might be causing them. Like Alex, you may find yourself using a variety of coping strategies to ignore your body's feedback. And that's completely understandable. If you don't know what else to do, you're doing your best to survive. Alex was a thirty-something former CEO sitting in first class, with extensive access to medical professionals and consultants, but surprisingly, the strategies he was given simply *numbed his symptoms* and kicked the can down the road.

Our bodies are resilient. If we skip one meal, we might feel depleted, but we can recover. Just like one bad night of sleep might knock us off our game, but we'll be back to ourselves in a few days. That sounds like a good thing, right? Not so fast.

When we're experiencing consistent stress without recovery, we begin to live with a net drain of energy. Then we naturally turn to more creative strategies to keep us going, but that's a losing game. These coping strategies work for a hot minute, but soon enough, they bankrupt our energy reserves.

Coping mechanisms start with good intentions: to get relief, accomplish a task, fulfill a commitment, or just keep moving in your busy day. Used regularly, they can become misguided attempts to manage stress. As we covered in Chapter 3, research shows that stress causes or exacerbates more than 80 percent of all illnesses.[2] The problem with stress is that it's such a generalized term. What does it really mean when someone says, "I'm stressed out"? It could mean, "I was in back-to-back meetings, skipped lunch, and now I'm famished." It might mean, "I'm frustrated because I don't think the changes in technology are making my work more efficient—in fact, they're slowing me down." Or "I'm stressed" could be the result of feeling emotional after learning about your child struggling in school or an aging parent's diagnosis of dementia. There are many underlying causes of stress, but what's universal is that they all manifest physically in your body.

Common coping strategies include reaching for a glass (or bottle) of wine; retail therapy; loading up on caffeine, sugar, or carb-heavy foods; numbing yourself with drugs; binge-watching shows; surfing the internet; or overworking. I can personally attest to the two 16-ounce ice-cold Mountain Dews plus a king-sized Snickers bar strategy (highly effective in the short term). It was a way for me to say yes to yet another hospital shift and override my lethargy, while also avoiding disappointing my colleagues.

What is your number one coping mechanism (comfort food, beverage, or behavior) that allows you to avoid listening to your internal physical signals? For example, after the failure of an important project, maybe organizing every closet in your home serves to prevent you from sinking into a deep well of disappointment. Maybe the high of accomplishing everything on your to-do list helps you feel worthy and needed by others. Maybe a carton of Häagen-Dazs coffee toffee ice cream soothes your post-breakup heartache.

If you're beginning to recognize your own coping strategies, don't be disheartened. Honor the ways you've survived challenges. I like to thank my coping mechanisms. They've helped me endure the roller coaster of life. So begin by patting yourself on the back and having a little fun as you creatively name the strategies that have gotten you through difficult times:

- **Chocoholic:** chocolate makes anything better

- **Busy Bee:** cleaning the kitchen, organizing your closet, doing laundry, keeping eternally busy, so you don't have to deal with the actual issue at hand

- **Timeless Taskmaster:** staying up all hours of the night to get your to-do list ta-done!

- **Forbidden Foods:** eating foods to comfort yourself that boomerang into immediate guilt upon swallowing

- **Mini-Series Marathons:** binge-watching your favorite shows to escape your own reality

- **Work Even Harder:** taking on any available work rather than dealing with the drama at home

- **Riding the Gossip Train:** using the drama of someone else's life to avoid your own

- **Lost in Gaming Reality:** disappearing into a world where you have power, even if it's in the form of a magic sword

- **Aspirational Retail:** buying clothes in the size you hope to be one day

- **The Midnight Gambler:** getting an adrenaline high from betting, whether it's sports, casinos, the lottery, or the stock market—with money you don't have

- **Neon Light Lover:** being in love with *falling in love*; starting and ending a series of relationships to achieve the repeated high—then crashing down

- **Run It Off:** running *from* something else—such as avoiding a conflict, task, or feeling an emotion

Yes, you read that right. When overused, even activities that seem healthy, such as running, can become numbing strategies. Trust me, I'm not knocking you for going on a run. Shortly, we're going to spend a whole chapter on the benefits of movement. But *why* you run matters. And whether you're running *toward* something (e.g., better health or feeling strong) or *away* from something (e.g., a challenging conversation or a hard decision) is an important distinction. If you run to relieve the stress of a conversation you've been avoiding, you may feel better on the run, and it may actually put you in a more grounded place. But here's the key: you still need to *have the conversation* to resolve your stress. Otherwise, you are merely running away from the much-needed discussion. And no matter how many runs you go on, that angst will still be draining you. Even the healthiest coping strategies can become a net energy drain if they're being overused to avoid another aspect of life; it's the motivation driving your action that matters most.

My point: these strategies work—at least for a few minutes—to shift your body away from uncomfortable sensations. If you're really good at powering through, they might even work for months, years, or decades.

Once you've identified your unique coping mechanisms, ask yourself: *What does this strategy allow me to accomplish? And what does it allow me to avoid?*

In what ways are those short-term strategies undermining you in the long run? Maybe that extra glass of wine to take the edge off after a crazy day actually makes you more fatigued the morning after. Maybe that cup of coffee in the afternoon is costing you a good night's sleep. It's time to recognize how your coping strategies impact you over time, so gather your courage, and let's shine a light on how these habits might be impeding your well-being.

The truth is your coping mechanisms aren't meant for the long haul. They are a summer fling that turned into a bad marriage. Call these strategies what you will—survival, indulgence, maybe even necessary relief—and thank them for accompanying you on your journey—because it's time for you to spend a little less time together.

I know what you're thinking, *My day is too busy. I don't have time to pause.* This might sound counterintuitive, but there are times when *slowing down actually helps you speed up.* Everyone has time to pause for at least one minute. And that minute can start to change the relationship with your body and help you think more clearly.

My favorite way to hit pause is with a technique Dr. Jim Gordon taught me—soft belly breathing. It's a short breathing exercise—and you have to breathe anyway, right? I'm just asking you to become aware of *how* you're breathing. Take a moment to feel your ribs, noticing how much of your chest cavity is occupied by your lungs. On an overscheduled, frantic day, when you're running around trying to do five more errands than humanly possible, you're barely using the top few inches of your lung capacity. Guess where the best oxygen exchange occurs? *At the bases of your lungs.* And you wonder why you feel so exhausted by the end of the day.

When you actually slow down your breathing, not only do you get better oxygen exchange but your diaphragm engages to help you. Your diaphragm is a thin umbrella-shaped muscle positioned below the lungs and above the stomach. When you deepen your breathing, your diaphragm flattens to accommodate the air and triggers your vagus nerve. This stimulates a parasympathetic (relaxation) response, slowing down your heart rate and lowering your blood pressure, telling your body it is *not* in danger. This signals more oxygen to go to the outermost part of your brain (the cortex) so it can think clearly and come up with creative options. As a bonus, slow, deep breathing soothes those uncomfortable signals coming from your body, reducing your pain and anxiety. And when your cells get more oxygen, they're able to produce more energy!

Deep breathing may happen in a yoga class or on a run, but during your daily routine, it doesn't usually happen without your focused attention. While doing this exercise, I close my eyes to eliminate visual stimuli. Some people prefer to lower their gaze, but not close their eyes completely. Please do whatever is most comfortable. Let's practice it right now, so you can experience the difference.

Soft Belly Breathing Exercise

Place the palm of your hand on your relaxed belly. Let gravity pull your shoulders down. Slowly and deeply inhale, allowing your abdomen to expand, and become aware of your hand moving outward. As you exhale, allow your belly button to move back toward your spine. Notice your hand moving inward. Repeat this sequence three times, paying attention to any shifts in your body's sensations. Notice if your level of relaxation has changed. (For a video of this exercise, go to *intuitiveintelligenceinc.com/pbmresources*.)

You can use soft belly breathing first thing in the morning, before an interview, during a tense meeting, in the boardroom, at a stoplight, or at the dinner table—any time, not just in a crisis situation. Remember, the more you practice a new habit, the easier it is to use in a stressful situation. The next time you're in a challenging conversation, a contentious meeting, or heavy traffic, interrupt your body's stress cycle by consciously taking a few deep breaths and noticing how it helps you relax and think more clearly.

Body Scan Exercise

The second step is not just to use soft belly breathing to relax but also to become aware of what is happening inside you. As you breathe, slowly and deeply, scan your body from top to bottom, noticing any areas of tightness or relaxation, tuning in to how your body communicates. With your next slow, deep breath in, bring your attention to the top of your head. Does your head feel heavy or light? Is your jaw

(continued)

53

(continued)

clenched? What about your neck and shoulders? This is often a place where people carry the weight of the world. Shrug your shoulders up to your ears and allow gravity to pull them down. Notice if one shoulder feels different than the other, or if they feel similar.

Gently bring your awareness to your chest. Pay attention to your rib cage expanding and contracting with each breath, protecting your heart and lungs all day long without your conscious awareness. Notice if you can feel your heart beating. Where are your hands placed? Are they warm or cool? On your next inhale, gently breathe into your abdomen, allowing it to expand. As you exhale, move your belly button toward your spine. When you soften the muscles of your abdomen, all the muscles of your body relax. Is there any tightness in your hips or pelvis?

Moving down into your legs, notice if the right one feels different than the left, or if they feel the same. And then gently move down into your knees, calves, and shins. With your next inhale, bring your attention to your ankles, heels, and the balls of your feet—until you get all the way down to your toes. After taking a few minutes to breathe and gently focus on different parts of your body, notice if there's a shift in how you feel. (The Body Scan video is also available at *intuitiveintelligenceinc.com/pbmresources*.)

Over time, these exercises will help you become familiar with the feedback your body is giving. For example, when you're engaging externally with someone, consider also getting curious about your internal body signals at the same time. When you notice a particular sensation (constricting or relaxing), consider taking note of what's happening externally, such as *where you are*, *who you're with*, and *the topic of conversation*. These data points are valuable information that are related and can help you identify what else is going on inside (clues to your thoughts, emotions, values, etc.), which we'll cover later.

You are now equipped with the tools to interpret the physical signals from your body. The more quickly you tune in to them, the easier it will be to navigate your world and your other levels of energy. Listening to the body's quieter, lower intensity messages will allow you to make minor adjustments, whereas if you override these early signals with coping mechanisms, they will get louder and last longer. And eventually, you will need to make bigger adjustments to get back on track.

Sometimes these signals from your body indicate an emergency health condition. Sometimes they tell you that you're chronically depleted. And sometimes, they just want to chat. It's your job to tune in, recognize your body's unique patterns, and put them into context to know what to do next.

Learning to listen to your body's messages earlier and treating the signals you receive as valuable data will allow you to navigate stress more effectively and sustain your performance over the long term.

It's time to take a quick inventory of your physical energy.

PHYSICAL ENERGY ASSESSMENT

Your physical energy thrives on consistency, following biological rhythms and regular nurturing. It requires being tuned in to the unique language of your Body Map for any subtle clues so you can adjust as needed. On a scale of 1 to 10, where 1 is "not satisfied at all" and 10 represents "extremely satisfied," how would you rate your satisfaction around self-care in each of the following areas?

- Energy

- Food

- Sleep

- Movement

We'll learn about each of these and discover what next steps are best for you.

CHAPTER 5

STRESS AND HORMONES

After burning out, I made huge strides in both my awareness and my focus on self-care. I credit these changes to another pioneering functional medicine physician that Dr. Gordon introduced me to in 2005, Dr. Mark Hyman. His ability to make complex topics profoundly simple and his depth of knowledge on not just *preventing disease* but also *optimizing my physical wellness* astounded me. I was so inspired that I asked him to become my personal physician. Through this partnership, I began eating better, sleeping more soundly, and even weeding out toxic relationships—both personally and professionally. But in the summer of 2007, I began noticing that it was hard to make it through the day. I had trouble getting out of bed and sometimes felt tired and wired. I consulted a few of my colleagues, who commented, "You sound like you could benefit from an antidepressant." By then I knew it was time to make another appointment with Mark. Upon hearing my symptoms, he said, "The first thing we have to do is to restore your circadian rhythm. You've gotten much better over the past few years, but your adrenals need a chance to reset—and that starts with a regular wake-sleep cycle. Either I'll put you on stress leave again, or you need to ask your chief to take you off all night calls."

I was stunned by this radical recommendation. How could I be a hospital physician and not take night calls? That was the most dreaded part of our work, potentially staying up all night admitting patients and taking care of emergencies. Each of us had a set number of night shifts per month. If I was taken off night calls, everyone else on my team would have to shoulder the additional burden.

As you can imagine, my request to hospital leadership that I stop taking night calls went over like a lead balloon. Ultimately, these symptoms became one of the factors that led me to realize my livelihood as a hospitalist was compromising my health. So a few months later, I made one of the scariest choices of my life: I gave up my tenured physician partnership and embarked on the next part of my healing journey.

What symptoms have made you wonder if you're burning out? Do you not feel as though the weekend is enough time to recharge your battery to start the next week? Are you tired, but when it's time to sleep, you feel wired and unable to relax? Do you feel drained, out of gas, and like you just don't have the momentum to make it through your day or week?

YOUR STRESS-FIGHTING SUPERSTARS

If you've been feeling more depleted than usual, are having trouble sleeping or are unable to function at your normal pace, your hormones might be out of balance. These are common symptoms of chronic stress. The body's stress-fighting superstars are your thyroid gland and your adrenal glands. They produce hormones that help you function during times of high stress and regulate your overall level of physical energy. But when the stress fighters are overused and out of balance, they are no longer able to meet the demands to produce additional stress-fighting hormones. When these glands become overstrained themselves, they begin to contribute to the symptoms of burnout that can eventually lead to disease. In fact, if put under enough stress, our body's stress fighters can actually become the stress-inducers.

Your Adrenals: The Emergency Response System

Let's start with the tiny organs gracefully perched on your kidneys, which are called your adrenal glands. These two powerhouses produce a family of vital hormones that modulate your body's stress response, your sex hormone levels, and your salt and sugar balance. Your adrenal glands are responsible for releasing hormones called adrenaline and cortisol that decrease inflammation and modulate the body's stress.

When I say respond to stress, a few examples would be the following:

- **Physical stress** of working long hours; fueling yourself with a diet of carbs, sugar, and caffeine; feeling tired and wired; not sleeping enough to allow your brain and immune system the time needed to repair

- **Mental stress** of trying to keep up with a hectic schedule, deadlines, work, and home expectations

- **Emotional stress** from the shame of imposter syndrome, financial anxiety, loneliness

- **Relational stresses** resulting from toxic work dynamics, political divides, social media, marital issues, tending to aging parents or children who need additional support

- **Spiritual stress** of feeling lost, disconnected from your higher purpose, or not feeling valued or appreciated (at work or at home)

Adrenaline and Cortisol

Your adrenal glands produce two key hormones that help you navigate stress and burnout: adrenaline and cortisol. When out of balance, you can feel perpetually tired, wired, or both. Chronic stress overtaxes the adrenals and interferes with your hormonal balance.

1. **Adrenaline.** Think of adrenaline as the short-acting hormone that responds to the stress of an acute emergency (fight, flight, or freeze), which results in the immediate dilation of pupils, elevation of blood pressure, and diversion of blood to your larger muscles, so you can navigate any high-stress situation.

2. **Cortisol.** Think of cortisol as the longer-acting version of adrenaline, allowing you to adapt to elevated stress over time. It has different functions, such as reducing inflammation; diverting digestion of fat, carbs, and proteins to create energy; regulating blood pressure; and controlling your wake-sleep cycle (also known as your circadian rhythm). Cortisol levels fluctuate. We experience the highest level upon waking, and then it drops throughout the day until it reaches its lowest level while sleeping. See a graphical representation of the typical rise and fall of cortisol within a 24-hour period indicated by the circles in Figure 5.1.

FIGURE 5.1 **Diurnal Cortisol—Normal**

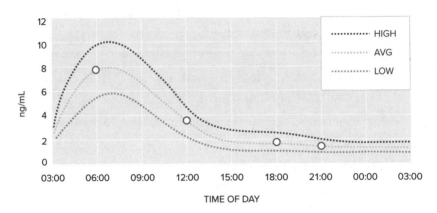

During chronic exhaustion or burnout, your cortisol levels can be depleted across the board and can look more like the circles in Figure 5.2.

FIGURE 5.2 **Diurnal Cortisol—Burnout**

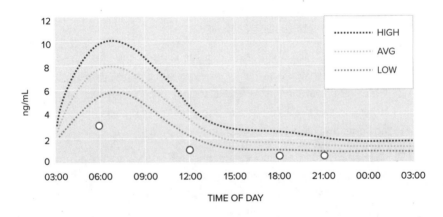

The danger is that, without adequate cortisol, you can't respond to the normal stresses of daily life. You end up feeling tired and exhausted most of the day, which then leads to using short-term stimulants—sugar, caffeine, alcohol, carbs—that eventually impact your long-term health.

What do you do if your physical energy levels are consistently low? *Consider this your warning:* There is no situation in which a net energy drain is sustainable, not in your bank account, not in your relationships, and certainly not biologically.

If you've been under prolonged stress at work or at home, you may feel as though, despite your time off on the weekends or on vacation, you can no longer recover. With ongoing chronic stress, your adrenal glands are no longer able to mount the normal response, so cortisol levels fall. Without the normal rise and fall of cortisol, several symptoms of burnout ensue.

If you're curious about how your adrenals are doing, ask yourself the following questions:

Adrenal Gland Quiz

1. Do you have trouble sleeping? Or do you experience underlying fatigue that persists no matter how much you rest?   Y / N

2. Are you finding it harder to handle stressful situations?   Y / N

3. Have you noticed that you are not able to think as clearly as you used to?   Y / N

4. When you change positions from lying or sitting to standing, do you feel weak or light-headed?   Y / N

5. Have you noticed a decrease in your sex drive?   Y / N

6. Do you crave salt or sweets?   Y / N

The more questions you answer yes to, the more likely it is that your adrenals might be working overtime or not working as they should be. If you would like to learn more, please check out *The Doctor's Farmacy* podcast, episode #38, titled "Wired and Tired: Fixing Adrenal Burnout."

If you know you spend more time in your sympathetic nervous system (accelerator), start to balance it out more with your parasympathetic system (brake). Incorporate one or more of the following on a daily basis:

- Hot bath—to relax your muscles and reduce cortisol

(continued)

(continued)

- Massage—to relax your muscles and improve blood flow

- Meditation—to slow down your thoughts

- Soft belly breathing—to stimulate your parasympathetic nervous system

- Waking, sleeping, and eating at the same times each day—to restore your circadian rhythm (natural wake-sleep cycle) and hormones

- Getting out in nature

- Gentle, regular movement, such as yoga, stretching, or walking

Your Thyroid: The Body's Engine

Your thyroid gland is located in your neck, near your Adam's apple. It regulates the metabolism of *every single cell in your body*. If you think of your physical body as a vehicle, think of your thyroid as the engine. How well the thyroid functions determines the horsepower of that engine. It's critical.

The thyroid gland is part of your endocrine system. It does more than just produce thyroid hormones that regulate your metabolism and body temperature. It also controls the function of your heart and muscles. It powers your digestion and brain while also playing an important role in bone health.

You produce two forms of thyroid hormone: active T3 and inactive T4. Eighty to ninety percent of the thyroid hormone produced is inactive T4, but in order to exert its effects, T4 must be converted into active T3. But just like a good action movie, there are many ways this process can be foiled. Prolonged stress (leading to other hormonal imbalances) and nutritional deficiencies (in selenium, iodine, vitamin D, or zinc) can adversely impact this critical conversion from T4 (inactive) to T3 (active).

When your thyroid levels are low, the brain senses this and stimulates the production of a hormone called thyroid stimulating hormone (TSH) to notify the gland that the body needs to produce more thyroid.

Ten percent of the general population, mostly women, suffer from thyroid dysfunction.[1] Many patients go undiagnosed, and even those who are diagnosed are often not adequately treated.

This is perhaps because there is some controversy about how to best test and treat thyroid disease. The standard approach I learned in medical school was to check the TSH, and if it fell within the normal range (approx. 0.5–5.5 IU/mL), there was no need to treat it. But my own experience changed my mind. My TSH level was 5.0 (so it was high but within the normal range), and I struggled with cold intolerance, hair loss, extreme fatigue, and weight gain. It wasn't until Dr. Hyman got my TSH level closer to 1.0 that my energy returned and my symptoms normalized. I now pay great attention to physical symptoms as my guide.

After that eye-opening experience, I began exploring different options to test and treat thyroid disease. After more than 20 years, I've come to the conclusion that using a functional medicine approach for addressing chronic disease is not only more comprehensive but also an extremely effective way to address thyroid dysfunction—without waiting until alarm bells go off.

You might be wondering if your thyroid is functioning well. If you'd like to know, take a quick quiz.

Thyroid Quiz

1. Do you experience your nails to be brittle or coarse?   Y / N

2. Do you notice your hair thinning (on your head or the outer third of your eyebrows)?   Y / N

3. Do you experience temperature sensitivity—feeling cold when others are not?   Y / N

4. Do you have muscle fatigue, pain, cramping, or weakness?   Y / N

5. Do you have trouble with memory, concentration, or brain fog?   Y / N

(continued)

(continued)

6. Do you have trouble losing weight, or have you recently experienced unexplained weight gain?   Y / N

7. In the morning, do you wake up tired and have trouble getting out of bed?   Y / N

8. Do you suffer from constipation (not having daily, soft, formed bowel movements)?   Y / N

The more questions you answered yes to, the more likely you could be struggling with a compromised or underactive thyroid. If you don't address these issues, then it can be counterproductive to try to care for your body in other ways. It's like trying to drive in first gear on a highway—pretty soon your engine will give out. (If you would like to watch some videos to better understand how your thyroid functions, check out the *The Doctor's Farmacy* podcast, episode #603, titled "How to Treat the Root Cause of Thyroid Problems.") To get professional help, consider finding a functional medicine practitioner. If you would like to explore functional medicine, go to the website for the Institute for Functional Medicine (*www.ifm.org*) and select the link for *Find a Practitioner.* Then enter your zip code to find a provider near you.

PARTNERING WITH YOUR BODY

Can you recall a time when you weren't perpetually exhausted? Other than vacation, when have you felt well fed, well rested, and completely energized? Remember, it's not sustainable to function on fumes and live from one vacation to another. It doesn't solve the problem, and you're only setting up your body for massive energy drains that will lead you to burnout or worse yet, to developing a physical health crisis.

With the epidemic of burnout sweeping our world, please reconsider what accomplishment and success truly mean. Rather than overriding your physical signals, are you willing to listen attentively and partner with your own body first?

Until now, you may have performed to meet outside expectations. That's important. By also listening within, you'll receive important clues from your body that lead to biological harmony with your environment. As you honor the signals your body is sending, you can maximize *feeling good* as you *do good* in the world. This requires a new perspective, one that includes your own health and wellness.

Imagine what feeling good on a physical level everyday would feel like and allow you to do in the world:

- How would it feel to jump out of bed excited to start your day?

- How differently might you respond to stress at work?

- How would it be to experience vitality, energy, and connection with your loved ones?

- How would it change your mood?

- How would it feel to have the energy to explore your dreams?

Developing a new relationship with your body will change everything. Since we've already established that what *got you here* likely isn't going to get you *where you want to go*, it's time to ask yourself, are you pushing through your body or are you partnering with it?

How you nourish, rest, and work your body directly affects the health of your adrenals and thyroid. Without those two functioning at optimal levels, your journey is bound, at some point, to hit a dead end.

To heal burnout, you need regular practices that will recharge you and create a net gain of energy, helping your stress-fighting organs heal so they work for you rather than against you. That is what a partnership with your body looks like.

Investing in feeling physically well and creating biological homeostasis has a ripple efffect on every other aspect of your life. In the next few chapters, you will gain clarity around what physical self-care can support you, specifically in regard to nutrition, sleep and movement.

CHAPTER 6

FOOD AS FUEL

When I say that paying attention to your food, hydration, sleep, and movement are foundational to strengthening your physical energy, I'm not telling you anything you don't already know. Yet *knowing* can be a world apart from *doing*.

You know the drill: the day starts by waking up not feeling rested, so you hit snooze a few more times than you'd like. Getting everyone fed and out the door sometimes means that you skip breakfast yourself. With 30 seconds to spare, you arrive at your meeting feeling exhausted—and it's only 9 a.m.

If you're at the office, maybe you brush past a frazzled colleague, avoiding eye contact so you don't have to engage. While struggling to remember key data for a presentation, you spill coffee on your keyboard—and by 2 p.m., your stomach is growling, so you grab a pastry from the break room. The rest of the day is spent working on ironing out unexpected complications to finalize a project. You are the last to arrive to pick up your tearful child, who takes an oath of silence all the way home. Feeling energy-depleted, you think, *Today was rough. I can barely get my job done, not to mention, I'm the worst parent in the world. I'm not working out or cooking tonight. We all deserve a treat.* To reward yourself for getting through the day, you make a pit stop to grab a pepperoni pizza and two liters of soda. An hour after dinner, your energy crashes. And finally, as your head hits the pillow, you feel tired and wired, begging your mind to shut off about all that needs to happen tomorrow—only to hit snooze again in a few short hours.

If your life feels like *Groundhog Day*, please know it doesn't have to be that way. You have the power to break the cycle. And when you do, a day spent feeling rested, energized, and satiated will be nothing out of the ordinary for you.

You can improve many of the physical symptoms of burnout by simply paying attention to your nutrition. We seldom make the connection between how we *fuel* and how we *feel*. How well we nourish our bodies affects us not only physically but also on a mental, emotional, social, and spiritual level. If you're a parent, you are well aware of the euphoria-followed-by-meltdown your little one experiences after consuming cupcakes, ice cream, and the innards of a piñata. (Psst, parents: if it's true for your kids, it's true for you, too).

WHEN FOOD IS ON THE BACK BURNER

As toddlers, we were naturally tuned in to our physical needs. And those around us were acutely aware of the consequences of ignoring those needs. When we got hangry, cranky, tired, or unreasonable, it wasn't rocket science—we just needed a snack, a burp, a nap, or a poop. As we grew into adults, we were socialized to be polite. We adapted our internal physiology to what was happening in our external environment. We needed to wait until the meeting was over to take a restroom break. An extreme example of this comes to mind from my internal medicine residency days. We used to sarcastically say to one another, "Eat when you can, sleep when you can, pee when you can," as if it were normal that our biology should be secondary to anything else happening in the hospital.

Surprisingly, I wasn't taught to prioritize prevention, wellness, or optimal health in my medical training. My tenure at SUNY Buffalo medical school from 1994 to 1998 was primarily focused on disease and the physiological breakdown of the human body. I received a total of four hours of training in "nutrition." Two of those hours were dedicated to learning how to bypass the digestive system in a patient who had just undergone abdominal surgery and provide them with intravenous (IV) nutrition, called total parenteral nutrition (TPN). We jokingly referred to our patient's TPN bags—the white liquid hung in plastic bags flowing steadily into their veins—as IV hamburgers and milkshakes, and made comments to one another such as, "We would be more efficient if we just prescribed ourselves TPN. That way we wouldn't have to waste so much time chewing and eating."

We spent the remaining two hours of nutritional education learning how to insert a nasogastric tube (NG tube) down the throat of a patient who recently had a stroke and couldn't swallow. I guess our nutritional training was more about bypassing the body's digestive system, rather than learning how to leverage its miraculous healing powers.

So naturally, when patients would ask me about food, supplements, and the latest information on how to detoxify their bodies, I dismissed their questions and hoped it was a passing fad. I remember once actually saying out loud, "It doesn't really matter what you eat."

Yep, you read that right. With a straight face, I told my patients that what they put in their bodies—three to five times a day—wasn't that important. Truthfully, at the time, I didn't know any better. For decades, what I put into my own body was an afterthought.

Thanks to my patients' repeated inquiries about how nutrition might help them, I began wondering what role nutrition had played in the demise of my own health. I eventually made the time to attend a five-day workshop titled "Food as Medicine." I learned about Dr. Mark Hyman's detoxification program where he had done preliminary research with 1,000 patients (noted in the research as N=1,000). They completed his medical symptoms questionnaire (MSQ) and then followed his 10-day nutritional program, which included eliminating processed and prepackaged meals, gluten, diary, caffeine and sugar. And instead, they began easing whole foods and hydrating with herbal teas and lemon water. After 10 days, they reported a 62 percent reduction in symptoms. I was astonished. (You can find the MSQ and his exact program in his book *The Blood Sugar Solution: 10-Day Detox Diet*).

I wondered if food could actually change the symptoms that I had begun to tolerate as normal: post-nasal drip, difficulty sleeping, fatigue, reflux, constipation, and midsection weight gain. Even post-burnout, I didn't recognize these symptoms as anything out of the ordinary. They were simply part of modern-day life. But what if that wasn't actually true?

WHAT'S WITH GLUTEN AND DAIRY?

I understood why Dr. Hyman was asking me to cut out processed foods, caffeine, and sugar (you'll learn more about those). But how was I going to part with my morning bagel, cream cheese, and chai latte?

I wanted to better understand what gluten was and why it mattered. I learned that gluten is a protein naturally found in wheat, barley, spelt, rye, triticale, and kamut. In the latter part of the twentieth century, to improve yield, the farming industry began to produce hybrid varieties of wheat. In conjunction with that, over the last 50 years, there was also a dramatic rise—400 percent—in celiac disease and nonceliac gluten sensitivity affecting 8 percent of the population.[1]

It turns out our "modern gluten" has been shown to cause symptoms such as fatigue, brain fog, headaches, depression, allergies, sinus problems, irritable bowel disease, reflux, joint pain, skin diseases (acne, eczema), and autoimmune diseases.[2]

Dairy? I could live the rest of my life happily eating only cheese and ice cream. The thought of giving them up for 10 days was the biggest barrier. I needed a good reason. Well, it was waiting for me. To my dismay, I learned dairy was linked to congestion, post-nasal drip, sinus problems, eczema, asthma, acne, irritable bowel syndrome, constipation, and rheumatoid arthritis.[3] Consoling myself that it was only temporary, I decided to take the leap, embark on *my own experiment* (what I refer to as N=1), and follow Dr. Hyman's 10-day detox program.

My energy returned. My reflux disappeared. I slept better. My post-nasal drip went away. My bowel movements became regular. I lost five pounds and felt better overall. I went from being a skeptic to being a believer.

MY N=1 RESISTANCE

To say I was surprised is an understatement. Not by the dramatic results—as much as how difficult it was for me to accept that *something so basic was foreign to me*. I was baffled as to why I had experienced so much resistance to the idea of food as medicine (or poison) for my biology. On top of that, how could such foundational ideas not be mainstream?

As I journaled and spoke to colleagues, I recognized that over my lifetime there had been a gradual, yet dramatic, shift of *where I placed my trust*. I had somehow lost connection to the wisdom of my young self that innately trusted my body and tuned in to my physical needs—eating when I was hungry and resting when I was tired.

Somewhere along the way, I had made the seismic shift to relying solely on **external data** (my training, education, other people's opinions, and double-blinded placebo-controlled trials with large numbers, such as N=10,000 participants) and had forgotten to consider the importance of my own internal experience. I had stopped trusting N=1, my **internal data**, which included my body's signals, my lived experience, and my inner wisdom.

When making decisions, this experiment gave me a profound understanding of how important it was to include *both* external and internal data. I had grown so used to only paying attention to external data that I needed to turn up the volume of my internal data, making the sound of my own inner GPS slightly louder than the voices of those around me. Since then, I've been on a life-changing journey, exploring the link between food and physical symptoms—not only for myself but for countless others.

PUTTING FUEL IN YOUR VEHICLE

What about *you*? How easy is it to consume an entire bag of potato chips and not savor a single bite? Are you someone who finds yourself in the middle of a hectic day, suddenly realizing that you're starving? How often do you devour the nearest source of calories, simply to stop your stomach from growling?

The problem is that when you're depleted, it's hard to make good choices. In fact, it's nearly biologically impossible. How can you? You're literally in survival mode, willing to take energy from the nearest available source. Whether it's your coworker's candy jar, a bag of chips to get you through back-to-back video calls or eating cereal for dinner, you just need to get by.

When you're on the edge of burnout or perhaps burned out already, N=1 is essential when it comes to food. That's because, if you're like most people, you've probably ignored your physical energy for too long. You must become aware of your daily food choices and what might be influencing your symptoms. This will give you the power to change how you feel.

To get clear on what you're using to fuel your body, you can try a simple exercise. For three days, keep track of what you eat, snack on, and drink. No judgment. Just compassionate observation. Think of it as your very own N=1 experiment.

. . . .

If you're interested in doing a deeper dive, I've also
included a library of fantastic books, podcasts, and other
resources at *intuitiveintelligenceinc.com/pbmresources*
that will aid you on your journey.

. . . .

WHAT'S THE DEAL WITH FOOD?

Nutrition is not taught in primary education. And I am living proof that the current generation of physicians have received minimal training on the proactive role that food can play in healing. Those who are newly graduating have begun to have classes such as Food as Medicine, but nowhere near what we will need to turn this epidemic around. No wonder there's an immense amount of confusion about the importance of food in our health. Dr. Mark Hyman of Cleveland Clinic Lerner College of Medicine says:

> How food is processed and preserved has dramatically shifted over the last 50+ years, and we're only now starting to realize the impact these changes are having on our health. Without knowing it and without being told on the labels, we have been ingesting substances that disrupt our digestive system or that our body simply cannot process. Some of the biggest offenders are artificial sweeteners, high-fructose corn syrup (HFCS), and trans fats. With the increased pace of our world, the demand for packaged foods that last on the shelf, the time-saving convenience of eating out, and an onslaught of ads from the food industry, so many of us have been persuaded into eating simply to ingest calories rather than to nourish and heal our bodies. One thing is for sure— all calories are not created equal.

That's interesting, considering many weight-loss programs count *only* calories or points, rather than paying attention to the quality of the nutrition being ingested. Obviously 100 calories from french fries have a different nutritional value and impact on your body than 100 calories from a sweet potato or broccoli.

Our reliance on heavily processed or fast foods has led us to eating calorie-rich, nutrient-poor foods that send our bodies the wrong biochemical signals. Instead of providing the nutrients that run our metabolic machinery efficiently and effectively, the information being provided leads to dysfunction and disease. The fact that two-thirds of all our calories come from only four food sources—corn, soy, wheat, and rice—contributes to this. Also, a lack of biodiversity in our food is leading to more nutritional deficiencies—which results in an enormous energy drain.

With so much conflicting information on nutrition, it's easy to be confused. Let's start with some general guidelines that support your biology and have helped me, my colleagues, and thousands of patients nourish our bodies. There is plenty of data about the foundational foods that enable the body to heal and function optimally. Rather than categorizing foods as "good" or "bad" or feeling deprived, reframe the experience of eating and turn yourself into a researcher, discovering what's in the learning lab of your pantry.

The following are some quick guidelines to delineate two important topics:

- What your body needs to heal

- What interferes with that process

These simple guidelines will take no more than a few minutes of your attention each day. The benefit is that in less than one month, your body will start to feel better and your stress-fighting abilities will improve. Dr. Hyman says it so simply, "Just take out the bad stuff. Put in the good stuff. And let your body do what it needs to do to bring you back into balance." Let's break that down into some practical steps.

1. Take Out the Unhealthy

Begin by eliminating three items: HFCS, trans fats, and sugar. (The first two aren't even real foods.) HFCS bypasses your biological feedback loops; increases cholesterol, triglycerides, and blood pressure; and causes insulin resistance,[4] which can lead to obesity, heart disease, diabetes, and cancer.

HFCS can be found in everything from ketchup to pancake mix. (Just read the ingredients on any box or squeeze bottle in your pantry.) The average person consumes approximately 73.5 pounds of HFCS per year. This sweetening preservative is easy to find. Sometimes it's listed as HFCS or simply as corn syrup. Of course, if you cook your own food, you bypass HFCS altogether.

Trans fats are liquid oils turned solid to preserve the shelf life of foods indefinitely. The most well-known version is Crisco, but the secret to finding them is knowing that any hydrogenated or partially hydrogenated oil is a trans fat. According to Harvard Medical School, trans fats increase harmful

LDL cholesterol, reduce beneficial HDL cholesterol, create inflammation, and contribute to insulin resistance. For every 2 percent of calories from trans fats consumed daily, the risk of heart disease rises by 23 percent. Trans fats have been banned in some countries as well as in certain US cities due to their well-researched harmful effects.[5]

Don't trust the "Trans Fat Free!" hype on food labels or the nutrition facts on the side of boxes. If you want to know what's really in your food, you *must* look at the ingredients list.

In 2006, the food industry and the government struck a deal—if something had less than 0.5 g/serving of trans fat, the product could be advertised as having 0 grams of trans fat or trans fat free! To outsmart the new rule and avoid changing any of the ingredients in their products, some food manufacturers merely doubled the number of servings on the outside of the box. If, for example, a product with 5 servings had 1 gram/serving of trans fat, the food manufacturers kept the recipe identical, but changed the exterior packaging to say the same product contained 10 servings, hoping you wouldn't notice.

How do you detect when there's trans fat in a product that advertises 0 grams of trans fat? Easy! By taking a few seconds to read the actual ingredients list. Look for any hydrogenated or partially hydrogenated oils.

Other Oils to Stay Away From

More recently, the elevated use of a category of vegetable oils (derived from seeds like canola or rapeseed, safflower, cottonseed, corn, soybean, peanut, grapeseed, and palm) while OK in small amounts can contribute to various symptoms and diseases when taken in larger quantities. This is the food industry's latest attempt to make food cheaper. Sadly, many restaurants use these refined oils rather than pure olive, avocado, or coconut oil. Another good option is ghee (refined butter). Keep these delicious options in mind for your own pantry.

Now about sugar. I know, I know—I love it as much as you do! Sugar has gotten you through many emergencies, propped you up during a long day or night, but let's look at the bigger picture here—namely, that the average person consumes 180 pounds of sugar per year. That's approximately a half pound per day.

Added sugar often shows up in large amounts, not just in foods, but also in drinks. Look, when you're feeling burned out, you'll take energy any way you can get it. You may even crave a sugar-caffeine buzz in the form of a Red Bull, a grande caramel latte, or my former favorite, an ice-cold 16-ounce Mountain Dew.

The problem is—what gets you out of a crisis can have longer term, unintended consequences. The short-term boost of sugar causes your adrenal glands to work harder and raises your insulin and cortisol levels, contributing to belly fat. Did you know that abdominal fat increases your risks of metabolic disturbances, heart disease, and type II diabetes?[6]

Often, we know when we're consuming a ton of sugar, like the 39 grams of sugar in one can of soda. But sometimes, sugar can be hidden in what seem like "natural" or "healthy" options. For example, instead of grabbing a soda, you might want to be healthy and choose a juice drink instead. Unfortunately, this choice could have you downing a whopping 40 grams of sugar! Don't let advertising and the nature picture on the label fool you.

When you're working to improve your body's physical energy, it's important to read labels and know what nutritional fuel you're choosing. Discover the hidden forms of sugar in your food by looking on the ingredient label for items ending in -ose, such as maltose, sucrose, and dextrose, or sugar alcohols, which typically end in -ol, such as xylitol, mannitol, or sorbitol. These items can contribute to symptoms of gas, bloating, or loose stools. These hidden ingredients can seem surprising at first, but now you have the information you need to avoid getting tricked by marketing gimmicks.

Some less obvious culprits are white rice, white bread, and white pasta, which, once in your system, are immediately processed into sugar. These fluctuations in your blood sugar levels may give you quick energy in the short term, but will deplete your energy and health in the long run.

2. Put in the Healthy

On the simplest level, focus on adding healthy carbs, healthy proteins, and healthy fats to your daily regimen. By "healthy," I mean clean, whole, unprocessed foods that come directly from nature.

To get started easily and ward off emergency snacking, carry good food with you. No matter where you find yourself—in an office, on a plane, at school, or in your own home—having healthy, delicious snack options readily available is a must. Combine a healthy fat, carb, and protein, just like you would in a meal, to keep your blood sugar and energy consistent throughout the day.

Here are a few of my favorites:

- **Fresh fruit and nuts,*** such as apples with nut butter (pecan butter or crunchy almond-hazelnut butter are tasty) or a banana with a handful of raw almonds

- **Fresh veggies with hummus or guacamole**

- **Black or green olives**

- **Sliced avocado** drizzled with fresh lemon juice and sprinkled with sunflower seeds

- **Grass-fed beef jerky** (alone or with nuts, olives, or cut veggies)

* If you're curious about the sugar in your fruit, that's what the nuts are for! Eating fruit in combination with protein helps slow down the release of sugar in your system. And yes, fruit is Mother Nature's sugar, so pay attention to how much you consume.

. . . .

Healthy Options

Here are some general categories that will hopefully spark a few new ideas:

HEALTHY CARBS
(the largest food group many of us eat)

- Whole grains (amaranth, quinoa, brown rice, bulgur, millet, buckwheat, steel cut oats, Bhutanese red rice, to name a few)

- Fruit

- Vegetables

- Beans

- Nuts (also a good source of protein and fat)

- Seeds (also a good source of protein and fat)

HEALTHY PROTEINS

Animal Protein (organic, pasture-raised, or grass-fed)
- Eggs

- Meat

- Poultry

- Fish

Plant Protein
- Legumes (beans, lentils, peas)

- Nuts (almonds, pistachios, walnuts, hazelnuts)

- Seeds (chia, hemp, pumpkin, sesame, sunflower, flax)

HEALTHY FATS

- Fish

- Olives and olive oil

- Coconut

- Avocado

These high-quality foods provide many vitamins, minerals, and anti-oxidants. Ironically, food manufacturers try to fortify their processed foods with these same nutrients to make them seem more natural and healthy.

One easy way to be confident that you're getting a wide variety of nutrients from plants on your plate is if you look down and see a colorful rainbow of fruits and vegetables. They will work to power your metabolic machinery, helping you think clearly, maintain consistent energy throughout the day, and even sleep soundly.

. . . .

Fun Fact

Have you ever noticed that nourishing whole foods, such as fruits, vegetables, and proteins, are located around the perimeter of the grocery store, while processed and packaged items tend to be placed in the center aisles? When shopping, think about how much time you'll save if you don't have to go up and down every single aisle.

. . . .

Shifting how you think about food can sometimes feel overwhelming. It's a big commitment to change how you shop, how you cook, and what you eat. Start small and use what you've learned here as a guide to make your next shopping list. Once you're accustomed to eating and shopping along these lines, then focus on adding some organic foods and fiber (nuts, seeds, avocados, berries, and whole grains). For more on which foods are most important to buy organic, see Figure 6.1 below.

FIGURE 6.1 Organic Versus Nonorganic

DIRTY DOZEN Eat Organic: These 12 fruits and vegetables are the highest priority to eat organic.	THE CLEAN 15 Eat Nonorganic: These 15 fruits and vegetables are safer to buy nonorganic.
Strawberries Spinach Nectarines Apples Grapes Peaches Cherries Pears Tomatoes Celery Potatoes Peppers	Avocados Sweet corn Pineapple Cabbages Onions Sweet peas frozen Papayas Asparagus Mangoes Eggplants Honeydew melons Kiwis Cantaloupes Cauliflower Broccoli

DETOX: TAKING OUT THE TRASH

One reason your body may be stressed is that it has not been properly detoxed. The word "detox" may make you think of anything between drug rehab and a green smoothie. I'm happy to tell you that what I'm talking about is your body's natural process of *taking out the trash*. Being a reliable partner to your body and helping it with its daily chores are especially important when you've experienced prolonged stress, which causes your body's natural biological systems to get bogged down.

On the most basic level, your cells require certain nutrients and must eliminate waste to function properly. So, who's tasked with taking out the daily trash for all 37.2 trillion cells in your body? Lucky for you, Mother Nature's got it handled. Your body's waste management system has five main pathways, and you can actively engage with each of them to ensure they are operating optimally:

- **Lungs.** Your lungs breathe in fresh oxygen and exhale carbon dioxide. If you take deep, slow breaths throughout the day, exhaling completely, you'll be amazed how much clearer your mind will be. This is your body's life force. Remember, in Chapter 4, you learned soft belly breathing, which is great for this!

- **Kidneys.** Your kidneys help filter your blood and as a byproduct, create urine. Drinking plenty of water will help your body flush out any toxicity you've taken in, whether it's caffeine, alcohol, medications, and more. If drinking water seems like a drag, jazz it up with a slice of cucumber, fresh mint, lemon, or lime!

- **Colon.** Your large intestine serves as a holding container to reabsorb water and release leftover solid waste from the digestion of your food intake. Eating lots of fiber every day will make that process easier and faster.

- **Liver.** The most obvious detoxification powerhouse is the liver (in pharmacology, we spent much time learning about how it clears medications, drugs, alcohol, and other substances from the body). Refrain from overburdening your liver. If you are a good candidate, and your medical provider recommends it, you could also consider supplements to support your liver function.

- **Skin.** The largest organ of detoxification is the skin. In the hospital, we focus more commonly on the skin as the vehicle to absorb substances like nitro paste to treat a heart attack. But as much as the skin functions to absorb substances, it also detoxifies the body through sweat—a huge benefit of daily exercise! In fact, exercise accelerates four detox pathways. Think about it: when you move your body, you breathe more deeply, drink more water, sweat it out, and just by moving around, your poop moves closer to the exit door too!

A little-known tip: bookend your days with a boost in the morning and a detox at night. For example, in the morning, I make a delicious rainbow smoothie to give me a steady flow of energy. Here's the recipe in case you'd like to try it yourself:

Rainbow Smoothie

½ cup water (or decaf green tea)
1 cup nondairy milk (hemp, almond or coconut)
1–2 tablespoons chia seeds, whole or ground
¼ teaspoon cinnamon
⅛ teaspoon ginger (dried or fresh)
½ cup frozen blueberries
½ cup frozen strawberries
½ cup frozen mangoes
1 cup packed favorite greens
½ cup ice to thicken (optional)

Blend to desired thickness and enjoy!

And at night, I either soak my feet in hot water (while watching my favorite show) or take a relaxing hot bath to unwind and release any toxins. You'll find how I create this spa-like ritual in the next chapter on sleep.

If you're ready to support your body and clear the overload of stress and waste in your system, there's another N=1 experiment you can try at home. Write down any physical symptoms you're experiencing and give them each a level of intensity from 1 to 10, where 1 is very infrequently with a low level of intensity and 10 is consistent with a high level of intensity. After 10 days of removing unhealthy ingredients, eating nourishing foods, and better supporting your natural detox pathways, do the same physical inventory exercise again. What's changed? (For those who are interested, you can find more information in Dr. Mark Hyman's book *The Blood Sugar Solution: 10-Day Detox Diet*, the plan I followed back in the day.) I can't think of a less invasive, more cost-effective way to reduce symptoms and elevate your physical energy.

For those of you who are ready for a deeper dive, you may have heard about an ancient Indian science of health and well-being called Ayurveda. This discipline believes in the inherent wisdom of the human body to repair, regenerate, and heal itself. Ayurveda describes our increasing pace of life, lack of sleep, use of technology, and consumption of processed food as a few causes of stress that create an imbalance in our natural waste management system, resulting in a variety of diseases. Ayurveda is built on the principle of eating the right combinations of foods while also accelerating your body's pathways of detoxification in order to bring you back into balance, followed by proper rejuvenation. I personally spent a life-changing three weeks at an Ayurvedic Centre Sitaram Beach Retreat in Kerala, India with Vignesh Devraj, MD, and experienced this profound healing practice myself to reduce inflammation and optimize my body's physiology. If the healing art of Ayurveda intrigues you, I highly recommend it.

WHAT ABOUT SUPPLEMENTS?

Supplements are a $159-billion industry and growing. There's a lot of controversy around their quality and usefulness because supplements aren't regulated in the same way that pharmaceutical drugs are. As a physician, my initial concerns included:

Do supplements really work?

Do they just create expensive urine?

Is this a way for doctors to make extra money?

I hate to sound like a broken record, but why didn't anyone mention this in medical school? Well, that last question wasn't entirely true. In conventional medicine, we focus on the extremes—too much or too little—and pay much less attention to the middle—what's optimal. For example, we were tested only on what diseases resulted from extreme depletion of a nutrient, such as how a severe lack of vitamin D leads to rickets or osteoporosis. Once again, our attention remained focused on crisis care. But since we can address signs of depletion and fatigue earlier, why *wouldn't* we?

Supplements are just that, they supplement your healthy food choices and are especially needed today because of the nutrient depletion in our soils and the fact that there is a lot more trash for our bodies to take out (the chemicals we're exposed to in our environment, including those in processed foods, plastics, personal care products, etc.).

Supplements are a simple way to provide your body with what it might not be getting from your lifestyle and food choices. Supplements are not an excuse to *not eat healthy*, they just support your digestive system in doing its enormous job.

A lot of research has been done around supplements, but make sure you check *who conducted the research* and *who funded it*. Since this is an unregulated industry, all brands are definitely not created equal. The following are some important ways to recognize high-quality supplements:

- They are manufactured at drug manufacturing levels.

- They have third-party independent verification, so that someone else has verified that *what the bottle says is in it is actually in it!* For more guidance on evaluating supplements, see the fact sheet "Dietary Supplements: What You Need to Know" from the National Institutes of Health.[7]

  - At the very least, minimum standards of certification include GMP (Good Manufacturing Practices) and USP (United States Pharmacopoeia).

  - If you have any questions, check *www.consumerlab.com*.

- Use clean products, meaning they are free of fillers, binders, coloring agents, and lactose (e.g., dairy).

- Make sure the products have some basis in science, have been studied in clinical trials, or have a long history of use without adverse side effects. Don't jump on the latest fad.

At a minimum, you'll likely need these three supplements:

1. A quality multivitamin and mineral combination

2. An absorbable magnesium and vitamin D, which keep bones strong and reduce bone loss as we age

3. An omega-3 fatty acid (fish oil) to help improve brain and heart health

Always ask your doctor or provider to do the tests to figure out if you have optimal levels of all the basic nutrients you need to thrive. WARNING: as I've mentioned, conventional physicians are excellent practitioners when your body breaks down—that's acute crisis care—so unless your provider has invested in additional training or has a deep passion for wellness and prevention, they may not be the most up-to-date on how to upgrade your body to become a high-performance vehicle. For chronic conditions and to optimize my health, I consult functional medicine practitioners who have been trained as traditional health professionals and in addition, have completed two more years of training focused on the nuances of optimizing your biochemistry. As I mentioned in Chapter 5, to locate a functional medicine provider near you, go to *ifm.org* and put in your zip code. If you're unable to find the right provider, Cleveland Clinic has an entire functional medicine department.

Based on my personal N=1 experience and treating patients with this approach, quite frankly, it's astounding that conventional medicine has not yet made the connection between our food and our health. Luckily, they are slowly waking up.

Speaking of waking up, I will tackle the importance of good sleep in the next chapter.

CHAPTER 7

SLEEP YOUR WAY TO HEALTH

D o you think sleep is a waste of time? If so, you're right—specifically if you're referring to what's *not* getting done on your *external* to-do list. After all, when you're slumbering, your inbox is expanding. Here's what you might not know: your body has its own *inner* to-do list. And over time, with the absence of sufficient sleep, the body is unable to recover and slides down the slippery slope of burnout.

Your body can likely handle one poor night of sleep, but as soon as you slip into a regular cycle of insufficient sleep, you end up with a deficient biological ecosystem that cannot easily be repaid. If you or someone you love has ever had to cope with credit card debt, you're familiar with this never-ending struggle. Trust me, paying down the interest on your sleep is just as challenging.

When was the last time you had a good night's rest? Do you hear yourself saying, "Well, it looks like it's going to be another late night?" or "I'll just catch up on my sleep over the weekend?" Whatever the case, if feeling tired and exhausted has become the norm, you may not even question it anymore.

For so many of us, sleep deprivation has become a way of life. According to the Centers for Disease Control and Prevention (CDC), an estimated 50 to 70 million Americans suffer from ongoing sleep issues and a whopping 1 in 3 adults have reported not getting enough sleep every day.[1] Whether you're burning the midnight oil to meet critical deadlines, managing young children afraid of the dark, or finding yourself up at night feeling anxious, your adrenal glands are likely on overdrive and you're experiencing a depletion of the precious energy your body needs to function optimally.

You've heard me describe a few of my past coping mechanisms—add *not sleeping enough* to the list. Working 36-hour shifts as a hospital physician was a major physical energy drain. But at the time, I wasn't concerned about the long game; I was just trying to get through the day (I mean, night). Worse, I had judgments about people who took proper care of themselves by getting enough rest like, *There's so much to be done. How can you be focusing on yourself right now?* And just like that, my mind bullied my body into believing that my inner world (lethargy and brain fog included) didn't hold the same importance as my outer world (taking care of my to-do list and patients).

Do *you* judge people who prioritize sleep as lacking drive or, worse yet, lazy? Often, how you relate to sleep goes back to your childhood and the relationship your parents or caretakers had with their own sleep. Was bedtime a sacred ritual with storytelling and cuddles? Or were there few rules around bedtime? Were you made to feel guilty for sleeping in? When I was young, I remember my parents wanting me to get out of bed and not waste the day. When I slept in, I felt guilty, like I was being a slacker.

If these attitudes and habits sound all too familiar, it's important to understand how vital rest is to your overall wellness. Sleep is not a frivolous activity or a nuisance. It's a non-negotiable step toward your health and healing. You will burn out without proper rest.

CALLING IN THE EXPERT

I'm not an expert on sleep. And if there's anything I've learned since my recovery from burnout, it's to *ask for help* when I need it. So I reached out to my dear friend Dr. Param Dedhia. I thought I was a good Indian child, but Param has me beat. He started out as a physician, educator, and researcher at Johns Hopkins, until he followed his passion to become an integrative health physician and director of Sleep Medicine, Obesity Medicine, and Executive Health at Canyon Ranch. Since then, he's gone on to create a private practice and a platform to share insights on health, longevity, and sleep.

Over the past 15 years, Param and I have had many in-depth conversations about the value of sleep, so I'm going to give it to you straight from the expert's mouth.

QUESTION 1: WHY DO WE NEED SLEEP, ANYWAY?

"Many of us mistakenly think that sleep gets in the way of our productivity. Nothing could be farther from the truth," Param says. "So much magic happens while we're sleeping. Sleep honors us physically, mentally, emotionally, socially, and spiritually—every single night."

While you're sleeping, here's what's happening:

- **Physically:** The body produces growth hormones, testosterone, and other proteins to perform cellular repair and build immunity to fight infection.

- **Mentally:** You're integrating your experiences from the day and committing them to memory. Quality sleep resets your mental clarity and focus so that you can be fully present to tackle the next day.

- **Emotionally:** While you sleep, your body flushes the limbic system of the brain, literally processing and letting go of challenging emotions so you can meet the next day with an expansive and open heart.

- **Socially:** A good night's sleep allows you to feel rested so you can be present for others in your waking hours.

- **Spiritually:** When fully rested, you have access to your creativity and the desire to explore what gives your life deeper meaning and purpose.

According to Param:

"What's important to remember biologically is that while you sleep, you're doing three important functions:

1. Repairing your muscles and immune system

2. Consolidating your memory

3. Emotionally processing the experiences of the day

The invention of electricity changed our sleep patterns. It allowed us to stay awake long after sunset. So our days are longer and nights are shorter.

If we force ourselves to stay awake longer than we should, a drag in our performance and mood usually follows. That's because chronic sleep deprivation alters the brain's executive functioning and consequently alters performance, making it more likely we'll make errors, from something simple, like forgetting to respond to a text message, to something harmful, like getting into a car accident."

Think about what happens when you get sick. All you want to do is lie in bed and sleep, which is exactly what our bodies need to do.

"Even when we aren't sick, we have the opportunity to heal while we sleep," Param highlights. "We improve our heart health, our mental performance and memory, our emotional stability, our creativity, and our capacity to be present for others."

Quantity

"For the vast majority of adults, the ideal amount of sleep is seven to nine hours. That allows enough time to go through the body's sleep cycles in order to recover," he continued. "There are exceptions—but you'd be amazed at the number of people who think they are the 10 percent exception. And to them I say, 'OK, you can get by with less, but why not give yourself the gift of a little more as an experiment to see how you feel?'"

Seven to nine hours may feel like a lot, especially between working and caring for family, making time to exercise, and *finally* doing something to relax at the end of the day. Who has time to squeeze in that much sleep?

Param says, "Simply move in the direction of health by adding an additional half or full hour of sleep." So if you're used to getting five hours of sleep, try five and a half or six hours. Then pay attention to how you feel and perform.

"You may not feel all the benefits from a single night of optimal sleep," Param cautions. "Give yourself at least 10–14 days of more sleep and you'll likely notice a positive change."

Just like a 10-day detox diet, it's a no-risk, low-cost, high-yield, N=1 experiment with your body.

Quality

While it's relatively easy to tell how *long* you're sleeping, it's harder to tell how *well* you're sleeping. Unless you're lying awake most of the night staring at the ceiling, you may think your sleep quality is bad if you're not sleeping for seven or eight hours straight. But that's actually not the goal.

"It's natural to wake up briefly multiple times a night and not even be aware it's happening. And by that, I mean just a brief arousal, where you momentarily wake up to reposition or roll over, not lying awake for hours counting sheep," Param explains.

QUESTION 2: WHAT DOES IT MEAN TO GET QUALITY SLEEP?

Param says:

> Quality means allowing for all stages each night—none of them are optional. Each cycle lasts for 90 to 120 minutes, and in between these cycles are when brief wake-ups may occur.
>
> There are two types of sleep stages:
>
> 1. Rapid eye movement (REM)
>
> 2. Non-rapid eye movement (NREM)
>
> NREM is further divided into three stages—N1, N2, and N3— and each is associated with certain brain activity. None of these stages is a luxury! Each is incredibly important to your body's ability to function optimally over time.

Stages of Sleep

Here are the stages of sleep.

NREM

- **N1: Transitional / Light Sleep.** This stage is when you move from wakefulness to sleep. It is very brief. You are in between being awake and being asleep. This is when you really start to unwind and relax into falling asleep.

- **N2: Light Sleep.** This stage does a little bit of everything from head to toe: the muscles relax, the heart rate and breathing rate slow, and your body temperature starts to dip. Brain activity begins slowing down. Your organs start to repair after working all day. Don't make the mistake of thinking light sleep doesn't count.

- **N3: Deep Sleep.** This stage is when greater repair and regrowth occur. This is when your body's doing all that hard work to repair any sore muscles from physical work or exercise, and clearing, strengthening, and upgrading your immune system. Memory consolidation occurs as well, allowing you to retain all that you've learned throughout the day.

REM

- **Dreaming.** Dreams are incredibly important for processing challenging emotions. So that festering anger at a snarky colleague, your disappointment at not getting a raise, that car that cut you off today— all of that gets released during your dreams.

Param continues, "If you don't get quality sleep, you are missing out on some stages. And if you're sleep deprived, your body can rearrange the order of these stages. Your REM cycle can start sooner because your body wants to prioritize clearing heavy emotions, before it gets to physical repair. And get this, if the body has to choose between physical healing and emotional processing, *emotions are the higher priority*." That's why a lack of sleep is harder on your physical body and undermines your immune function's ability to fight infection.

"Over time, eventually, *all* the stages of sleep will suffer. Your memory and thought processes won't be as effective, your immune function will decline, and your emotions—well, let's just say, you'll be much more irritable, quick to anger, or even weepy. It's different for everyone."

QUESTION 3: WHAT ARE THE BARRIERS TO GOOD SLEEP?

Before anything else, you need to address any potential physical issues, like sleep apnea, restless leg syndrome, pain, hormonal shifts, or bladder issues. Once you've dealt with those, then you can move on to other common hindrances. On average, the two issues Param sees most often are, first, not planning your days to include your sleep and, second, expecting sleep to arrive like a present from Santa.

"Start with planning your entire day as an integrated experience," he advises.

As humans, we're meant to be *diurnal*. That is to say, despite living in a world that is running 24/7, we're not *nocturnal*. It's not normal for us to be staying up late or working the night shift. Unfortunately, getting to sleep early is not always an option. Physiologically, we function best when we follow a routine, falling asleep and waking at a consistent time each day.[2] All of which comes down to circadian rhythms. In fact, the 2017 Nobel Prize was given to the scientists who unveiled circadian rhythms.

Traditional Chinese medicine and Ayurvedic medicine have always prioritized the timing of sleep, but Western medicine has only begun to publish it over the past 20+ years. Think of your circadian rhythm as your internal clock, regulating your 24-hour wake-sleep cycle. There are a series of hormones, such as cortisol and other chemicals in the body that cause you to wake up each morning and help you fall asleep each night. Your need for sleep *increases* over the course of the day and *decreases* overnight, which causes you to wake up in the morning.

Biologically, our sleep is supposed to mirror the rise and fall of the sun. Not surprisingly, exposure to artificial light can disrupt your circadian rhythm and adversely impact your sleep drive. I also have a tendency to want to stay up late and get up late, but it's not good for my sleep cycle.

Pushing yourself to stay awake and ignoring your body when it tells you it's tired are going to negatively impact your physical energy, your focus, your ability to fight infection, and your overall health.

Though an ideal sleep schedule varies from person to person, Param suggests going to bed between the hours of 9 and 11 p.m. and waking up between 6 and 8 a.m. Routine and consistency are the key to developing good sleep habits. Set a wake time and bedtime that you can follow, and then stick to them (gradually adding more time if you've been in the habit of sleeping less than seven hours). As you adjust, don't be surprised if it takes a while to actually fall asleep. Drifting off requires transition; you can't force it.

"Busy people expect to just lie down and magically drift into slumber," Param comments. "Especially if they've been struggling with a sleep deficit for some time. Their bodies need their help because they aren't used to falling asleep easily. I like to think of going to sleep as tapering off from the day. Unless you're so exhausted you absolutely collapse, you don't automatically shift from your *world of doing* into a *world of dreaming*. It's more natural to ease your way there. To taper, choose activities or habits that help you wind down, rather than rev up."

QUESTION 4: HOW DO WE GET BETTER SLEEP?

"It's a matter of partnering with your biology and preparing for both the days *and* nights," Param says.

Daytime

Here are some quick tips that will guide you during the daytime to help you sleep better:

- **Sunlight.** Whatever your preferred clock, get exposure to bright light first thing in the morning. This triggers a cascade of brain chemicals to promote energy and wakefulness. Conversely, at the end of the day, it's best to limit light exposure as darkness triggers the release of melatonin and other chemicals that help you fall asleep.

- **Exercise.** You may be surprised to know that getting *30 minutes of daily physical exercise* is also critical to keeping your circadian rhythm balanced. Movement releases more adenosine, which goes to your brain and helps you sleep.

- **Caffeine.** Limit your intake to the first half of the day, as many people take time to clear caffeine from their bodies. Caffeine in the second half of your day could have you making extra trips to the bathroom at night. Unfortunately, caffeine also blocks adenosine, the chemical generated from working out that promotes deeper sleep. It's a double whammy.

- **Nutrition.** Eat whole foods at regular intervals throughout the day to help maintain balanced, sustained energy. Also *eat dinner at least three hours before bedtime* to allow your body to prioritize emotional processing and detoxification, as well as cellular and immune system repair (rather than using its energy to digest a meal).

- **Emotional processing.** The very best cure for insomnia is getting to the root of your anxiety or stress. Learning to navigate challenging emotions, such as disappointment, anger, and grief will help solve your sleep issues in the long term. If you have a thought, worry, or concern, but you don't address it during the day, those stressful emotions will be waiting for you at night. Learning to forgive, accept, and let go of past grievances are powerful emotional and spiritual practices that will help you sleep better at night. Your emotional health is tied directly to your physical well-being. You may want to check out my audiobook, *TalkRx: Five Steps to Honest Conversations That Create Connection, Health, and Happiness*, which provides a practical toolkit to communicate, lean into healthy conflict, and navigate your (and other people's) emotions effectively. A variety of other approaches, such as somatic healing, Internal Family Systems (IFS) therapy, Compassionate Inquiry therapy, cognitive behavioral therapy, and group therapy are also very useful.

- **Prepare your environment.** Reducing clutter in the bedroom can help create a calm environment, as can lowering the temperature. Since each person is unique, experiment to figure out what works best for you.

Nighttime

Here are some quick tips that will guide you at night:

- **Reduce stimulation.** Avoid stimulating activity two hours before bed. (e.g., watching TV, surfing the internet, answering emails). Avoid having any kind of screen in your bedroom. Turn off all devices at least 30 minutes before bedtime. Blocking the blue light from your screens is simple and will help you sleep better. Designate your bed for sleeping and sex only.

- **Avoid substances** that can interfere with sleep, including:

  ○ Alcohol, caffeine, sugar

  ○ Antihistamines

  ○ Stimulants (e.g., Ritalin)

  ○ Steroids (e.g., Prednisone)

  ○ Headache medication (e.g., Fioricet has caffeine)

  ○ Cold medications (containing pseudoephedrine, phenylephrine)

- **Set yourself up.** Keep your bedroom completely dark with black-out shades. Or you can use a sleep mask to prevent unnecessary light from disrupting your sleep. Use ear plugs made of soft silicone to block out sound. Consider lighting some candles or playing soft music. Do whatever you need to feel more at peace.

- **Ritual.** This is probably the most important step. If you think of bedtime as tapering off the excitement of the day, a ritual will help you train your brain to recognize that it's time to relax. A sleep routine is important for your physical, mental, emotional, social, and spiritual well-being. It signals that it's time to wind down before sleep. It's as simple as relaxing your body with a detox foot bath or full bath.

Detox Bath Recipe

Fill a bucket or full bath of warm water and add:

1 cup Epsom salt (has magnesium to relax muscles)
1 cup baking soda (alkalizes your system)
10 drops of lavender essential oils (reduces cortisol levels) or eucalyptus oil (stimulates immune function, clears sinuses, prevents snoring)

- **Clear your mind.** Keep a journal and pen next to your bed so that you can:

  - Record your plans for the next day, reducing your anxiety for the morning

  - Write down any unresolved worries so that after a good night's sleep, you can come back to them at a later time

  - Jot down three experiences that happened during the day that you're grateful for

- **Sounds that soothe.** Listen to:

  - Restful music

  - White noise to help you eliminate outside sounds

  - Gentle guided imagery to help you taper off your day

- **Tea ritual.** Drink warm lemon water or a cup of chamomile tea, although not too much and not too close to bedtime, as trips to the bathroom could interrupt your sleep!

QUESTION 5: BUT WHAT IF I'M *STILL* NOT SLEEPING?

If you establish a healthy sleep routine and still can't seem to sleep well or long enough, you may need additional support. There are a number of remedies available. It can take time to find the right sleep regimen for you. I always recommend starting with the lowest dose of any treatment and working your way up as necessary. Table 7.1 offers general guidelines and is intended for educational purposes only. It's essential that you consult with your medical practitioner prior to taking them. Supplements and medications serve only as a bridge, intended to provide temporary relief for insomnia, but they're not meant for long-term use.

TABLE 7.1 **Supplements and Medications**

DRUG	WHAT IS IT?	HOW IT WORKS	SIDE EFFECTS
Melatonin	Hormone produced by the body; originally used to resolve jet lag	1 mg used for time zone shift and 3–5 mg used for hypnotic effect; under-the-tongue tabs so it enters your system quickly	Sometimes results in a hangover the next morning or very vivid dreams; most do not have quality control
5-HTP	Chemical the body makes from an amino acid called tryptophan	Lifts mood	Sometimes results in a hangover the next morning. Can cause serotonin syndrome in patients also taking SSRI antidepressant medication.
Magnesium glycinate	Relaxes twitches, cramps, and spasms; lowers stress	200–800mg/day	Too much can cause loose stools
Cannabidiol (CBD)	Cannabis has 500+ chemicals, and one of them, THC, gives a dissociative effect; CBD has anti-inflammatory effects.	Tinctures placed under the tongue; allow 15–60 minutes for efficacy. Start low and go slow. Speak to knowledgeable professionals who can educate you.	With prolonged use, there can be a reduction in REM. Note: I am not advocating smoking, vaping (inhaling hydrocarbons into lungs can be toxic), or eating as edibles (takes 2–6 hours for absorption, therefore easy to overconsume).

DRUG	WHAT IS IT?	HOW IT WORKS	SIDE EFFECTS
Antihistamine (e.g., Benadryl)	Blocks release of histamine, reducing allergy symptoms, such as watery eyes, nasal congestion, and itchy throat	Benadryl is a sedating antihistamine, which means it will likely make you drowsy.	Can last in the body for 36 hours (therefore, it is best not to use every night). It can build up fogginess in brain, bladder retention, constipation, and dryness of the nose and throat
Trazodone	At low doses, can be effective at your histamine receptors; nonaddictive sleep agent to help you fall and stay asleep; promotes deep sleep	Has a short half-life of 3–6 hours	Note: also used as an antidepressant in larger doses
Zolpidem (Ambien)	Efficacy for 4–5 hours; a non-benzodiazepine agonist	Faster onset than Lunesta	Dizziness, hallucinations, sleepwalking, and sleep-talking; with prolonged use, there can be a reduction in REM sleep
Eszopiclone (Lunesta)	Slower release and longer activity (7–8 hours); a non-benzodiazepine agonist	Slower onset than Ambien; works longer	Metallic taste; with prolonged use, there can be a reduction in REM sleep
Zaleplon (Sonata)	Short-acting (1–2 hours) non-benzodiazepine agonist	Used for sleep onset or return to sleep for middle of the night awakening	Dizziness, amnesia, imbalance, and confusion. Given rapid onset and clearance, the pharmacokinetics may set this up for fewer side effects than Ambien or Lunesta.

"So many people come to me saying, 'I've tried sleep hygiene. It didn't make a difference,'" Param said. "Then I ask them if they've gone through the steps I've outlined for them. And if so, how long did they give it? These health concerns develop over time and they also take time to resolve. It's just like with nutrition—you can't eat one salad and declare yourself a healthy eater. This is about building a new approach to your sleep." (If you're interested in learning more about your relationship with sleep and doing your own personal sleep history, please go to *intuitiveintelligenceinc.com/pbmresources*.)

As with all transformation, slow and steady wins the race. Don't try to radically change your sleep schedule overnight. It can be as simple as creating a welcoming space to rest and reward your body for a long day by giving yourself a little more time to sleep each night.

By getting a good night's sleep and listening carefully to your body, you are giving it the time it needs to complete its inner to-do list, which will not only amplify your at-work performance but also allow you to be present and engaged with those you love.

CHAPTER 8

THE JOY OF MOVEMENT

Our natural state is being in harmony with our biology and nature's rhythms. Back in our hunter-gatherer days, we were constantly on the move. We chased after prey, ran away from predators, and walked for miles in search of food and fresh water. We built shelter and carried children. We ate when we were hungry (or when we successfully found food), and we slept when we were tired or when the sun went down. But since the Industrial Revolution, physical labor has been replaced with mental labor. The plow was set aside in favor of the desk—or nowadays, the laptop and smartphone. We didn't have to make time for exercise. Staying fit was a by-product of our way of life. Unfortunately, that's no longer the case, but it doesn't mean movement is any less important for our biological well-being. In fact, it does you a world of good.

THE BENEFITS OF MOVEMENT

Research has shown that daily movement serves as a powerful brain and mood-booster, sleep-improver, and physical energy-enhancer. Exercise has important implications for our physical, mental, and emotional health. Wherever you begin making changes, it will positively impact other aspects of your health and life. All energy levels influence one another.

Here are a few fun facts that will (hopefully) inspire you to move:

- **Better night's sleep.** Exercise uses a cellular energy currency called adenosine triphosphate (ATP). When you exert yourself physically or work out, ATP breaks down into adenosine and three phosphates. That adenosine goes to your brain and promotes more sound sleep.[1]

- **Elevate your mood.** Exercise has been revealed to be as effective as antidepressants in elevating mood.[2] Thirty to forty minutes of daily exercise (jogging was most commonly studied) raises your feel-good endorphins and levels of serotonin and norepinephrine (the two neurotransmitters that most antidepressants work to increase).

- **Improve memory.** Functional magnetic resonance imaging (fMRI) studies show that 10 minutes of mild exercise resulted in immediate improved performance on a memory discrimination task and increased connectivity between the parts of the brain focused on thinking and memory.[3]

The CDC states that *everyone* benefits from a moderate amount of daily activity.[4] This activity can consist of longer time periods with lower intensity, such as brisk walking for 30 minutes, or through more intense, shorter time periods, such as 15–20 minutes of jogging or interval training.

What's important to remember is that there are three types of movement essential to long-term health and well-being:

1. **Aerobic exercise** strengthens the most important muscle in your body, your heart. The goal of aerobic movement is to elevate your heart rate to 70 to 80 percent of your maximum heart rate (MHR).*[5]

2. **Resistance training** builds strong and healthy muscles, bones, and joints. After 30 years of age, muscle mass declines by 3 to 8 percent per decade.[6] *You have to move it or you lose it.* Muscle plays an important role in metabolism as well.

3. **Flexibility** is important to stretch your muscles, increase your range of motion, and reduce injuries. Flexibility and balance become even more critical as you age, preventing falls and allowing you to remain independent.

---

* You can calculate your MHR by subtracting your age from 220.

THE CHALLENGE

When you're maxed out or burned out, exercise is usually the last thing on your mind or, on the flip side, the only survival strategy you have. I'm not going to lecture you about your wasted gym membership or your dust-covered Peloton bike. Trust me, I get it. I have to come up with all sorts of ways to trick myself into moving my body. Jogging and lifting weights sometimes feels like a form of punishment. But I'm happy to tell you that because I've struggled so much to be consistent with exercise, I've figured out a variety of ways to get my body moving that feel good and are *fun* to me.

Some lucky people naturally gravitate to exercise and movement and use it to blow off steam. It's a powerful way to recharge and boost your endorphins (the feel-good hormones that flow after a good workout). You might even be the type of person whose normal weekend activities consist of preparing to participate in triathlons, marathons, and other athletic challenges. If you have a regular movement routine, congratulations! This may be an effortless area of energy gain for you.

ALL OR NONE

So many of us approach movement like we do everything else, with an all-or-none mentality. Upon moving to California in my early thirties, I realized that I had put on 10 extra pounds that weren't coming off so easily. Mortified that I no longer fit into my favorite jeans, I signed up for the Wildflower Triathlon. I raised money for the Leukemia & Lymphoma Society and spent four months training for a 1-mile swim, 25-mile bike ride, and 6-mile run on the hilliest course in the country. I threw my poor body, which had sat in a chair, motionless for more than a decade of higher education, into the extremes of training for a triathlon. In the process, I lost those 10 pounds—but I also put unnecessary stress on my body. It's important to pay attention to consistency, as opposed to what you can brag about on social media.

Which scenario sounds most like you? Are you someone who thinks, *If I'm going to run, I'm going to run a marathon because what's the value of a 5K?* Or over time, have you become a version of yourself you don't recognize—perhaps, not moving much at all? Maybe you're somewhere in between.

To lovingly tend to this area of life, you don't have to be an ultra-marathoner or devoted yogi. All you need is a willingness to integrate movement into your life in a balanced way. Most important, honor wherever you are now.

Even if you're someone who exercises regularly, it still might be helpful to reflect on the distinction between *listening to your mind* versus *honoring when your body has had enough* and not pushing yourself to extremes. You endurance exercisers are experts at overriding your body's signals. If you're an extreme athlete, your mind might be saying something like:

I'll rest when I'm dead.

This body was made to be used.

Don't be lazy.

When you notice yourself thinking these types of all-or-none thoughts, that's the moment to pause and tune in to your body so you can stop the habit of overriding it. See what the experience is like when you make a different choice. You can expect it to feel awkward and uncomfortable at first. But take a few minutes to breathe deeply and really tune in to how your body is feeling and what it needs.

Dramatic physical signs include constantly feeling run-down, being unable to recover over the weekend, or getting sick more often than you used to. These are clear signs that your immune system and adrenals are depleted. When you're this exhausted, taxing yourself further by forcing a workout or overexercising will only exacerbate the problem.

MOVEMENT CAN BE FUN

You already work hard. You don't need more work. But I bet you could use more joy and play in your life. So why not make moving your body an activity you look forward to?

Exercise is often an opportunity to bring fun into your day, yet so many people view it as a chore or an item on their to-do list. The goal is to find movement that evolves with your body's capabilities and energizes you. If dancing is what brings you joy, why are you forcing yourself onto a treadmill or burning yourself out on CrossFit, marathons, or high-intensity boot camps? The secret is paying attention to what you're naturally drawn to.

When you were young and no one was telling you to exercise, how did you spontaneously move in your body? When I was a kid, I was a gymnast.

I must have been six or seven years old the first time I saw the magic of Nadia Comăneci using her body to defy gravity. I was spellbound by her graceful back handsprings, twists, and flips and how she effortlessly landed on the mat with chest forward and hands held high. I inquired about the possibility of my own gymnastic endeavors, and my parents enrolled me in a local Tumbling Tots program. Soon I discovered how pliable and pretzel-like I could become—doing back walkovers anywhere there was space and handstands against any wall that didn't have artwork. I fell in love with gymnastics. Even while off the mat, I would never be idly standing and talking to someone; instead, I would place all my weight on one leg and slide the other leg up to form a triangle on the side of my standing leg's knee. Sometimes, I would even show off my balancing capabilities by stretching both hands above my head, placing my palms together, and exclaiming, "Look, Mom, no hands!" It wasn't until many years later that I realized in yoga, this was called tree pose. When I was chatting with a friend, I would stretch my legs wide in front of me or go into the splits. Twisting my body into a pretzel and doing cartwheels on the lawn was exhilarating. For the next five years, I competed and brought home first-place blue ribbons at nearly every event.

As I grew in age and height, gymnastics was, unfortunately, no longer an option for me. You can imagine my delight as an adult when I discovered yoga because I still got to do the splits and headstands, just in a much more stationary way. I refer to yoga as "gymnastics for big kids"!

What about you? Was there a time in your life when you played and moved naturally in your body? What clues can that time give you about ways you might like to move now?

As a child, I also enjoyed learning ballet, tap, and jazz, so it's no wonder I love music and group dance. A few years ago, I discovered Qoya, a group class that combines yoga, free dance, and feminine movement—my version of "dancing for big kids." Qoya is done with a group of women. Ladies, if you're interested, you can find a sample Qoya class at *intuitiveintelligenceinc .com/pbmresources*.

Initially, I found myself a little self-conscious dancing in a group. But after a few classes, I let go of my self-consciousness and realized that the relational and emotional connections made the experience more exciting and energizing than when I exercised alone. I liked the variety; each class was a new experience with different music and different people. And I eventually realized that everybody was more concerned with themselves—they weren't even paying attention to me.

Is there a way to combine your favorite activities into fun forms of movement? If you aren't quite sure, go through the following questions to gain more clarity.

Partner with Your Body Exercise

Please answer a few questions to get you thinking about what will inspire you to partner with your body. Circle the answers that resonate for you.

1. **What motivates you to move?**

   Accomplishment / setting goals

   Health

   Losing weight

   Physical appearance

   Playing with kids / grandkids

   Remaining agile / flexible with age

   Other _____

2. **Who are you competitive with?**

   Yourself?   Yes   No   Sometimes

   Others?   Yes   No   Sometimes

   Yourself and others? Yes   No   Sometimes

   Other _____

3. **What settings inspire you to want to move your body?**

   Your home

   The gym

   A fitness studio

Nature / outdoors

Other _____

4. **With whom do you prefer to exercise?**

Alone

With a pet

With a trainer

With a partner / friend

With a group / team

Other _____

5. **What do you like to do while working out?**

Focus on the parts of my body I'm exercising

Let my mind rest, wander, or zone out

Socialize or talk on the phone

Listen to music or a podcast

Watch news, politics, or my favorite show

Read or study

Other _____

6a. **Do you have any injuries / limitations?**   Y / N

6b. **If you answered yes, how can you best support your body?**

A brace / supportive gear

Low-impact movement (on land or in water)

Physical therapy

Develop flexibility by stretching

Education and / or getting a trainer

Other _____

KNOWING YOUR LIMITATIONS

Of course, it's important to know your body and adjust accordingly. I learned tennis by playing with my dad every Saturday morning. In his late forties, I remember how heartbroken he was when he began experiencing discomfort in his knees. So instead, he reinvented himself and became a nonstop golfer. (My all-or-none tendencies were definitely passed down from my dad.)

Or you could be like Jacob, who was a competitive biker until, at age 65, his hips started giving out. So instead, he started kayaking and then joined thelocal rowing team. Now he has a community of septuagenarian competitive paddlers!

There are always ways to move your body, even after injuries or the challenges of aging creep in. In those difficult times, if you tap into your creativity, you'll be able to come up with inspiring options.

Take a look at some fun ways you can move your body. And circle any that catch your eye or look interesting. Trust your intuition that whatever you're drawn to is the right one to try next.

Ways to Move Your Body

When it comes to moving your body, there are various options, depending on your preferences.

INDIVIDUAL
- Cycling
- Dancing
- Rollerblading
- Running
- Stationary biking
- Walking

WITH A PARTNER
- Pickleball
- Catch
- Racquetball
- Squash
- Sex
- Tennis

WITH A TRAINER
Boxing
CrossFit
Gymnastics
Jumping rope
Lifting weights or kettlebells
Sit-ups and / or push-ups

WITH A TEAM
Baseball
Basketball
Field hockey
Football
Hockey
Lacrosse
Soccer
Softball
Rugby
Volleyball

IN A STUDIO
Barre
Bootcamp
Dance
Karate
Kickboxing
Pilates
Pole / belly dancing
Qi-gong
Spin
Yoga

IN NATURE
Hiking
Mountain biking
Rock climbing
Horseback riding

IN THE WATER
Canoeing
Kayaking
Scuba diving
Stand-up paddleboarding
Surfing
Swimming / diving
Water aerobics
Water-skiing

IN THE SNOW
Cross-country skiing
Downhill skiing
Snowboarding
Snowshoeing

OTHER

_____

_____

_____

_____

_____

_____

_____

More movement means more energy across the board. But I bet for some of you, there's still that pesky voice at the back of your mind, saying, "I don't have the energy for exercise. I'm exhausted, remember?" Fair enough. You need to have the physical energy to get yourself moving. That's why it's essential to focus on assessing your nutrition, sleep health, and stress hormones first, and then adding movement in ways that energize you rather than deplete you. Listen to your body. I promise you will see benefits in just a couple of weeks. And once exercise becomes routine, you'll be on your way to healing the physical symptoms of burnout.

PHYSICAL ENERGY REASSESSMENT

Remember that quick physical assessment you did at the end of Chapter 4, where you rated your satisfaction from 1–10 in each of the following four areas, where 1 was "not satisfied at all" and 10 was "extremely satisfied"?

- Energy

- Food

- Sleep

- Movement

Now that you know more about your physical energy, it's time to get a little clearer.

1. For the areas you rated less than a 10, ask yourself, what would make that area a 10? For example, you might answer with:

   - **Energy:** "I gave myself an 8 because I have good energy and love what I do, but my energy wanes around 2 p.m. for the rest of the day. What would make it a 10 is making sure I schedule 15 minutes between appointments to rest, recharge, and refuel in order to keep my energy levels consistent throughout the day."

   - **Food:** "I am at an 8, as I nourish myself with whole foods regularly and have gotten into a great routine of preparing food. What would make it a 10 is if I made one new delicious, healthy recipe each month for variety and creativity."

- **Sleep:** "I'm at a 6. What would make it a 10 is setting a bedtime of 11 p.m. and creating a spa-like sleeping environment so I would want to get into bed at 10:30 p.m. to read and settle in. That would make sleep more enjoyable, instead of a chore."

- **Movement:** "I give myself a 5 because I enjoy it when I exercise, but I'm not consistent. What would make this area a 10 is daily stretching and creating a regular routine that I enjoy. I don't have to work out every day for my score to be a 10, but I do need to be in nature to feel good. I would also love a technological device to measure my movement, sleep, and heart rate variability to see how they improve."

2. Overall, on a physical level, are you experiencing a net gain (+) or a net drain (−) of energy?

☐ net gain (+)   ☐ net drain (−)

The way you determine this is by looking at your answers and also checking in with your Body Map. If you feel a constriction or tightness in your body as you answer these questions, you likely have a net drain in this area. If you have a feeling of openness, ease, or lightness in your body as you answer these questions, this energy level is likely a net gain for you. We'll do this at the end of every section.

Go ahead. Take your time to finish your physical re-assessment. I'll wait.

Every small improvement in your partnership with your body helps. And as your physical energy grows, so will the energy in *all* areas of your life. In the next section, we'll investigate how to recover lost mental energy, which starts with becoming aware of your thoughts.

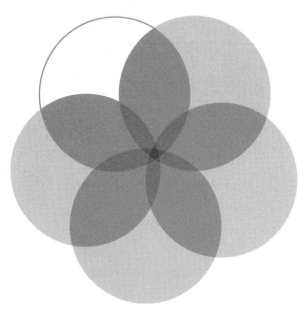

PART II

MENTAL ENERGY

CHAPTER 9

MENTAL ACROBATICS

You already learned that I won blue ribbons for tumbling on the gymnastics mat, but what you might not know is that I also engaged in mental acrobatics with equal dexterity. Anytime I heard a colleague needed a day off, I chimed in with, "Sure, I'll do it!" Yet anytime I needed help, I thought, *I'm not going to bother anybody. I'll just stay late and do it myself.* When I didn't feel treated fairly, I would tell myself, "Don't make such a big deal out of it. It might make her mad if you say anything." And if I discovered I was being gossiped about, rather than confronting it, I would avoid conflict by simply pretending no one had said anything at all. Trying to suppress my thoughts drained me of mental, emotional, and relational energy.

It took only one hour with Roger for him to diagnose me with a severe case of people-pleasing. As you remember, my journey with him was cut short by the healthcare insurance company not being willing to pay for our sessions because I wasn't taking the antidepressant medication he had prescribed. So I began navigating my own healing journey. I knew a major factor draining my precious energy was my inability to communicate effectively, advocate for myself, and lean into healthy conflict. Therefore, one of my many steps forward included attending a series of communication workshops. They taught me the power of changing my thoughts to heal my social energy drains. I began feeling more confident and was ready for a more intense experience.

Monthly for an entire year, 10 of us enrolled to be interns in an advanced communication and leadership program. The curriculum was focused on mastering the art of high stakes conversations. Eight months in, we'd developed a deep sense of mutual trust. But somehow, I still felt like I wasn't really close to any of my co-interns.

I remember we were practicing something called a fishbowl, which was an exercise where you state the unedited truth. (I know—ouch.) Our facilitator, Kris, prompted one us to speak about any thoughts that were arising in us. That would start a domino effect of conversation about whatever came out. Meanwhile, our colleagues were sitting around the two of us in a circle intently watching the show (hence, the fishbowl).

Kris began, "Neha, why don't you start with how you're feeling right now."

A little startled, I responded, "It's weird, despite being with you guys one weekend a month for the past eight months, I still feel a little disconnected and lonely. Yeah, I guess that's what's coming up for me."

"Katie, why don't you share with Neha any thoughts that you have in response to her current experience?" Kris prompted.

My fellow intern Katie began, "Neha, I mean I really like you. And I want to know you better. But it seems like there's not really any space for that to happen. You show up for our program just on time or often a few minutes late. And when we get a break or go to lunch, you immediately rush to check your phone. It seems like there's not enough hours in the day for what you have on your plate. Kind of like you're in a constant panic. Honestly, I want to be closer to you, but well, I experience your energy as chaotic and swirling—kind of like the Tasmanian devil—you know, a *crisis-in-motion*."

I immediately felt nauseous, and my throat constricted. My initial reaction was to muster everything I could to defend myself. *You have no idea how many responsibilities I have. I'm doing the best I can. And all you can do is criticize me!*

But I was also a good girl who wanted to please everyone and impress my peers—and according to the rules of the fishbowl, I had agreed to stay open and thank her. So I replied, "Thanks for your feedback, Katie."

And then my underlying fears of being judged or doing something wrong erupted into a cascading waterfall of tears down both cheeks.

Katie leapt out of her seat to try and undo the damage she saw unfolding, but this wasn't Kris's first rodeo. She knew exactly how this emotional scenario might play out and gently directed Katie back to her seat.

"Katie, it's your job to compassionately speak your truth and trust that Neha is strong, resourceful, and capable enough to hear it. Please have a seat, and both of you, take a slow deep breath in . . . and out. And another.

And another. That includes all of you compassionately witnessing this. Something important just came up for healing, and it's our job to be present as both Katie and Neha experience the emotions moving through them."

A few moments later, Kris asked, "Neha, how are you doing?"

Each time I tried to speak, the result was even more tears combined with dry-heaving. Kris came over and gently rubbed my back, while another intern ran to grab more tissues.

Here's the truth: Katie was right. She had so clearly articulated what I experienced but never had words for. In an attempt to prove my worth, I had put myself on a constant treadmill of *doing*, perfecting my workaholic coping strategy. For the most part, society rewarded me for it. But that moment in the fishbowl revealed the cost of running my life that way.

Over time, I realized how incredibly valuable her feedback was. Come to think of it, I had often wondered why, after moving 3,000 miles to the West Coast, I was so busy but hadn't felt close to anyone. This is when my perspective on the power of giving and receiving feedback began to change. What if, instead of defending myself, I could be open to feedback and experience it—and maybe even thank the person for having the courage to give it to me?

Katie's visual about spinning uncontrollably was profound and caused me to become aware of my body in space and consciously slow down. I even began to speak more slowly. Over the next few months, my peers came to me one by one and told me how brave I was and expressed the changes they were noticing. Could it really be that slowing down could help me strengthen my connection to others, and ultimately speed up? If so, then it was time to evolve my protective thought patterns that had served me for decades but now were keeping me from what I wanted most—authentic connection to others.

THOUGHTS ON REPEAT

Often, we develop ways of thinking—a set of well-worn thought paths, if you will—to adapt to and survive stressful situations, and we continue to follow those paths even after we have moved on from those settings and no longer need those mental strategies. For instance, your current state of busyness or overwhelm may have started with a simple thought, such as *Of course, starting a family adds stress to my life. I'll adjust over time.* Or perhaps you thought, *No big deal. I can take on a few new clients. It's only a couple of additional hours per week. And I definitely need the money.*

Becoming aware of our mental strategies and thought patterns allows us to assess if they are still serving us or just stressing us out. When you slow down enough to notice them, you'll see that many automatic thought patterns can be a potent source of stress. And they might not even be true anymore. These old patterns will exhaust you and lead you toward burnout.

You may have outgrown some of your thought patterns, just as you do with clothing, friend circles, and phases of life. If you recognize outdated thought patterns, it's important to first acknowledge how your mental strategies have served you. They have gotten you where you are today. The key, just like in the stock market, is knowing when it's time to let go of them.

For example, when I went on stress leave from the hospital, ironically, what I feared most was being alone with my own thoughts: how I was a total failure and would inevitably be rejected by others. I mean, could there be worse feedback to receive than what I interpreted my colleague Roger's message to be when he told me my 16 patients would be seen, just not by me? I interpreted that to be: *You can go home now. We've got other physicians who can do this. You're easily replaceable.* This was my greatest fear: that somehow I was not needed, wanted, or special.

You can imagine my shock when I realized how my ways of thinking had, in fact, contributed to the chronic understaffing at my hospital. Because whenever there was a problem, I saved the day. I said yes to additional shifts when I really should have said yes to a good night's rest. Why would they hire more people? They had me to fill any staffing gaps. Have you ever had a relationship like that, where the harder you tried, the harder it got?

I was making fear-based decisions that people wouldn't be pleased or impressed with me (and subconsciously, that if I didn't volunteer and make myself useful, I wouldn't be valued). These thoughts were draining my mental energy and undermining my ability to truly be a good team player.

On medical leave, I remember thinking, *This way of thinking may have worked for decades, but clearly it's not working anymore.* Once I recognized how outdated my behavior was and that my mental programming was actually having the opposite effect I desired, I realized that if I changed my thoughts, then maybe I had the power to change the outcome. I had already experienced this with Katie following that life-altering experience in the fishbowl. By being open to feedback and being willing to acknowledge the truth, my resulting relationship with Katie and the other interns had dramatically shifted and we all became much closer.

Examining my thoughts around self-care seemed like the best place to start. If I made myself a priority, I wondered, *Could I transform self-doubt into self-confidence?* I made an agreement with myself: I was going to get 7 hours of sleep per night, eat whole-food-based meals, and walk at least 30 minutes each day. And when I was at those communication workshops, removed from my regular life, I actually *kept my word to myself to prioritize my own self-care!* I was taking important steps to becoming *me-powered.*

My self-care incrementally began extending into my life in between communication workshops. I began sleeping better at night, which made me more efficient and pleasant during the day with my patients and my team. And because I was no longer overextending myself, the need for additional help on our medical team became obvious. After having to cover the night shift themselves on New Year's Day, the leadership team miraculously came up with the budget to hire the appropriate staff required—something they had said for years they couldn't do.

Who knew that by facing my fearful thoughts and realizing I could say yes to myself, instead of another shift, I could actually help solve the staffing issues? In the short run, there was discomfort, as I learned also to take into account what my own biology needed. In the long run, we all benefited—the hospital, my colleagues, and especially the patients.

What are your thoughts about your burnout or physical symptoms? Perhaps you beat yourself up for being so tired and not being able to get everything on your to-do list done. Maybe you think it will get better once things change at the office or the kids move out. Maybe you tell yourself to keep at it no matter what because *success requires struggle.*

Your brain may be giving you outdated information—and you may not have realized it. Just because you have certain thoughts doesn't mean you shouldn't re-evaluate them. You get to consciously choose your thoughts. I'm going to support you in becoming aware of how to identify thought patterns that contribute to burnout and assess whether they're helping or hindering you. Then you get to decide what to do with them.

When I took interest in what was going on in my head, I was able to shift how I related to myself. This was most obvious in my self-talk, the silent conversations I had with myself. When I made a mistake, instead of, *You idiot, why did you do that?* I noticed myself saying, *You've been working hard, Neha. You're doing the best you can. If you need a break, take it.* I gradually shifted my self-criticism to self-compassion, and I began to treat myself as I would a dear friend. This may not sound like much, but it was a game changer!

If you want to free up some mental energy and reduce your stress, it's crucial to examine the way your highly developed brain could betrying to protect you. Outdated thought patterns can drain your energy and undermine your relationships—which, for those of you who value efficiency—only requires more of your energy to repair.

Since our thoughts happen automatically, rarely do we get curious about where we've made assumptions and put ourselves or others in a box. As you translate what you observe into thoughts, it's easier than you might think to confuse fact with fiction. Yes, I said fiction. In the moment, it can be hard to distinguish what you observe from what you *think about* what you observe. It's fiction until you verify whether it's true or not.

FACT (DATA) VERSUS FICTION (THE STORY YOU MAKE UP)

The way we view the world is greatly influenced by our childhood, upbringing, culture, and past experiences—the happy memories as well as the traumatic ones. That's the blueprint upon which we also form our thoughts in the present moment. It's essential to understand the difference between what we observe—*raw, objective data* such as the body language, tone, and words of those around us—versus *interpretations of that data*, such as what you or the person using them meant to convey.

For example, if you're giving a presentation and you see someone yawning, you may assume they're not engaged by what you're saying. What you might not realize is that they made attending your presentation a top priority, despite their low energy due to their wife recently having a newborn and being on baby duty the night before.

We all interpret external data, all day, every day. We do it on autopilot—and make the big mistake of assuming that other people think and live *the way we do*. Everyone has their own backgrounds and past experiences—all of which impact the way they think. Because we're all so different, most of the time, our interpretation of what other people are thinking is wrong! Staying curious and examining our thoughts is an easy way to regain mental energy.

It's time to distinguish data (facts) from our interpretation of the data (thoughts). By objective data, I mean facts that come in through your primary physical senses (sight, hearing, taste, touch, and smell) or what a video camera would capture. A video doesn't interpret the facts to mean anything specific. It merely documents and records them. For example, security camera footage in a building could show smoke, people coughing, people walking or running out of the building, or perhaps someone slipping after stepping in a puddle.

In addition to body language that a video camera picks up, your body's more advanced internal data-collector might detect the smell of smoke, feel the heat, and taste soot in your mouth. From all of this, you would probably guess that the building is on fire and everyone needs to evacuate. That may very well be an accurate interpretation of the available data—but you don't know for sure yet! Maybe it's a fire that has recently been put out. Or it could be the building next door, and you should remain in this building to stay safe.

A common culprit of losing mental energy is that we misinterpret data, are misled by assumptions, make judgments, and fail to get curious about what else the data could mean. Let's explore another example:

- If you see an invite to a meeting pop up on your calendar and you think it is about furthering a cause you are passionate about, you'll likely look forward to attending (energy gain).

- If you see an invite to a meeting pop up on your calendar and you think it's to cut vacation time, budgets, and bonuses this year, you may not look forward to going (energy drain).

The only data in this scenario is that an invite popped up on your calendar with a date, time, and place for a meeting. Everything else is a story you made up about the data you observed. In any given situation, the brain wants to make sense of the facts around it. That's its job! But sometimes the computer system of your mind short-circuits and jumps to conclusions. If you accept your interpretations as fact, you won't ask the most important questions: Is how I interpreted this data true? Is it not true?

The answer? You don't know yet.

Take another common example from work. Suppose it's a Friday morning, and while eating breakfast at home, you receive an email from your boss saying, "Due to unforeseen circumstances, we're down a team member today." Your inner dialogue might go something like: *I bet it's Jay. Last week, I heard him telling Clara that he's working too hard. The reason he knows that is because it's midsummer and he's still pale as a ghost. I bet he went to the beach. I'll need to handle the extra sales calls and client complaints on top of my own workload. My day is going to be miserable. Jay is so inconsiderate. Yet again, I won't have time for lunch, and I don't think scarfing a chocolate chip cookie and downing an energy drink are going to get me through this one.*

So what were the **facts**?

- It's Friday morning.

- I received an email from my boss saying: "Due to unforeseen circumstances, we're down a team member today."

- I overheard Jay tell Clara that he's "working too hard and he knows that because he's still pale as a ghost."

And what were the **stories you made up** (a.k.a., the potential fiction)?

- *I bet I'll have to handle the extra sales calls and client complaints.*

- *Jay is at the beach.*

- *Jay is inconsiderate.*

- *I won't have time for lunch today.*

- *I'm not sure a cookie and an energy drink will get me through this.*

- *My day is going to be miserable.*

Until you have a chance to communicate with your boss directly to find out who called out, you have *no idea* if any of those stories are actually true. This is when miscommunication, assumptions, gossip, and judgments take hold, and mental energy goes swirling down the drain.

When you have a knee-jerk reaction because you think you already know exactly what's happening, *you* can actually be the *source of misunderstanding*, manufacturing drama and spreading rumors. This can lead to not only your mental energy drain but sometimes to a collective social energy drain among your colleagues.

Remember, you don't know what's actually happening until you ask. So *get curious, not furious*. Curiosity allows you to hit pause, gather more information about a situation or person, and expand your perspective—rather than blindly believing the stories you make up about them.

Let's play out what actually happened that day. You showed up at the office and ran into Jay, who happily greeted you in the elevator. Your boss called a team meeting and shared that Clara's son fell down the stairs and had a dental emergency.

Did you need to cover for Clara? Was your day ruined? Did you have to miss lunch?

No, because your boss hired a temp for the day. And although the day was busy, Jay asked you to lunch, during which he told you that he's transferring to the San Diego office because he just can't take these New England winters any longer.

You will never know whether your initial interpretations (stories) are true unless you decipher fact from fiction. It's often beneficial to unhook from your automatic thought process and get curious. This applies not only to your thoughts about others but also your thoughts about yourself—your own *self-talk*.

THE CONVERSATIONS WITH *YOU*

Self-talk can seem like background noise, but don't be fooled. These thoughts expand—or limit—what you think is possible in your job, your relationships, your health, and your life. One way you form self-talk is through personal experience. For instance, if you were successful at something, you might have decided *you are capable of anything*. When you were eight years old, maybe you won the scavenger hunt at your bestie's birthday party. Rewarded with a life-sized stuffed panda bear, you decided, *I'm athletic and talented*. Or two decades later, at your friend's wedding, maybe a raucous crowd circled you, hooting and hollering as you showcased your latest dance moves, so you thought, *I'm a ladies' man!* Experiences such as these can often result in self-talk that expands what we think is possible and empowers our mental energy. Expanding beliefs include thoughts such as, *I'm hardworking. I'm smooth. I'm kind. I'm hopeful. I'm beautiful. I'm a strong leader. I'm a good parent. I can do anything I put my mind to.*

On the other hand, perhaps you tried certain activities that didn't have the outcome you had hoped for and decided, *I'm a disappointment* or even worse, *I'm a loser.* If you got injured while running a race, you may have thought, *I'm clumsy and weak.* If you didn't do as well as you wanted on a test, you may have thought, *I'm stupid.* These seemingly innocuous thoughts are potent drains of mental energy.

Many societies tend to focus more on limiting beliefs rather than on expansive thinking, and this begins when we are still toddling around in diapers. A majority of the feedback that toddlers receive is "No," "Stop it," or "Don't do that." This emphasis on negative feedback leads to an imbalance in our self-talk as we're forming our perspectives and what we believe about ourselves. Growing up hearing our caretakers focus more on what we *shouldn't* do rather than what we *should* may have contributed to thought patterns that produce tragic stories in our heads—long after those voices are gone.

Whether you are consciously aware of it, the external voices of the people who surrounded you growing up have likely had a huge influence on your internal self-talk. For example, if you were embarrassed in front of your third grade class by being the last one picked for kickball, you may have interpreted that to mean *I'm not good enough.* If you had a parent look over your report card that had all As and one B and comment, "Why did you get a B in English when you always get As?" you may believe that *you're a failure and you must continuously achieve to earn love.* If there's an ongoing pattern of someone close to you putting you down, criticizing your looks, or questioning your judgment, that may make you believe that you constantly need to prove yourself in order to be worthy. Ingrained energy drains like these are important to identify and repair; otherwise, they bleed into many aspects of your life and wreak havoc.

One way I explain this to parents is: when you speak to your kids, notice whether you are meeting them with criticism or compassion because your *external voice* will eventually become their *internal voice.*

What were some of the most common phrases from your parents, your mentors, and your leaders that have stuck with you? Take note if any of those thoughts result in energy gains or drains. If you remember, we began the book with more general phrases I heard as the underlying message from those around me, at work and at home:

Do more with less.

Faster is better.

Success requires struggle.

After listening to those messages for so long, my burnout taught me that maybe there is a limit to how much I can do alone, maybe faster isn't always better, and that perhaps together (meaning bridging my inner world and my outer world, and asking for help from others) might be a better option.

Your self-talk often dictates the rules you live by, such as *I'm too old, I'm not hip enough,* or *I'm not assertive enough.* We all have our own versions of this. Do any of these self-limiting beliefs sound familiar to you?

- *I'm not rich enough.*

- *I'm not successful enough.*

- *I'm not thin enough.*

- *I'm not witty enough.*

- *I'm not disciplined enough.*

Many of us have a version of the "I'm not good enough" narrative. But these thoughts have often gone unchallenged. Whatever your version of this self-talk is, pay attention to whether it's a limiting or expanding belief. When you have a certain thought, notice the bodily sensations that go along with that thought. If you discover you're feeling tense, heavy, or constricted, that thought is likely a limiting belief that is draining your energy. On the other hand, if you notice yourself feeling open, light, relaxed, or uplifted by certain thoughts, they're likely attached to an expansive belief.

Let's go a bit deeper. How strong is your inner critic? You know that voice in your head that never lets you make a mistake, that's way too hard on you—fueling your fear of failure. How has that voice been speaking to you about your current symptoms and stress load?

Mine shows up most obviously when I'm presenting to a large audience, when someone questions my underlying intentions or judges my performance harshly online. Sometimes it shows up when someone accuses me of not being considerate or informs me that I've made a mistake that might have inadvertently caused harm to someone else.

Bring to mind a time when you received a strong or unexpected reaction after sharing your opinion.

- What are the most common phrases that run through your mind?
- Whose voice/s do those phrases remind you of?
- How old were you?
- What did it mean about you being loved or not?
- What did it mean about whether you belonged or not?
- How did it impact your self-confidence, self-esteem, and willingness to take risks?

The good news about your inner critic is that you can retrain it—by recalibrating how it interprets and processes both the external and internal data it's receiving. Believe it or not, you can transform your inner critic into your best friend forever (BFF). Once you do, this alignment will give you a continuous stream of mental energy. For example, when I gain weight, rather than beating myself up and thinking *I'm getting fat*, I now replace that thought with, *Thank you, body—for expanding to absorb the stress I couldn't. I'll take over as soon as I am able.* The result? Compassion for how stressful my life has been. Acknowledgment for how hard my body has worked. Knowledge that I am the one in charge to change it. An elevated mood. More resilience. Inspiration to take new action. There are plenty of challenges that you encounter in life. There's no need to pile more on top of that by being cruel to yourself. Be kind to yourself. Recognize how hard you are working. And treat yourself with honor and respect. The way you treat yourself teaches other people *how you expect to be treated.*

Initial Three Thoughts Exercise

Now that you're getting the gist of deciphering fact from fiction, let's examine some of the topics that impact you most in your work. Below, note your initial three thoughts about each topic. Don't overthink it. Write down whatever comes to mind first, whether it's about yourself or others.

BURNOUT

1. _____

2. _____

3. _____

MONEY

1. _____

2. _____

3. _____

MAKING A MISTAKE

1. _____

2. _____

3. _____

EXPRESSING EMOTIONS

1. _____

2. _____

3. _____

GIVING OR RECEIVING FEEDBACK

1. _____

2. _____

3. _____

(continued)

(continued)

Read through your answers. Then use these five questions to gain important insights:

1. What patterns do you notice?

2. Do any of those thoughts stem from voices in your past?

3. Which thoughts are facts?

4. Which are fiction (assumptions or the story you're making up)?

5. Which thoughts are negative self-talk that leave you feeling depleted or drained?

What's most important is to recognize if you see any patterns that will provide clues about valuable information you might be missing (like facts about a situation or person). This is an opportunity to identify patterns. If you're up for going a bit deeper, take the final two steps.

6. Label each thought as fact or fiction based on whether or not you have objective data to verify it.

7. Draw a star next to the thoughts that are the most stressful or draining for you.

The stories you create matter. When you make assumptions and judgments, or let your inner critic run unchecked, whether or not you consciously realize it, the result is a huge mental energy drain. Your thoughts determine how well you're able to navigate communication and conflict. I promise, your thoughts (self-affirming or self-deprecating) can make or break any aspect of your life: your performance, your relationships, your career trajectory, your dreams, and even your legacy. The good news is: you have the power to change them.

MENTAL ENERGY ASSESSMENT

To change your thoughts, you have to know what they are. It's time to make the *subconscious* conscious!

1. What three thoughts run on repeat in the background of your mind, especially related to your workload or life responsibilities?

2. What percentage of the time do you focus on:

    *   Repetitive thoughts, worries, or regrets?

    *   Wanting to change other people's actions and behaviors?

    *   Wishing the world was different than it is?

3. What do you think about the stress levels at work and in your life? How much time and energy do you lose stressing *about* your own stress?

4. What do you think about *asking for help*?

5. What thoughts empower you?

    Can you identify which of your thoughts contribute to anxiety, insomnia, a lack of productivity, or mental exhaustion? These are important clues that reveal unresolved conflict or mental strategies that no longer serve you.

By simply illuminating the thoughts that are occupying your mental real estate, you are taking the first step—gaining awareness—which will catalyze your ability to change them. Now you will know where you are experiencing potholes in your journey and draining unnecessary energy as you try to find detours around these limiting beliefs. As you reflect on your *Initial Three Thoughts* exercise, identify which ones are serving you, slowing you down, or stressing you out. Then we can heal them together!

CHAPTER 10

YOUR THOUGHTS SHAPE YOUR EXPERIENCE

W hat if this isn't the right outfit for the event? What if the technology doesn't work? What if the audience isn't engaged? What if there's traffic en route to the venue? What if I express my opinion and people don't agree? What if I don't know how to answer their questions? I'm too overwhelmed to handle this. I'm just going to screw it up. It's better if I back out now because odds are—it won't work out anyway.

In the previous chapters you learned how to identify your Body Map, distinguish data from the stories you make up, and observe the quality of your own self-talk. Let's integrate this data to discover your thought patterns, which shape how you interpret any situation. There are three main thought patterns: personalization, projection, and generalization.

- Personalization is *self-focused*.

- Projection is *other-focused*.

- Generalization is about *factors bigger than either party involved*.

Once you understand how you form your thoughts, you'll be able to navigate any situation in your life with more confidence.

Our thoughts are how we interpret the world around us and within us. We wouldn't have the ability to reason, analyze, or debate one another without them. But they're not always the most helpful. Let me clarify: they're *trying* to be helpful. Your brain is attempting to make meaning of what's happening while also protecting you. But due to past experiences, some of the thought patterns you rely on may have been formed as an escape route from perceived harm. For example, if you raised your hand in grade school to answer a teacher's question, and your response was met with, "Nope. Wrong answer. Anyone else?" as your peers pointed at you, whispered to each other, and giggled, you may have thought, *I'm never raising my hand again. Everybody thinks I'm stupid.* Long after you've left that classroom, if any of those thought patterns got stuck on repeat, you might shy away from *any* opportunity to speak in public. This is one of the ways mental stress can consume your energy and rob you of opportunities later in life.

These days, the dangers we encounter are rarely life-threatening; instead, they threaten our sense of belonging, security, and self-worth. We defend ourselves against anything that might indicate that we may no longer be a valued member of the tribe.

For example, suppose you have been working like crazy and despite burning the candle at both ends, you make a mistake on a project. Months later, it shows up on your performance review as the reason you're not getting promoted. Place a check mark next to the following phrases that would most closely reflect your initial response:

- *I'm a failure. I'm definitely getting fired.*

- *I didn't realize how tired I was. I should have asked for help or an extension.*

- *My team doesn't value me. They don't know how much I do.*

- *Not everybody had to work the weekend. I wonder if we all had similar workloads?*

- *Is leadership aware that we came in on time and under budget?*

- *With insufficient resources and staff, how does the organization expect us to get anything done?*

- Other _____

  _____

  _____

Your initial response to your performance review can reveal which common thought pattern(s) you default to:

1. **Personalization:** when you make it about *you*

   - *I'm a failure. I'm definitely getting fired.*

   - *I didn't realize how tired I was. I should have asked for help or an extension.*

2. **Projection:** when you make it about *someone else*

   - *My team doesn't value me. They don't know how much I do.*

   - *Not everybody had to work the weekend. I wonder if we all had similar workloads?*

3. **Generalization:** when you make it about *something bigger* than you or someone else

   - *Is leadership aware that this project came in on time and under budget?*

   - *With insufficient resources and staff, how does the organization expect us to get anything done?*

Each of these thought patterns are necessary and can be helpful. In fact, when all three are used together in a healthy and balanced way, the combination often provides a comprehensive view of *what is actually happening.* Let's explore them one by one.

THOUGHT PATTERN 1: PERSONALIZATION

Personalization is when you're focused on *your contribution* to an outcome. A healthy use of personalization leads you to acknowledge how your action (or inaction) may have contributed to the outcome of a situation. This thought pattern works well when it supports you in taking personal responsibility for your contribution.

For example, suppose you made lunch plans with a new colleague, Carlos, to meet at The Grill on Wednesday at 12 noon. You arrive at 11:55 a.m., eager to get to know him better. You order an iced tea while you wait. As you finish your drink, you glance at your watch. It's 12:17 p.m. You check your phone. No missed calls, texts, or emails. If you're using a healthy form of personalization, you might think:

- *Maybe I got the days mixed up.*

- *I wonder if I'm at the right place.*

- *I should have confirmed that we were still on.*

If these are the types of thoughts you have, you're likely someone who defaults to checking *your personal accountability* first. That's great that you focus on yourself—because this is a key part of every exchange. And a healthy use of personalization will have you owning your part in any situation.

What About Narcissism?

Before we go further, I'd like to clarify an important point. Because personalization is self-focused, I often get asked—is it a form of narcissism? Entire books have been written about narcissistic behavior. In a nutshell, I think of narcissism as someone caring *only* about themselves and behaving in manipulative ways to further their own self-interest— sometimes at any cost. A key feature of narcissistic behavior is the inability to empathize with others.

On the other hand, personalization refers to a form of self-reflection that allows you to become aware of how you showed up in a situation and take personal accountability. You have the ability to understand how your behavior(s) may have impacted those around you.

To reduce stress, you may find yourself overusing or underusing personalization without even realizing it. Let's examine what happens if you're overusing this thought pattern.

Too Much

When you *overuse* personalization, it can easily transform from personal accountability into self-blame—taking too much responsibility. This happens when you interpret situations, conversations, and other people's reactions or behaviors to be *a reflection of you*—even when they are not. An overuse of personalization will send you into a tailspin of confusion because what's happening may not have anything to do with you. And you won't understand why, despite "taking more accountability," nothing improves. There's a big difference between *taking ownership* and *blaming yourself*.

Let's revisit the example of Carlos. When you overuse personalization, you might think:

- *I knew I wasn't important to him.*

- *I must have said or done something that upset him.*

The internal dialogue of this thought pattern sounds something like this: *Whatever is happening must be a result of something I said, did, or didn't do.* It's true that what you say, do, or think will have an impact. But those who have this as their default perspective view other people's behavior and general mishaps as their own fault.

Blaming yourself for something that has nothing to do with you can come from a variety of sources, including childhood trauma. For example, if their parents didn't get along or got divorced, children sometimes wonder what *they* did wrong. They can blame themselves for something that had nothing to do with them.

One way people compensate for feeling unworthy is to hold unreasonably high expectations of themselves. Whether it's striving in athletics, academics, or at work, this external effort is a common way humans try to make up for a perceived lack of self-worth. Sometimes, this can also be associated with perfectionism.

Perfectionism is measuring yourself according to whether your performance or outcome was flawless. This fear-based behavior reveals a high level of control and low level of self-trust. Often, perfectionism results in critical thoughts about yourself and others, missed deadlines so you can fix that *one last detail*, and despite valiant efforts, a pervasive sense of underlying dissatisfaction. The predominant thought with perfectionism is *"If it's not perfect, it's not good enough."*

Perfectionism is an extreme self-focus that at times can keep you stuck and hinder your ability to collaborate, rather than accept your limitations and move forward with ease and grace. One way this shows up at work is through micromanaging. At home, this is sometimes described as helicopter or drone parenting.

You might be wondering what the difference is between the *pursuit of perfection* and the *pursuit of excellence*. They are related concepts. They just have different points of focus.

Excellence is striving to give *your* very best effort. It's about directing your full presence and energy into whatever you do. Here's the key: you want to do that while also allowing yourself (and others) to be human and learn from mistakes. With excellence, you work hard and possess the self-trust to take risks, and if an undesirable outcome occurs, you give yourself and others grace to absorb the lessons in order to change course.

How do you know whether you're focused on perfectionism or excellence? Ask yourself, on whom are you focused? Is this more about what *others think of you or how something appears*? Or is it about *you* giving something your all?

If you have perfectionistic tendencies, recall a time when your pursuit of perfection led to diminishing returns with yourself and with others. Here are a few examples of typical perfectionistic thoughts:

- *I never do anything right.*

- *I can't believe I forgot—I'm such an idiot.*

- *It's not good enough. I need to start again from the beginning.*

When personalization is used in a way that's harmful, you compare yourself to others and feel *less than*. For example, if you have two higher-education degrees, you think, *there's someone with three*, just so you know there's always *more* you could be doing. If you have a certain amount of money invested, you think, *there's someone who has more, got a better rate of return, and will be able to leave a greater legacy than me*. If you're really good at this type of personalization, you'll even compare yourself with your younger self. Yep, that version of you that you didn't even value back then, but now seems so attractive, youthful, and smart!

You may not think this is a big deal, but it has an enormous impact on your career, your relationships, and your willingness to take risks to create the life you want. For example, if you hear about a position at work opening up that sounds like your dream job, but you think, *I went to a public school, so I doubt I'll be selected,* so you don't apply. Or after losing an important client, you don't even bother going after other opportunities because you think, *it'll just be a waste of time* or *they'll probably go with somebody else anyway.* If this behavior resonates, you may have a case of *imposter syndrome.* Despite excellent performance reviews, along with countless compliments from friends and colleagues telling you how talented and amazing you are, you still have an underlying dread that at any minute, you'll be revealed as a fraud. Imposter syndrome is more common than you think.

Overusing personalization will leave you in a downward spiral of insecurity, with the constant need to please or measure up to others. This thought pattern will keep you from taking risks, going for your dreams, and focusing on what truly matters. Worst of all, it will leave you in a never-ending state of longing—eternally dissatisfied. You use the accomplishments of others in combination with your perceived inner deficiencies as fuel to continue striving. If this is a cause of energy depletion for you, help is on the way.

Too Little

When you *underuse* personalization, you're avoiding accountability. The most common way this can play out is blaming another person or the system—and feeling powerless to change the outcome.

For example, I underused personalization when I didn't recognize my part in enabling the understaffing issue at the hospital by taking on more shifts than I could handle. I felt like a victim when I didn't see how I played a role. The danger to *underusing* personalization is that you don't realize that you have the power to change the outcome, at the very least, for yourself. In any situation, if you're not interested in your part and instead are complaining and waiting for someone else or an organization to take ownership, you'll likely end up feeling stuck. And stuckness is the fast lane to energy drain.

Personalization Energy Drain

You take too much or not enough accountability for your part in a situation, leading to beating yourself up, propping up your self-image, comparing yourself to others, or blaming other parties or the system.

Personalization Energy Gain

Your brave action of taking accountability will often inspire *others* to show up and take responsibility for their part in a situation. You end up with not only a gain of your own mental energy but also a bonus: stronger connections with others and an increase in relational energy as well.

Next, let's explore the second thought pattern focused on *others*.

THOUGHT PATTERN 2: PROJECTION

Projection is when you focus on how *another person's contribution* influenced an outcome. A healthy use of projection leads you to understand the impact of someone else's action (or inaction). This thought pattern works well when it supports you in understanding how someone else's words, behaviors, or actions contributed to a situation ending up the way it did. It's important to use curiosity and generous intent.

Let's go back to the example of Carlos being late for lunch. If you were using healthy projection, you might think:

- *I wonder if Carlos forgot.*

- *Maybe Carlos isn't feeling well.*

- *I bet Carlos wasn't sure if our plans were confirmed.*

Healthy projection is an important aspect of mastering communication in any scenario. However, sometimes, in an attempt to reduce stress, you may find yourself overusing or underusing projection without even realizing it. Let's start by examining what overusing projection might look like.

Too Much

When you *overuse* projection, it can quickly turn into a toxic blame game. In the same scenario in which Carlos was late, you might think or say to someone else:

- *Carlos is so rude and disrespectful.*

- *He doesn't value other people's time.*

- *He's inconsiderate, absent-minded, and disorganized.*

When you jump to conclusions, you're overusing projection. Just think of all those Monday morning quarterbacks rehashing Sunday's football game. Doesn't it come so easy to identify what a colleague, friend, or partner got wrong? When projection is used without generous intent and includes criticism without curiosity, then it quickly becomes blame.

Blame can be the great escape hatch to get out of trouble. When you were young, did getting scolded sometimes feel like the end of the world? Did you ever play the game "Pin the Blame on Your Sibling"?

Blame often comes easily because the stakes are lower—it's not about you. It's about someone else. If it's not your fault, *you* still get to belong. It's no wonder that as adults, many of us have developed a habit of projecting statements that sound like:

- It's *your* fault.

- *You* messed up.

- *You* made me do it.

- Why did *you* do that?

People overuse projection for a good reason: to create a sense of control and safety. Overusing projection is often rooted in fear and is about self-protection. It can be uncomfortable to feel disappointment, rejection, or anger. Rather than learning how to process these challenging emotions, it's much easier to deflect that discomfort on to others. This happens when people judge others and make someone else bad, wrong, or 100 percent responsible for an outcome. Overusing this thought pattern is far too common and causes disconnection and high stress in relationships—both at work and at home.

For example, if someone made a mistake, thinks they are in trouble, or believes they might receive a poor evaluation or even lose their job, they may use projection to deflect responsibility. Unfortunately, this defense mechanism is often a successful strategy.

Occasionally, people are direct and say their projections out loud to the person they're in conflict with. However, most often, people voice their grievances to a third party or simmer in silence. If they voice their grievances to others, it becomes a wildfire of gossip that undermines trust. The worst part is that the person being blamed often doesn't even know there's a problem—until they hear it from someone else at work, at home, or in the neighborhood. This can feel like a betrayal and fuel the fire of stress and division. If they simmer in silence, this can lead to poisonous resentment and a feeling of powerlessness. Making assumptions or judging people without being curious creates an *us versus them* mentality and results in feelings of separation and isolation.

Have you ever heard yourself, a colleague, or a friend making any of these statements:

- He's sloppy.

- She's in it for herself.

- He always thinks he's right.

- They slept their way to the top.

- Can't depend on him; he never contributes anything.

- Don't ask her to do it; she's incompetent.

- She's too set in her ways. She'll never change.

When projection is used as a way to gain or retain power over another person, it's called *gaslighting*. This is an intentional, manipulative, and deeply harmful way of creating self-doubt in someone else. The goal of gaslighting is to make another person or other people not trust their inner GPS and question their own lived experience and intuition. It may seem minor at first, but over time, it has the devastating effect of *eroding the victim's self-trust*.

Gaslighting is more common than you think. Here's an everyday example: Suppose your colleague takes credit for a project you worked on together. When you protest, he looks you in the eye and says, "I did 90 percent of the work the week you were on vacation. Did you want 10 percent of the credit?" This can be confusing, and you might find yourself feeling guilty and thinking, *Did I really do only 10 percent of the work?* Because you were away the first week of the project, a seed of self-doubt sprouts and you decide to let it go. You have young children and need to leave at 5 p.m. to pick them up from day care. You have told the team that when necessary, you're happy to come in early or work from home after the kids are in bed. On the next collaboration, when once again you are not mentioned as a key contributor, you approach your colleague, who replies, "You leave every day at 5 p.m. on the dot. Those of us who are really dedicated to what's happening stay late to work on critical elements of the project, so we should get the credit for making it happen." You find yourself questioning the value of your contribution, despite the early mornings and late nights you have invested.

Once this type of interaction becomes a pattern, over time, when something goes wrong—at work or at home—your default may become to assume it must have been your fault. The gaslighter's manipulative overuse of projection then leads to the victim overusing personalization. As you can see, this is a vicious cycle, and if it sounds familiar to you, please speak to a mental health professional to learn more about gaslighting.

While I have described these as two distinct thought patterns, personalization and projection are often intertwined in relationships. As you might have noticed, if someone underuses personalization (by not taking accountability), they often overuse projection (blame). So yes, underusing personalization and overusing projection can both lead to blame.

Too Little

On the other hand, sometimes people underuse projection. While it's not as common as overuse, underusing projection has its issues, too. You miss a big part of what happened—the other person's reaction, response, and contribution to a situation. You may underuse projection because it is uncomfortable to hold someone accountable for their role in an undesirable outcome. For example, a parent who wants to be friends with their child might not say anything when the child acts out, doesn't complete their chores, talks back, or even lies. A common reason people underuse projection is to avoid conflict and maintain harmony. But this is false harmony and results in a short-term energy gain followed by a longer, more substantial social energy drain. True harmony only comes from a willingness to compassionately speak your truth. And authentic communication in relationships is what creates lasting energy gain.

Projection Energy Drain

When projection is used to deflect personal responsibility or to blame another person, it creates an *us-versus-them* mentality that causes confusion and depletes energy. On the other hand, when projection is underused to avoid conflict entirely, although there's a short-term energy gain of momentary peace and harmony, it will result in a long-term energy drain because you are not addressing and resolving the real issue.

Projection Energy Gain

When projection is used wisely, with curiosity and generous intent for the other person, it illuminates an expanded perspective. This allows for a balanced and thoughtful approach to resolving conflict and learning from an experience—together.

. . .

Next, let's explore the third and final thought pattern, which is focused on how outside circumstances can play a role as well.

THOUGHT PATTERN 3: GENERALIZATION

Generalization occurs when you assume that external factors, bigger than either you or another person, influenced an outcome. It's often true that the reasons for a delay or unexpected event can be due to *matters outside of either party's control.*

An example of this from our earlier scenario with Carlos would be if you thought:

- *I wonder if there's heavy traffic on the freeway.*

- *Maybe he got stuck at work.*

- *Maybe his car broke down.*

When used in a healthy way, generalization accounts for external factors that could be influencing a situation. That's one part of the equation. So rather than the limited perspective of *how you contributed* to a situation (personalization) or how *another person did* (projection), this thought pattern allows you to identify what *other factors* may have contributed to the outcome (generalization).

When you realize there are many possible ways this could have happened, it will allow you to remain curious and open in your exchange with Carlos. Let's say he finally arrives at 12:25 p.m., you might say something like, "Hi, Carlos, I thought we were meeting at noon. What happened?"

And he may reply, "Oh no! I thought I was five minutes early. I had 12:30 p.m. down. I'm so sorry to keep you waiting."

No matter which of these thought patterns you defaulted to, if you approach the scenario with personal accountability, curiosity, and generous intent, you can see how easy it is to have an open and curious exchange to get to the root cause of what happened. And it may be something totally different than you had even come up with!

Outside influences *do* play a role in our lives. Have you ever been late because of traffic? Have you ever had a flight delayed by bad weather or mechanical issues? And on the other hand, have you ever used outside influences as an excuse for something that was genuinely your doing—like when you overslept and were late for a scheduled appointment, and rather than taking ownership, you used the oldest trick in the book and blamed it on some "uncontrollable" factor: the parking lot was full, my earlier meeting ran late, or the school bus driver forgot to pick up the kids? If you've turned to these types of excuses, go easy on yourself. Just *call yourself out* and make a different choice next time.

In organizations, generalization is good for identifyingtrends, alignments or misalignments such as:

- Global shifts influencing certain markets

- Systemic factors shaping future business

- Policies and norms that support or don't support an organization's highest values

In interpersonal relationships, generalization can provide context for why a situation turned out the way it did. For example:

- Someone being late to dinner or the movies because they had a last-minute child-care scheduling conflict

- A friend not being able to pay you back because their employer's electronic payment system malfunctioned

- An international speaker missing their keynote presentation time slot due to an extra-long line at immigration

But just like the other two thought patterns, when you overuse or underuse generalization, dysfunction ensues.

Too Much

When you perceive an issue, such as a toxic work environment, to be "out of your control," it's easy to overgeneralize. Maybe you want to avoid conflict by not saying *who is really responsible*, so you blame the system, the process, or whomever is not in the room. Maybe you feel helpless because your company prides themselves on a culture of politeness. The problem is that when you overuse generalization, you begin to *believe* you have no control. And this can leave you feeling demoralized, indecisive, and powerless. When you're overwhelmed and don't think your input or contribution can make a difference, it only further exacerbates your stress and depletes you of energy.

For example, on my hospitalist team, we had countless conversations about how our experience would be different *if only management had to work under our same circumstances*. Despite these conversations, when we were understaffed and had no one to cover the night shift, I readily volunteered. Part of the reason I did this was to avoid short-term conflict and my fear of abandoning my patients. I felt like I had no way out because I had taken an oath to serve. I had to blame someone for my exhaustion, so the organization's poor leadership was an easy place to deflect my blame. When I got stuck in a pattern of overgeneralization, I couldn't see my own part in what was happening and didn't realize I had the power to say *no*. I was volunteering for those extra shifts; no one was making me take them.

Can you see how my *overuse* of personalization, in taking too much accountability, was enabling a dysfunctional system to continue? And on the flip side, can you see how I was simultaneously overgeneralizing by holding the system responsible? I bet you're starting to see how dysfunction in any of these areas can overlap with the others.

Too Little

When generalization is underused, you miss how the environment (or third parties) may have influenced a situation. For example, in June 2008, when I left my physician partnership to become an entrepreneur focusing on corporate communication, health, and wellness, I didn't take into account the external factors that could undermine my success. I had taken out a home equity loan to fund my new business endeavor but never imagined the possibility of a financial crisis, until September 2008, when banks were closing credit lines. Companies were no longer interested in health and wellness but were laser focused on downsizing the workforce. Then in 2012, the day the Affordable Care Act went to the Supreme Court, four hospital clients panicked and canceled my consulting contracts. I was aware of the current events but hadn't considered the link between the healthcare debate and my clients' fear of how it could impact their bottom line.

These economic and political factors beyond my control decreased my income and dramatically increased my stress levels. By failing to consider them, I nearly lost my company. Fortunately, I used this experience to take more personal accountability and gain clarity on how I might meet these new challenges. So I reinvented my business plan to help companies support employees navigating anger, anxiety, and burnout in the workplace. In addition, I realized the value of consulting across a wide range of industries. That way, economic shifts wouldn't wipe my company out. Last, I changed my contracts to require upfront payment to secure my time in advance.

Our lives are so complex that it's easy to get overwhelmed and feel paralyzed. This can have you wanting to focus on what you *can* control: yourself. And that's a good thing! But without also recognizing the bigger picture, you may be missing the expanded perspective necessary to understand the full context in which you're operating.

Generalization Energy Drain

When you use generalization to blame factors outside of your control, you can feel victimized and give away your power or you could miss key components that are influencing your situation. You may feel confused, not understanding why, despite your earnest efforts, you feel powerless. Or if you aren't aware of how external factors influence your situation, you may feel blindsided when your business or life take an unexpected turn.

Generalization Energy Gain

Engaging in healthy generalization provides an expanded perspective of how outside factors have influenced an outcome, enabling you to make comprehensive, clear, and effective decisions.

Congratulations! You now know how personalization, projection, and generalization play a role in your thoughts and interpretations of the world. Let's
apply these principles more specifically to your life.

Thought Pattern Awareness Exercise

Take a moment to go back to the questions you answered in Chapter
9 in the Initial Three Thoughts exercise. Use your answers there as the
basis for this exercise, which will help you become aware of how you
tend to form your thoughts.

1. Next to each thought, identify which thought pattern it is by
   writing (P) for personalization, (PR) for projection, and (G) for
   generalization. It might be a little tricky to label them if you've
   never categorized your thoughts this way before. Give it a try
   anyway. Feel free to write down more than one pattern or a
   question mark if you are unsure. This exercise will help you
   notice if you tend to lean more heavily toward a certain thought
   pattern as your predominant way of thinking.

2. Once you complete this, take a broader look at your thought
   patterns. Are a majority of your thoughts focused on yourself
   (P)? Mostly about others (PR)? Or about the system in which you
   work or live (G)? There's no right or wrong answer.

3. Place a (+) next to the (P), (PR), or (G) if you think there's a
   possibility you're overusing them and a (−) if you think you may
   be underusing them.

Balancing Your Perspective Exercise

If you have marked a thought as personalization (P), to balance it out ask yourself two additional questions:

- What might be happening for the other person that I haven't thought of? (projection)

- What outside factors beyond those identified could be at play? (generalization)

If you wrote projection (PR) next to a thought, to expand your perspective ask yourself:

- How might my action or inaction have contributed to this outcome? (personalization)

- What outside factors beyond those identified could be at play? (generalization)

Finally, if you marked a thought as generalization (G), balance your perspective by asking:

- How might my action or inaction have contributed to this outcome? (personalization)

- What might be happening for the other person that I haven't thought of? (projection)

This expanded perspective will equip you to think more balanced, energy-gaining thoughts. Remember, the quality of your thought patterns will determine the quality of your communication—with yourself and with those you love and lead.

PUTTING IT ALL TOGETHER

A system—whether it's a company, a family, a community, or an entire society—is made up of people and is impacted by the ways in which we operate individually, how we work together, and the processes we develop to serve one another and ourselves.

Each of us must take accountability for our personal choices within these systems. You have chosen your friends and the kind of relationships you have with your family. You've chosen this job, with this company, in this city. I'm confident that there are good reasons you did this. Perhaps it was a combination of the following: the geographic location, reputation, pay, flexibility, opportunities for advancement of your interests, and proximity to your children's school or to family. You accept a regular paycheck, so you have made an ongoing agreement to be a part of that system. That means you're getting something you want in exchange for your skills, energy, time, and effort. I find it's helpful to remember the reason(s) you made that agreement in the first place, so you can feel more balanced in relation to the system.

You can influence certain aspects of your job, but there are other aspects that you cannot control. If the ones you can't influence are impacting your performance and satisfaction, then you may want to reevaluate *the choice you make every day to stay in that job* or try something new.

But before you make any rash decisions, it's time to take the next step to integrate your healthy and balanced thought patterns into having conversations with others—specifically on giving and receiving (or resisting) feedback. Let's tackle this challenge head-on.

CHAPTER 11

FEEDBACK IS YOUR FRIEND

I hate feedback. At least I used to.

People react to the idea of getting feedback in a variety of ways. Some create elaborate strategies to avoid having the conversation at all. Others listen but discount the validity of what they're hearing. Some show up for the conversation and then artfully deflect the blame onto someone else. Others preemptively take way more than their share of blame to avoid receiving criticism from someone else. Still others take the words to heart and feel deeply criticized. Most people don't know how to interpret and process this vital information.

A common knee-jerk reaction is to showcase only the highlight reel of our lives by not acknowledging, discussing, or revealing our flaws, mistakes, or mishaps. Except this results in a drain of precious mental energy in our everyday interactions. A majority of us have never been taught how to navigate the emotions that arise when we feel we've underperformed, made a mistake, or disappointed another. It is a rare and special human who seeks out and cherishes feedback. But that's all about to change.

In my experience, many people would rather live in denial than face the emotional discomfort of receiving feedback, preferring to focus solely on their strengths. Sure, I get it, having a conversation about what's not working can be uncomfortable. Avoiding feedback separates us in relationships, keeps us from knowing our blind spots and being as effective as we could be, and most of all, prevents us from growing, learning, and transforming our energy drains into energy gains.

What's your first reaction when someone says, "Hey, can I give you some feedback?" Do you cringe and brace yourself for a verbal assault? Are you open and curious? Or are you somewhere in the middle? Do your thoughts race, as you wonder, *what did I do?* I used to experience all of that. And sometimes, I still do.

People often bristle at the idea of receiving feedback because it can feel awkward or painful to have someone else 'expose your weaknesses.' But, in order to take personal accountability, it's important to acknowledge how others are perceiving us. Here's the key: whenever someone highlights a weakness, would you be able to receive it differently if you knew that *a weakness is just a strength overused*?

That simple change in mindset will transform your experience, which in turn will deepen your relationships, reduce your stress levels, and elevate your performance.

How do you do this? By using the Superpower Recovery Tool. There are five practical questions that we'll explore together. I have no doubt that once you master this tool, you'll be thirsty for feedback.

Superpower Recovery Tool

Answer these five questions:

1. Verbatim, what feedback did you receive?

2. What's the positive quality underneath? Describe what's good about possessing this quality.

3. When you are overly _____ (insert quality from question 2), what do you experience?

4. What's the mild opposite of the quality you named in question 1?

5. Refer to the original feedback you received. How might you pull back and transform your apparent weakness into your superpower?

Below is an example of how someone might answer the Superpower Recovery Tool questions.

1. Verbatim, what feedback did you receive?

    Answer: *"You're **arrogant**. You always think you're right."*

2. What's the positive quality underneath? Describe what's good about possessing this quality.

    Answer: *I'm **confident** and **self-assured**. I advocate for myself and speak up. I'm often willing to take control or lead a situation.*

3. When you are overly **confident** and **self-assured** (insert qualities from question 2), what do you experience?

    Answer: *Sometimes I experience a loss of connection and distance in relationships.*

4. What's the mild opposite of the quality you named in question 1?

    Answer: *The mild opposite of arrogance is humility and curiosity.*

5. Refer to the original feedback you received. How might you pull back and transform your apparent weakness into your superpower?

    Answer: *I could slow down, ask questions, and listen to the answers. Being open to other people's opinions will expand my perspective—transforming arrogance back into confidence.*

It's your turn. Refer to the Superpower Rebalancing Sheet in Figure 11.1 to see how these ideas apply to feedback people commonly receive, and try it for yourself! If you want a few more examples, watch "The Superpower Recovery Tool" video. You'll find it at *intuitiveintelligenceinc.com/pbmresources*.

FIGURE 11.1 **Superpower Rebalancing Sheet**

FEEDBACK ALONG THE LINES OF . . .	+ QUALITY UNDERNEATH	MILD OPPOSITE
Arrogant	Confident / self-assured	Humility / curiosity
Autonomous / lone ranger	Independent	Team-player / collaborative
Blaming others	Hold others accountable	Personal accountability
Conflict-avoidant	Maintaining peace / harmony in the moment	The ability to endure temporary discomfort to speak compassionate truth
Defensive / guarded	Self-protection	Open / receptive / trusting
Fearful / anxious	Vigilant / anticipatory	Self-trust / risk taking
Idealistic / optimistic	Positive / hopeful	Practical/ action-oriented
Know-it-all / self-righteous	Confidence	Curious / ongoing learner
Negative / pessimistic	Protective / cautious	Open / hopeful
Overly responsible	Personal accountability	Expand perspective to include others and the environment
Reactive	Move quickly	Thoughtful / responsive
Stubborn / inflexible	Determined / clear	Open / curious / agile
Sensitive	Caring / emotionally aware	Set good boundaries / holding others accountable
Slow / takes too long	Detail oriented / thoughtful	Efficiency and Effectiveness

FEEDBACK ALONG THE LINES OF . . .	+ QUALITY UNDERNEATH	MILD OPPOSITE
Indecisive	Cautious / careful	Decisive and clear
Noncommunicative	Independent	Expressive / communicative
Wordy / talk too much	Expressive	Clear, concise, good listener
Workaholic	Hardworking / dedicated	Balanced / well-rounded

How do you feel after reframing feedback as a strength overused? I hope you use this five-question tool as a simple way to transform any feedback into an energy gain. Your ability to receive and integrate feedback is an enormous advantage both at work and at home. Now it's time to check in on your overall mental energy.

MENTAL ENERGY REASSESSMENT

1. What are the top three repetitive thoughts occupying your mental real estate? If you're unsure:

   - Pay attention to what keeps you up at night.

   - What's on your mind first thing in the morning?

   - When you're showering or driving down the highway on autopilot, where does your mind wander?

2. What does your self-talk sound like? What do you say to yourself when:

   - You make a mistake?

   - You feel disappointed in yourself?

(continued)

(continued)

3. Which thought patterns are you underusing or overusing?

- Personalization (you)

- Projection (someone else)

- Generalization (bigger than you or someone else)

4. Have you ever received challenging feedback? Try using the Superpower Recovery Tool questions alongside the Superpower Rebalancing Sheet to transform that feedback into your underlying strength.

5. Overall, on a mental level, are you experiencing a net gain (+) or a net drain (−) of energy?

☐ net gain (+)   ☐ net drain (−)

The way you determine this is by looking at both your reassessment answers and also by checking in with your Body Map. If you feel a constriction or tightness in your body as you answer these questions, you likely have a net drain in this area. If you have a feeling of openness, ease, or lightness in your body as you answer these questions, this energy level is likely a net gain for you. We'll do this at the end of every section.

Every awareness in your partnership with your mind helps. And as your mental energy grows, so will the energy in *all* areas of your life. In the next section, we'll investigate how to recover lost emotional energy.

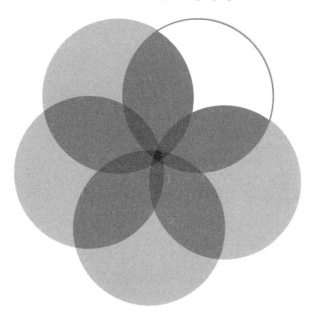

PART III

EMOTIONAL ENERGY

CHAPTER 12

EMOTIONS 101

Despite being in the business of life and death, "How to Effectively Navigate Emotions" wasn't a course in medical school or residency. Thanks to burnout, my energy and focus shifted to developing my own emotional intelligence. I became more confident in navigating the unknown as well as my ability to help others. In 2005, I followed through on the idea that I had expressed to Roger about using my burnout experience to educate and support my colleagues. So I organized and led my first group workshop called "Self-Care in Health Care" for oncology physicians, nurses, and staff. The purpose of the workshop was to reduce stress by improving teamwork and communication. One of the participants was Stan Mackey, an oncologist I had known for years. His introverted nature and matter-of-fact answers rubbed his colleagues and some patients the wrong way. He didn't seem to notice the wake he often left in his path. Personally, I loved consulting with him because he was a human encyclopedia of the latest research trials, and his mannerisms reminded me of one of my favorite professors. But his emotional IQ? Well, like many colleagues I've consulted with, Stan needed some support on that front.

Prior to the start of the group, I'd received plenty of pushback for combining doctors, nurses, and staff in the same workshop. The tension was palpable as individuals sidelined me in the hallway, commenting in a whisper:

- "Shouldn't the doctors and nurses be in separate groups? They won't say what they really mean."

- "What about power and hierarchy? Will there be repercussions for telling the truth?"

- "Whose crazy idea was this anyway? It'll never work."

On day one, the horror on one nurse's face was evident as she exclaimed, "You mean Mackey is in this group?! There's no way I'm going to stay if he's here." She crossed her arms in front of her chest, rolling her eyes. "One of us needs to leave, and it's not going to be me."

My instinct told me that powerful emotions like these, when processed and expressed in a safe environment, could be the catalyst for the camaraderie and psychological safety they so desperately needed. If I could teach this group how to navigate their emotions, they would have an opportunity to care for one another, which would no doubt ripple outward to patient care, other collegial relationships, and their personal lives.

Just then, Stan scurried in and occupied the last open seat in the circle of 10 chairs. He seemed to be deep in thought—almost like his body made it to the workshop, but his mind was still preoccupied by his previous patient.

I explained the basic guidelines of the group and that we would pass a green fabric heart filled with lavender to identify who had priority to speak. Most important, I asked that each participant focus on herself or himself. "It may be tempting to hope someone else 'gets it' or learns how to communicate better," I said, "but it's critical that you keep coming back to yourself. If each of you stays focused on your own experience, I can be sure that everyone in the room is accounted for."

After a couple sessions, I noticed that Stan was primarily giving one- and two-word answers.

Me: Stan, how are you doing today?
Stan: Fine.
Me: What's on your mind?
Stan: Nothing.
Me: Is there anything you'd like to discuss today?
Stan: Not really.

Each time he finished speaking, he would quickly pass the green heart to someone else. Only when I prompted the group to finish the sentence, "If I could speak from the heart, I would say . . ." did Stan venture beyond his one-word replies. With an expressionless face, he said, "I don't typically speak from the heart. I speak from the head and mouth. Thank you."

Noticing his rigid body language and awkwardness, I felt somewhat deflated. *He's going to be a tough nut to crack,* I thought.

Looking back, I can't really blame Stan for his discomfort. The topic of emotions is often nerve-racking. And most of us were never formally taught in school, at home, or at work how to cope with them—especially the challenging or uncomfortable ones.

EMOTIONS MADE SIMPLE

One of the most important aspects of emotions is that, no matter how uncomfortable or difficult they are, they can be simplified into *one word*—for example: joyful, confused, or betrayed. We'll talk about this concept more in depth shortly, but for now, I'll put in boldface various emotions throughout the chapter to assist you in identifying them and noticing how easy naming them can be. A few everyday examples include **anxiety** about never-ending deadlines and emails; **frustration** with uncooperative colleagues, clients, or family; **resistance** to changing our routines; and group text **appreciation** when we achieve milestones. There's the **joy** we receive from our children intertwined with the **irritation** we have with them, and the **pride** we have in ourselves combined with the **worry** and **disappointment** when there's a chance we may not reach our goals.

What makes emotions more complex is that they're tied to our physical sensations, such as muscles tightening, jaw clenching, or stomach turning (refer to the Body Map in Chapter 4). They can also be vague and overwhelming. This discomfort has many of us wanting to steer clear of emotions altogether. Because we don't know how to navigate them, they can easily confuse us, slow us down, or handicap our ability to think clearly and be decisive. However, once you understand what's happening inside and can articulate it, you will gain a new level of confidence in your relationships.

In the workplace, I've come to appreciate the apprehension around anything remotely perceived as touchy-feely or diplomatically labelled as *soft skills*. Eliminating emotions has a noble intention: empowering people to stay on schedule. That's understandable, considering how much our society values productivity and efficiency. Therefore, the goal becomes to avoid feeling any emotion that would slow us down or complicate our decision-making. In fact, many prefer to just *avoid feeling at all*. But whether or not we want to acknowledge them, emotions are an integral part of our daily experience.

The role of emotions, especially at work, may seem like a low priority. But once you realize they're driving some of our most desired outcomes—loyalty, motivation, camaraderie, engagement, collaboration, and innovation—you may change your mind. If you're thinking, *Who has the luxury to slow down and feel?* Soon you'll realize that you (and your teams) can't afford not to.

An emotion is a feeling or mood state that changes depending on how you are relating to the experience of your life at any given moment. I like to describe emotions as *energy in motion*. It's important to acknowledge all emotions and allow them to move through you, rather than letting them get stuck inside you. Emotions are important real-time data. They occur in response to your thoughts (conscious and subconscious) and often show up physically through body language, fluctuations in tone, or facial expressions. Because of this, sometimes other people will comment on your emotions even before you realize you're experiencing them yourself.

RULES ABOUT EMOTIONS

When you were young, you likely witnessed family members and people in your community react in unique ways to a range of emotions. There may have been spoken and unspoken rules such as:

- Just chill.

- We're in public. Now is not the time to be a drama queen (or king).

- Why do you always act like such a baby?

- Keep your head down and don't get involved.

- You have so much more than other people. There's nothing to be sad about.

Long after you left your family, you likely continued using that emotional blueprint that you didn't even know you had. As you transitioned into the workplace, you likely picked up even more "emotional rules" from your mentors, peers, and bosses. Often without even knowing it, you continued adjusting your emotional responses to fit in or at the very least, prevent conflict.

Consciously or subconsciously, when you avoid emotions, you lose the opportunity to identify, express, and heal yourself by experiencing them. When you stop your emotions from moving through you, that energy doesn't disappear—it has to go somewhere. Sometimes you may deflect it onto others. Or you can become reactive or defensive, undermining your own best intentions—without even knowing it. Often these emotions get stuck inside you, creating a steady drain on your energy, as you put so much work into *not* feeling anything. The irony is, rather than simply feeling and releasing them, you're hauling them around everywhere you go.

By leaning into our emotions, we can develop powerful relationships, make quick and effective decisions, and reconnect to the meaning and purpose in our work and lives—all keys to preventing burnout. This was my vision for the entire team when I formed the Self-Care in Healthcare group, Stan included.

The problem is when individuals like Stan are so tuned out of their own emotions, they don't even recognize them when they occur. Or they easily get overwhelmed by the sensations that accompany emotions, so they block out feeling anything at all. This need for control has them developing all sorts of coping mechanisms that lead them to disconnect from their own bodies and hearts—not to mention, those around them.

When physiological signals spike at the same time you're experiencing strong feelings, the combination can feel chaotic and unsettling. Emotions are inextricably tied to your body's physical sensations, such as heart racing, stomach turning, and palms sweating. In most cases, these biological responses are normal. They are how your body copes with change. The problem comes when we don't listen. The signals won't go away, like most people hope. In fact, they get louder.

Let's say you receive an email announcement that your leader has been promoted and you'll be getting a new boss that you're much less fond of. You may experience a sinking sensation in your stomach. Maybe you're barely able to breathe, realizing that you feel **panicked**. It's hard to think clearly when you're physically uncomfortable. But believe me, your thoughts and emotions are running the show. That's why it's so essential to practice becoming aware of them. You may be responding to some stories you've made up about others or protective self-talk in your head, which are generating challenging emotions of **fear** and **panic**.

In moments like these, it's completely normal to want to regain control and focus. Your brain may judge emotions as a threat. That's why you may suppress, deny, or reason away your feelings. But that's only when you don't understand their value. When you can effectively use the information coming from both your head and your heart together, your inner GPS emits a stronger signal and you know exactly what to do next.

EMOTIONS LIKE COMPANY

Besides causing physical discomfort, emotions can be difficult to navigate because we rarely experience just one at a time. Emotions, like teenagers, often travel in packs.

How does this show up in real life? Imagine you've just been promoted at work. Pure **bliss**, right? Well, not so fast. If you were applying for the job alongside a trusted colleague, there may be some **awkwardness** as well. You might even feel some unexpected **guilt**. What if your career advancement comes with the stipulation of needing to move your family to a new city, while your children are in the middle of high school? This good news might also come with feelings of **anxiety** (around attaining the next level of performance), **trepidation** (about uprooting your family), and **overwhelm** (by all that needs to be organized to make it happen).

When we have a limited emotional vocabulary, we usually opt for simplicity. Be careful not to get stuck in the "I'm **stressed**!" bucket. A lot of emotions will huddle together under the single umbrella of feeling stressed.

For example, if you're a single parent, and you say, "I'm stressed," you may mean one or more of the following:

- I have to work this weekend, and I feel **guilty** and **disappointed** that my kids will be babysat by their devices, rather than spending quality time with me.

- I didn't have time to buy groceries, and I feel **frustrated** and **ashamed** because I say how important health is, yet I'm grabbing takeout once again.

- It's my responsibility to bring snacks for soccer practice this week, and I'm **irritated** and **overwhelmed** because I'm physically exhausted and it's just one more item on the to-do list.

Being clear about what you're feeling will allow you to get the support you require and know what may need to change (even if it's simply in your thought patterns). By identifying the exact emotions present in a given situation, you gain a more complete picture of what's really happening. Much like the personalities assembled around the dinner table, this experience can feel like a "family of emotions." Once you decipher them, they will provide clues that, coupled with curiosity, will pave a clear path to your own heart and to those of others around you.

THOUGHTS VERSUS FEELINGS

Sometimes you can confuse your emotions with thoughts. While thoughts and emotions influence one another, they are separate and distinct. You're already familiar with three thought patterns: personalization (you), projection (other), and generalization (bigger than you or others). The story you choose to believe will determine how you *feel*. Remember in Chapter 10 when your friend Carlos was 15 minutes late?

If you *personalized* that experience by thinking, *I bet I'm being stood up!* You may have felt **rejected**, **hurt**, or **disrespected**.

If, on the other hand, you veered toward *projection*, you may have thought, *Carlos is so rude! Didn't his parents teach him any manners?* This thought may have led you to feeling **upset** or **angry**.

And finally, if your thoughts tended toward *generalization*, you may have thought, *Oh no! I hope he didn't get into an accident or have to stay late at work again.* In which case, the resulting emotion(s) may have been **curiosity**, **worry,** or **concern**. So as you can see, the power of changing your thoughts can have a powerful impact on how you feel.

There's a big difference between expressing what you're thinking and expressing how you're feeling. We often mislabel thoughts with phrases like these:

"I feel *like*" or **"I feel *that*"** plus a string of words that express an explanation, an opinion, a judgment, or a story. For example:

- "I feel *like* my boss was ignoring me."

- "I feel *that* my boss wasn't present."

Despite using the word *feel*, there was no emotion included in either of those sentences, just the thought that one is being ignored or the boss wasn't present. All it takes is inserting one word after the word feel such as *like* or *that* to derail expressing your feelings and instead be expressing thoughts.

In this same scenario, an emotion would simply be expressed by saying, "I feel" plus a one-word emotion, such as, "I feel **dismissed**."

The former two statements express thoughts, which imply an opinion or interpretation of what your boss was doing, whereas the latter is clearly expressing your emotional reaction. Be on the lookout for the simple words *like* or *that* inserted after the word *feel*. That's your warning that you're leaving your heart (emotions) and heading back up to your head (thoughts).

Another challenge: most people have a fairly limited emotional vocabulary. For example, they can identify when they're **happy**, **sad**, **glad**, or **mad**, but in reality, there are many more emotions, such as **curious**, **reluctant**, and **energetic**. On the next page, you'll find an Expanding Your Emotional Vocabulary Exercise.

Why should you care? Because expanding your emotional vocabulary will vastly improve your ability to articulate what you're experiencing. Knowing how to name emotions will also boost your confidence and clarity in decision-making, allowing you to communicate more effectively, and letting you connect more easily with others. Now that's an emotional energy gain!

UNEXPECTED CONNECTIONS

A little-known fact is that your *physical* and *emotional* issues are also related. Unaddressed emotions can result in intractable physical symptoms, such as headaches, insomnia, and pain. When we avoid or suppress our emotions, they can show up physically to get our attention. With strong emotions such as anger, we can find ourselves in fight-or-flight mode, which causes a chain of physiological effects, including a spike in heart rate, blood pressure, blood sugar, and cholesterol levels. In today's high-stress world, these biochemical responses have become a regular occurrence, which over time can create devastating outcomes for our physical health.

If going through a worldwide pandemic has taught us anything, it's that the invisible aspects of life, such as viruses, the internet, and yes, emotions, can be driving what's happening in the physical world. All physical ailments impact our mental and emotional health, and the opposite is also true.

A friend of mine, Arun Sardana, remembers having his first episode of tachycardia (heart racing) at the age of 12, while carrying his baby cousin up a spiral staircase in his grandmother's home. For many years, whenever he had anxiety, once again he would experience a fluttering sensation in his chest.

Expanding Your Emotional Vocabulary Exercise

Here is an emotional vocabulary list summarizing several common emotions. This is by no means complete, so feel free to add any others you can think of.

HAPPY	CURIOUS	CONNECTED	Skeptical
Joyous	Intrigued	Loved	Hopeless
Proud	Inquisitive	Grounded	Self pity
Elated	Wonderment	Ease	**POWERFUL**
Peaceful	Awe	Moved	Comfortable
Surprised	Alive	Touched	Confident
Ecstatic	Confused	Open	Eager
Generous	Puzzled	Nurturing	Energetic
Abundant		Trusting	Fulfilled
Grateful	**MAD**		Hopeful
Playful	Angry	**SAD**	Glad
Energetic	Annoyed	Depressed	Empowered
	Edgy	Lonely	Inspired
ANXIOUS	Irate	Lost	Engaged
Annoyed	Resistant	Unloved	
Exhausted	Frustrated	Disrespected	**ADDITIONAL**
Irritated	Hurt	Tired	**EMOTIONS**
Nervous		Exhausted	_____
Stressed	**FEARFUL**		
Overwhelmed	Scared	**DISAPPOINTED**	_____
Impatient	Apprehensive	Bored	_____
Apprehensive	Panic	Disgusted	_____
Distressed	Shock	Dejected	_____
Uneasy	Horrified	Uncomfortable	_____
Concerned	Reluctant	Uneasy	_____

When you read this list, notice:

1. Which emotions feel most familiar? Place a checkmark (✓) to the left of these ones.

2. Which ones do you have the most resistance to? Place an ✗ to the left of these ones.

(continued)

(continued)

To expand your emotional vocabulary, choose one of the emotions you checkmarked and circle two other words that describe that same emotion in varying intensity. For example, if I had placed a check mark next to *anger*, I might circle *irritation, frustration*, *upset*, *livid*, or *rageful*. A good way to think about emotions is on a spectrum of intensity. The following four examples in Figure 12.2 are of how emotions when left unchecked can grow bigger. Start from the center (in your peaceful heart) and then follow each emotion from the middle to the outer circle, noticing how each one increases in magnitude.

FIGURE 12.2 **Home Diagram**

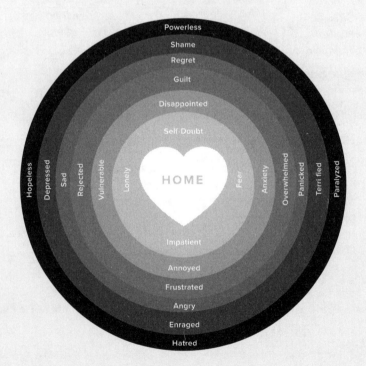

Bring to mind a recent emotional experience. Use the emotional vocabulary list to find words that best describe how you felt. It's OK if there's a family of emotions riding together; there usually is.

His physicians told him that it might be a congenital defect. They recommended cardiac ablation, a procedure to stop the electrical impulses likely causing the symptoms. They also advised him to avoid caffeine and spicy foods to reduce his stress.

Decades later, following his divorce, while discussing the trauma that children experience as a result of sexual abuse, Arun suddenly remembered that the first incidence of tachycardia happened the same day after he was sexually abused in a bathroom directly below the spiral staircase.

Since then, Arun has worked to reveal, feel, and heal that deep psychological trauma without any recurrences. He has gone on to create Karuna, an inner-child well-being educational platform to help heal others suffering from childhood trauma. As a side note, Arun now enjoys two cups of coffee and plenty of spicy food daily.

Arun's story illustrates the obvious overlap between the physical and emotional worlds, but so many of my colleagues continue to compartmentalize the body from the mind, heart, and spirit. Nobody did this better than Stan.

I needed to cut him some slack. Of all the medical disciplines, oncology is one of the most intense—in which every patient arrives with a potential death sentence. Stan was a good doctor. He cared for his patients with impeccable attention to detail, focusing on the latest scientific trials, treatment plans, and prognoses. My hope was to inspire him to see the interwoven nature of our physical and emotional health. I knew that to get there, he would need a lightbulb moment.

During week four of the group, the opportunity arose. Two participants were in a heated debate when I noticed the color of Stan's face change. After mediating their conflict, I turned to him and asked, "Did something happen while those two were talking? Did you feel any physical signals in your body?"

"No," he replied matter-of-factly.

"Well, I noticed your face getting flushed and your ears turning red. In fact, they still are. Can you feel what's happening?"

"No," he replied, slightly surprised.

I handed Stan the green fabric heart and asked him to hold onto it during our group from then on. "Next time I ask you if you can feel your body, but you can't, just say you can feel the weight and texture of this green lavender heart in your hand," I prompted him.

He hesitated and then said, "Sure, that sounds easy enough."

Even though Stan didn't realize it yet, he had taken the first step toward experiencing his emotions. With the simple gesture of holding the green fabric heart, he was about to tune in, rather than tune out.

AVOIDING UNCOMFORTABLE EMOTIONS

It's certainly easier to share the positive, happy experiences when we look and feel confident. Most people prefer to project an image of success, fun, and exceptionalism (the highlight reel of their lives on social media). Yet we're often less willing to expose our vulnerabilities: our failures, disappointments, or when we need help or assistance.

While you may think that you're more resilient without these challenging emotions, that's not the case. The most compelling lie we tell ourselves is that we can, as social researcher Brené Brown says, "selectively numb emotions" such as **pain, disappointment,** and **grief**. In fact, what actually happens is that we simultaneously dull the painful emotions while also reducing our capacity to experience pleasant emotions such as **joy, connection**, and **gratitude**. And then we wonder why we feel so **drained, disconnected**, and devoid of emotion in our lives.

All emotions are meant to move through you and provide valuable data. True resilience doesn't come from an emotion-free life; it comes from knowing how to surrender, experience them, and allow them to guide you.

For years, without even realizing it, Stan had become the master of cutting emotions out of his life. His definition of quality care did not include slowing down to ask his patients questions about their emotional journey with cancer, such as:

1. How are you adjusting emotionally to not working?

2. Are you feeling **supported** at home?

3. How do you feel about losing your hair?

. . . or any of the dramatic life changes that come with a cancer diagnosis. Stan was simply operating—as best he knew how—from his well-developed intellect.

One day in our group, a nurse confessed that her pending divorce was impacting her ability to be present with her patients and to function at work.

When I noticed Stan's face turning bright red again, I asked the nurse if she could pause for a moment.

"Hey, Stan, what do you feel in your body right now?"

"Nothing," he replied. As I pointed to the green heart in his hand, he continued, "Oh, yeah, I mean . . . I feel this heart in my hand, right?"

"Do you?" I asked. Noticing Stan's accelerated breathing, I got up and stood beside his chair. "Stan, is it all right if I put my hand on your back?"

He nodded. I could feel him sweating and trembling. "Great," I said. "How about if I put my other hand on your upper chest?"

Stan nodded again.

"OK. Take a deep breath and push my hands apart. Can you do that?" In that moment, slightly **surprised**, Stan realized he had the ability to override his panicked shallow breathing and resumed control with a nice, slow, deep breath.

After one minute of breathing that way, I asked him, "Stan, what do you feel now?"

He responded, "This time, I can feel the green heart cushion in my hand." Then he paused. "I can feel my feet on the ground." We all sat at attention— this was the most he had tuned in to his body in four weeks.

"And I can feel my stomach turning and constriction in my upper chest. Now I feel numbness in my arms and tingling. I haven't felt this way since my own divorce." He continued, "My wife left me because she said I work all the time and I didn't show up in our marriage. I don't know what she was talking about. I work every day to provide for her, the kids, and our life. My patients and colleagues love that I know the best treatments and can help them get better. It's probably better this way. I hope she finds happiness. I must say it's awfully lonely for me, though, to know she's not at home anymore—even if I'm never there."

After this unexpected burst of accountability, tenderness, and vulnerability, we all sat in silence. No one saw that coming.

"Neha, what's in this green heart anyway? I don't normally talk about my personal life."

I smiled, and began, "What you just shared is perfect. That green heart is the gateway to getting back into your body and letting your physical sensations guide you. I think for many years you've been relying pretty heavily on your head."

As the group continued, each person opened up, one by one. It was as if Stan's ability to be vulnerable and present gave them permission to share more freely, too. Stan wasn't the only one who hid behind his white super-hero cape, while tightly guarding his own heart. I witnessed each of these healthcare heroes lean in and connect to each other's humanity. Instead of rushing through, they slowed down and stayed present. This was a day to remember.

Despite what society has told us, it's not a weakness to express your emotions, be vulnerable, or acknowledge feeling exhausted or burned out. In fact, it's in your best interest to do so because it serves as the catalyst for your healing. Being able to identify and express challenging emotions—without judging them—provides you with a profound sense of self-trust, confidence, and control to navigate almost any situation. It also gets you away from feeling "stressed" to feeling what's really going on inside you. This ability doesn't just improve your work, it will also create ease in your otherwise chaotic day while making you feel more alive and connected to your life.

What do you do when you feel uncomfortable emotions? Slow, soft, deep, and focused belly breaths are a powerful tool to help relax and allow the energy to move through you. What's amazing about the life-sustaining power of our breath is that it's an automatic bodily function that *you also have voluntary control over*. When you don't take control of your breathing, you limit your ability to adjust, adapt, and feel. So if you're feeling discomfort, you have the power to change that . . . simply by slowing down and deepening your breath. Pause to take three soft, deep belly breaths. And if, like Stan, you spend more time in your head than your heart, finish this sentence to connect more deeply with your emotions:

"If I spoke from the heart, I would say . . ."

If you're not sure how to answer that, start with identifying your physical sensations or the thoughts running through your head. And trust that the right words will come to you.

THE IMPACT OF ACCESSING YOUR EMOTIONS

Close to the end of the workshop, Stan began opening up more about how his patients were impacted by his newfound emotional skills. From what he described, his approach to emotional engagement with patients was to choose his words carefully. He told a story about one of his favorite patients, a young woman who had lung cancer and had entered the active dying phase. Because he was more aware of his body's sensations, he could readily feel his own grief. She reminded him of his daughter. Instead of running to his next patient or ignoring the emotion, he let his eyes water as he said, "It's been an honor to be your doctor."

The patient grabbed his hand and squeezed hard. "Thank you, Doc. I can't tell you how much that means to me."

That seemingly simple gesture carried a profound impact on Stan. He was able to tolerate her emotional response because he was connected to his own feelings.

When one of the nurses commended him, he looked bashful and said, "Oh, it was nothing."

From the way he said it, with such pride and happiness in his eyes, I could tell that his "nothing" meant "everything."

When week eight of the Self-Care in Healthcare workshop arrived, I asked everyone to gather in a circle. I explained that we were going to end our time together with gratitude for one another.

Explaining why gratitude matters, I said, "I believe some of our deepest desires are to be heard, seen, and valued. We give an incredible amount to our patients, and this has been a time to slow down and share our hearts with one another to recharge ourselves.

"In the gratitude exercise we're about to do, the person holding the rose quartz stone will be receiving gratitude from the rest of the group.

"Now, does anyone want to hear something that isn't true?" I asked.

The room was silent.

"Good, because many people get uncomfortable in silence. And I don't want you to fill the silence by saying something that isn't true. So if there is silence, trust that it's because people are thinking about the best way to appreciate you, rather than deciding that it's because there isn't anything positive for anyone to say.

"For those on the receiving end of gratitude, your only job is to notice the physical sensations in your body, practice soft belly breathing, and believe what is being said about you is *true*. Allow yourself to take it in, practice receiving, and just say two words: thank you."

Slowly, we moved around the circle, and we finally came to Stan. He held the green fabric heart in one hand and the rose quartz stone in the other. He blinked a few times quickly, as if he was nervous to hear what was coming. One by one, each person told him how this time together helped them discover a man who seemed to hide behind his medical journals and use knowledge as a way to connect. Some expressed how they loved the bright and colorful soul that he was. Others spoke of his kind and gentle demeanor. Everyone referred to how much his vulnerability about his divorce helped them feel more connected to him.

Then the nurse who had initially expressed disdain toward him blurted out, "Stan, I have to say, I was wrong about you. You really do care—and you actually do have a huge heart."

Stunned, Stan replied, "I had no idea I hid it so well."

EMOTIONAL ENERGY ASSESSMENT

How do you feel now that we've waded into highly emotional waters? You've received a lot of information and reflected on the ways in which you navigate—or avoid—your emotions and the emotions of others.

To help you expand your awareness, answer a few questions that will highlight your emotional blueprint—the underlying patterns that were formed early in your life—that consciously or subconsciously drive how you navigate challenging exchanges.

1. Can you name the five most common emotions you experience?

2. Growing up, which emotions were OK and which were not OK?

3. What was your strategy for handling the ones that were *not OK*?

4. What emotions are OK at work?

5. What emotions are best left at home?

6. What emotions are taboo in social settings?

7. What emotions do you most avoid in others?

8. On a scale of 1 to 10, with 1 being not at all and 10 being extremely connected, how would you rate your ability to identify and express your emotions?

CHAPTER 13

ANXIETY: LIFE IN A PRESSURE COOKER

Remember the nurse who said, "If Mackey's in this group, I'm leaving," when she learned that Stan was going to be in the Self-Care in Health-care group? Her name was Tanya. It was probably obvious from her strong reaction that she had a history with Stan. Their working dynamic was handicapped by her chronic anxiety that often turned into anger in his presence. Early on in our group dynamic (before Stan's emotional breakthrough), Tanya was sharing how important it was to make sure the patients and their families felt cared for, and how much energy she and the other nurses put into protecting the doctors from that emotional burden. When I asked everyone to respond to what Tanya had just shared, there was an outpouring of love, support, and appreciation for her and all the nurses. Stan, in full introverted Stan-fashion, merely mumbled, "Thanks."

His one-word answer triggered Tanya's anxiety and anger. "Dr. Mackey, I have worked in this department for 10 years," she said, her voice trembling and her eyes filled with tears. "I do my best to make sure you all have *everything* you need, and despite all of that, you've never once addressed me by name. My name is Tanya."

Stan stared blankly at her, and it was clear to everyone in the group that she was right. He didn't know her name. I got up from my chair and, with her permission, put one hand on her upper back and the other on her upper chest just below her neck to ground her and help her slow down her breathing. I could sense how primal it was for her to feel overlooked. I also knew how much courage Tanya had mustered to speak truth directly to a work colleague in a position of authority.

"I . . . I'm sorry," Stan stammered. "You're right, the oncology nursing staff makes sure we have what we need. I never really notice unless something goes wrong. Tanya, I appreciate you and what you do to support our patients."

Within minutes, Tanya's decade of anxiety and anger deflated like a balloon and a sense of calm came over her. I returned to my seat. "You two have been working together for a long time. Tanya, is there anything you can think of that you admire about Stan?"

She shrugged. "Well, it's true that Dr. Mackey is one of our best doctors. I always know that when my patients are being seen by him, they'll receive the very best medical care. He never misses a detail and knows all the newest trials, so his patients have the best chance of surviving. Not to mention he takes on the toughest cases."

I smiled. "It sounds like you two actually make a great team. The patients are just as important to Stan as they are to you, Tanya. You just care for them in different ways, bringing unique and complementary skills to the table."

I turned to Stan. "What can you do to help make this situation better? What gesture might connect you to Tanya to express how much you appreciate her?"

He seemed perplexed for a minute, but then unexpectedly said, "What if we acted more like colleagues? And instead of Dr. Mackey, why don't you just call me Stan?" he inquired.

Tanya's eyes widened, and her breathing became more rapid and shallow. "Oh, I couldn't do that. You're a doctor, and I'm just a nurse. I can't . . ." as she froze with anxiety. Once again, I got up and stood behind her with one hand on her back, gently reminding her of her bravery, so she could continue.

I began, "Thank you for your suggestion, Stan. And thank you for expressing your fear, Tanya. It seems like the hierarchy in healthcare is getting in the way of you being able to connect with Stan. What if for a few weeks, you just think of his offer like an experiment and see what it feels like? If it doesn't work to call him Stan rather than Dr. Mackey, we'll come up with another option."

"OK," she hesitantly responded, visibly uncomfortable and skeptical of how referring to a physician by his first name could solve anything.

A few weeks later, as I pulled into the parking garage, I saw Stan and Tanya walking toward the hospital, laughing and joking, as they referred to each other by first name. These few weeks had solidified a bond of mutual respect and built a powerful bridge between them.

WHAT KEEPS YOU UP AT NIGHT

Honestly, who hasn't experienced anxiety? Maybe it starts with a little self-doubt or fear and before you know, it progresses into worry. If you're not paying attention, that emotion can grow into anxiety, panic, and maybe even paralysis. It's one of the most common emotions motivating us to work too hard and go too fast.

Common fears include:

- Disappointing another person (clients, leadership, family, friends, etc.)

- Logistics changing unexpectedly

- Public speaking

- Failure

- Making a mistake

- Missing a deadline

- Getting sick

- Not having enough money

- Not being where you think you should be at a particular stage in your life

Society has many judgments about anxiety, namely, that it's a sign of weakness, incompetence, or lack of confidence. What are your judgments (thoughts) about anxiety in yourself or in others?

WHY ANXIETY IS USEFUL

Anxiety is important data (like all emotions are) that can help identify areas where we might feel less confident, highlight what matters to us, and protect us from upcoming surprises. As an experiment, throughout this chapter, see if you can suspend your judgments about anxiety, and instead, notice the ways in which it can be a valuable asset.

Think back to your teenage days. In order to belong to a certain crowd, did you ever have a heightened awareness of what the cool kids were wearing or perhaps the need to excel in academics that inspired you to strive more than you would have on your own? If you were on a sports team, did you ever have performance anxiety that motivated not only your own achievement but also encouraged you to stretch yourself to further the team's success?

An upside of anxiety is that it can also motivate people to focus, prioritize, and take action to prevent something bad from happening. In the early months of the pandemic, for example, healthcare providers created elaborate systems to keep their families safe from potential exposure. Some arrived home and went straight to the laundry room to wash their scrubs and shower before reuniting with their families. Some even chose to physically separate themselves entirely to eliminate any chance of getting their family sick. Until we understood the nature of the virus, their actions likely protected many of their loved ones.

However (and whenever) anxiety might show up, this emotional state triggers the nervous system. Once adrenaline is released, an onslaught of physical symptoms may follow, including a racing heart, sweating, and tense muscles. Your level of awareness of your Body Map (refer to Chapter 4 for a refresher) will determine how early you recognize the symptoms. How intense do these feelings need to get before they capture *your* attention? If you're ever confused between two emotions, just get curious about your thoughts, so you can decipher how you're feeling. What stories are you telling yourself?

Beware: a common mistake people make is to confuse anxiety and excitement. Although they are both high-energy emotions, they are different because excitement comes with underlying thoughts of *optimistic anticipation* while anxiety is fueled by potentially *catastrophic thoughts*. For example, let's say you're about to give a talk to a new client. You notice your heart racing, a lightness in your chest, and your muscles tensing, while you think to yourself, *I hope this presentation goes great, so we can secure funding to expand into a new customer base!* This is a case of anticipatory excitement and potential opportunity. Let's say in the exact same situation, you had similar physical sensations but different thoughts, for example, *I better not mess this up! I'll be the laughingstock of the office.* Although you were experiencing similar physical signals, it can sometimes be difficult to identify exactly what's happening inside you. You are now equipped to know how your thoughts will help you decipher nuanced emotions.

WHY ANXIETY MIGHT NOT BE USEFUL

While anxiety can be useful, it can also undermine you, heightening your stress and draining you of energy. The two most common types of anxiety are acute and chronic.

Acute Anxiety

Acute anxiety is characterized by a sudden onset of fear, accompanied by elevated heart rate and blood pressure. Acute anxiety can show up as an immediate reaction to something that surprises you—ranging from getting cut off in traffic to being afraid of what might be wrong with your health. When a person gets overwhelmed by their anxiety, they can sometimes transition into having a panic attack, which is most obviously characterized by shallow, rapid breathing. In fact, they may be doing something called "reverse breathing," where they suck in their belly on the inhale and relax it on the exhale. This kind of breathing causes hyperventilation, which only makes the anxiety worse.

Two good examples of acute anxiety occurred during the Self-Care in Healthcare group: when one of the nurses began speaking about her divorce and Stan got flushed and his ears turned red, and when Tanya was trembling as she spoke about Stan not knowing her name, even though they'd been working together for a decade.

In the emergency department, I encountered many patients hyperventilating due to anxiety about what might be wrong with them. This was a great opportunity to get them to tune in to their bodies by putting one hand on their back and one hand on their upper chest near their neck and physically interrupting their swirling thoughts, while teaching them soft belly breathing as a tool to calm down. The bonus of being in the hospital was that they were hooked up to monitors and could literally witness their physiology changing in real time. They were fascinated to experience their heart rate, blood pressure, and breathing rates drift down to normal as their oxygen levels soared. "Thanks! I can't believe how easy it was to control my anxiety, Doc."

My satisfaction came from seeing how this simple exercise could transform anxiety into empowerment for them.

When anxiety shows up, get grounded in your body to shift how you feel. This will naturally prevent you from spiraling into a future-doom scenario. Consider soft belly breathing for yourself the next time you feel anxious and see if you have a different outcome.

Chronic Anxiety

Chronic anxiety is a constant low-level worry that lasts for six months or more. It makes it difficult to relax, and it begins to interfere with your ability to feel joy in your everyday activities.

People often wonder why they have ongoing anxiety. I like to explain chronic anxiety as *a failed attempt to control the future*. Sometimes anxiety is a strategy you developed in response to your family upbringing and your life experiences or a coping mechanism you use to stay safe. Anxiety also commonly occurs following traumatic experiences. For example, if you get into a car accident, you may find yourself in a state of hypervigilance each time you subsequently get on the highway, as a way to reassure yourself that it won't happen again. Or if you had a parent who experienced anxiety each time you left the house, you may think that loving others means you need to worry about them—even when they go out for a routine errand, like picking up groceries. The bottom line: if you don't reveal, feel, and heal your anxiety, that fear will likely be an emotional undercurrent, continuously draining you of precious energy.

As far back as I can remember, my mom had chronic anxiety around two independent and unrelated issues: meeting deadlines and wanting her children to be safe. Parents are protective by nature, but my mom took it to an extreme. Even in our twenties and thirties, when we were traveling to a family wedding or on vacation, my mother would request that both of my sisters and I traveled on separate flights. Why? Because if the plane crashed, at least she wouldn't lose all three of us.

WHAT'S THE WORST-CASE SCENARIO?

Anxiety drives us to think through potential worst-case scenarios, trying to prevent them from coming to fruition. This future-focused, fear-driven emotion is just trying to warn you about any potential surprises or adverse outcomes that might occur. But you can't control every aspect of life to protect yourself, your colleagues, or those you love. Anxiety is sometimes helpful, but other times, it merely serves as an illusion of trying to regain control. And once it becomes chronic, anxiety has definitely outlived its usefulness. Then it's time to assess the cost of it being a continuous mental and emotional energy drain. In fact, this type of consistent worry will often lead you to the very outcome you feared, a self-fulfilling prophecy.

For example, anxiety about your company's finances could balloon into worrying that your business will fail, which could then lead you to not invest in the resources needed to grow, and so—due to your own fears—it does fail. Then this experience makes you even more confident that you were right. This is an example of anxiety with a positive intention that can take you out of the present moment and cause you to make decisions based on fear rather than facts.

Where does anxiety show up in your life? Start with times when you feel low-intensity fear or self-doubt. Then reflect on what causes you worry, anxiety, panic, or even paralysis.

Back from the Future Exercise

If you acknowledge your anxiety, you can take steps to resolve your fears, putting preventive measures in place so you can feel more secure. Even chronic anxiety can be addressed by recognizing the underlying thought patterns and using them as clues to heal the root cause.

Whenever you feel yourself getting anxious, these steps will help reground you, expand your perspective, and allow you to be present in your current reality.

1. **Get Present**

    a. Notice any worrisome thoughts.

    For example, my mom might notice thoughts such as, *I hope my daughter is safe. I wonder if she is all right. She hasn't called yet today. What if she got into a car accident?*

    (continued)

(continued)

    b. Focusing your attention on your physical body is the quickest way to become present in the moment. Focus on gravity pulling you down, and feel the chair, couch, or floor supporting you; bring your body into the present moment. Practice soft belly breathing for three slow deep breaths or until you feel more settled (if you want a refresher, go back to Chapter 4).

2. **Name That Fear**

    a. Write down, "What if . . ." and finish that statement.

        My mother might write, "What if my daughter is hurt?"

    b. Leave two inches of space between each statement. You'll be coming back to it.

    c. Then write down, "What I'm most afraid of is . . ." and finish that statement.

        My mom might write, "What I'm most afraid of is not being able to protect her."

    d. Write as many of these statements as you can until you can't think of any more. By writing your fears down, you bring your mind into the present moment.

3. **Expand Your Perspective**

Go back to your list of fears and challenges and notice any limiting beliefs, stories, or unknowns there. One by one, write underneath each of those fears what the truth is in the present moment, for example, I am safe. Begin your statement with, "Right here, right now, the truth of the present moment is . . ."

        My mother might write, "Right here, right now, the truth of the moment is that I last spoke with my daughter yesterday, and she sounded healthy and happy. I haven't talked to her yet today. I don't know where she is. I have no data telling me that anything bad has happened."

4. **Reprogram Your Thinking**

   Now it's time to get creative! Create an "I am" affirmation to replace those fearful thoughts running on repeat in your mind. This short "I am" affirmation will help interrupt these ingrained brain pathways and create a simple and clear phrase that can reprogram your thinking. A powerful, clear, and concise statement will help you counteract your fears and keep you in the present moment of what's actually true.

   > My mother might write, "I am the mother of a capable, smart, and experienced daughter. I trust her."

5. **Ask Yourself: What Would Self-Trust and Courage Do Now?**

   What action would you take if you trusted yourself to handle what comes next? Write down whatever thoughts come to you. It may take time to make sense of what arises, and that's OK. Staying open is part of learning to trust yourself. You've got this.

   > My mom might say, "Self-trust and courage would have me focusing on what I need to get done today. If I'm worried, I can text or call my daughter to inquire if she's OK."

. . . .

To download an anxiety handout and see videos of clients being coached live, go to *intuitiveintelligenceinc.com/pbmresources*.

. . . .

Here's what most people don't realize—building self-trust is the path to healing anxiety. If you trust that whatever happens, you're resourceful and can figure out what to do next, you won't need to run endless loops of worst-case scenarios in your mind. By getting your body, thoughts, and fears back from the future and into the here and now, you will understand what's driving your chronic anxiety energy drain. Once you create powerful affirmations and reroute your thinking, you will be able to transform your anxiety into self-trust, boldly navigating the best path forward. You've taken yet another step forward to becoming *me-powered*.

CHAPTER 14

ANGER: WHEN WE EXPLODE

When people think of burnout, they commonly think of exhaustion, depletion, and overuse. They don't realize that anger could also be depleting their energy. I know that over the course of my own burnout, anger would often arise. It's an energizing emotion, to be sure, and it propels you but not always in the right direction. For me, it moved me forward . . . toward the cliff of burnout. I got annoyed with my colleagues for dumping work on me or not giving good patient handoffs. I got frustrated with leadership for not supporting us with enough staff. I got upset with the hospital for its unsustainable policies—occasionally, I even got mad at nurses who reported a patient spiking a fever at 4 a.m. (my confession to Roger in Chapter 2).

What's important about exhaustion is that it lowers your ability to endure stress and allows the more challenging emotions to rise, and anger is no exception—particularly if anger is an emotion that drove you in early childhood.

In Indian culture, it's a common practice to share child-rearing with extended family. In 1969 my older sister, Ritu, was born, and I followed shortly thereafter in 1970. To support my immigrant parents as they worked full-time, my grandmother (Nani) relocated to Michigan to take care of us. Then when I was three months old, my grandfather (Nana) received an opportunity to go to Africa on assignment with the United Nations. He requested that Nani join him. Everyone decided it would be best for Nani to go and take me with her.

Two years later, my mom and Ritu came to pick me up and bring me back to Michigan. To say I was heartbroken to leave Nani and Nana was an understatement. Apparently, I cried for nearly a month straight. I imagine my anger was from both fear and pain. It was nobody's fault. My grandparents took incredible care of me. My parents showed me nothing but love. And yet apparently I was so angry about being uprooted from my life there that upon my return to the United States, I refused to call my father "Dad." I was only two years old, and I would refer to him solely as *Hey you*. "Hey you, I'm hungry." "Hey you, I need potty." After a few months of anger and frustration on both sides, my father took two weeks off from work and spent every day feeding and playing games with me. Finally, I softened toward him and began calling him "Uncle." Thanks to his continued persistence, I eventually called him "Dad."

THE ROOT OF ANGER

Even though anger can be uncomfortable for the person experiencing it and those in the presence of it, it is not a "bad" emotion. Anger is not the real issue at hand, because anger is a secondary emotion. It's driven by fear, pain, or both. This intense feeling has many origins, but it often manifests to let us know when we're experiencing something as unjust or unfair. This internal alarm gives us an opportunity to express ourselves and take action in the service of what's most important to us. Whether anger is used to justify taking office supplies from work or get revenge on someone who has betrayed us, pay attention to what's driving the emotion to better understand what's happening.

At its heart, anger is self-protective, a means to regain safety. Whether you've articulated your boundaries or not, anger is also a sign that a line in the sand has been crossed. If this goes on over time, that anger will harden into resentment.

Just like in the Home Diagram in Chapter 12, the expression of anger can appear on a spectrum of intensity. If you catch it early, anger can show up mildly—as a slight irritation or annoyance. It may manifest physically in a variety of ways, such as finger or foot tapping. If the emotion is more intense, it may progress to being upset, feeling frustration, or outward hostility. This may become visible by your face flushing, a sharp tone, a raised voice, or swearing. Think: fists pounding, footsteps leaving, and doors slamming. Did your parents reserve the formal name listed on your birth certificate for moments like these? "Phoebe Marie Shaw, get down here right now!"

When you get angry, it means your thoughts (in response to something you've observed, been told, or remembered) have triggered a fight-or-flight response. This causes a series of biochemical reactions, including the release of hormones, most notably adrenaline and cortisol. Your heart rate and blood pressure rise, along with your blood sugar and cholesterol levels. This process readies you to handle any potential threats—real or imagined. Your body doesn't know the difference between a real thought or one in your dream. That's why when you're having a nightmare, in which you're being chased by someone or falling off a cliff, you wake up sweating, with your heart racing. Except when you open your eyes and look around, it's pitch black and peaceful. That's why it's so important to recognize when anxiety or fear are driving your thoughts. Don't put your body through the drama, unless it's real. That is a common way we lose precious energy.

ORIGINS OF ANGER

Anger can be startling and unmistakable. Many of us would prefer to turn our heads or cast aspersions on those who are angry simply because we don't know how to deal with anger ourselves, so we make the other person wrong for being upset. That's a mistake. When we witness others being angry or raise our own voice, we may come to harsh conclusions. *She has no control. He's so dramatic. I'm so negative.* On the other hand, anger can be viewed as a powerful display of authority. Those of us who had a parent who ruled by anger tend to feel this way. As a result, you might live in fear of anger or follow your parent's example of becoming angry to get your way.

When I'm working with an organization, I often encounter patterns of struggle between a manager and a team member. When I see this, I inquire, "Who, in your family of origin, does this experience remind you of?"

They usually protest. "What does my home life or my upbringing have to do with anything happening at work?" they ask.

"I know it might sound strange," I reply. "But your upbringing has as much relevance to how you're behaving as the clothes in your closet have on what you are wearing right now."

The environment we grew up in influences how we handle anger. Our reactions to adversity are often automatic, based on our past experiences and what was modeled in our upbringing. If you had a parent who would react by yelling when they were misunderstood, you could be the one who now publicly yells at a colleague when communication breaks down. If a parent did not express anger, you could be the one who now withdraws in silent resentment after not being taken seriously in a meeting. Your upbringing determines what you find acceptable when it comes to expressing or responding to anger. Another way this can show up is by you retaliating against what you experienced by choosing the opposite behavior from that of your caretaker. Everyone has their own unique response.

What is your relationship to anger? Are you someone who goes from 0 to 60 in less than 3 seconds? Have those around you mentioned your "short fuse"? If so, you are most likely saddled with unresolved tension in interpersonal relationships and / or a constant need for corrective follow-up conversations. If this is your style, anger is a short-term release valve that requires long-term cleanup.

Another option could be that you make a point to bypass anger by suppressing it within you and avoiding other people's explosive behavior at all costs. Do you put on a smile for others while secretly seething? Or maybe burying your feelings has become so commonplace that you hardly recognize just how deep your resentment is. If so, you are most likely carrying a heavy load of unexpressed emotion that is weighing on your heart and depleting precious emotional energy.

A third option is that you might find yourself somewhere in between. Maybe you express your anger passive-aggressively with snarky barbs, underhanded comments, or neighborhood gossip. Perhaps you vacillate between conflict avoidance and the occasional eruption.

Left unchecked, anger can quickly become a dangerous situation for those involved, transforming into rage and violence. The intensity of anger depends on many factors: what's happening, how triggered someone feels, the intensity of the experience, and the length of time they have been enduring a situation. However you navigate anger, it is worth taking inventory on how effectively you're utilizing this energy-fueled emotion—or not.

UNHEALTHY ANGER

Anger has a purpose. Our ancestors developed a biological ability to shift into fight-or-flight mode, which helped them survive in the wild. If there was an attack or some other threat, they would become fearful (or angry), and this biological mechanism was a prompt to either fight or run away from life-threatening danger. While our ancestors faced more basic threats to their survival, such as scarcity of food, prevalence of disease, and risk of violence from enemies, these episodes often resulted from Mother Nature or random events. And outside these experiences, they likely had periods that were peaceful.

But today's high-stress, fast-paced society is self-created, often leaving us feeling like we are constantly under attack. This is where our *do more with less, faster is better*, and *success requires struggle* mentality comes in. A brusque response from someone who is equally overwhelmed can feel like a slap in the face. A hot-headed driver cutting us off in traffic can spark the very same series of biological reactions as a genuinely life-threatening event. But our bodies were not designed to remain in a perpetual state of biological alarm that has become our current reality.

When I was practicing in the hospital, I witnessed the almost-daily effects of poorly managed anger. Those who are chronically resentful and furious experience sleep problems, high blood pressure, and digestive issues, to name a few ways that this hot emotion shows up in the body. Anger is not simply a challenging emotion—it's potentially life-threatening when left unchecked. Research shows that chronic anger is directly linked to an increased risk of heart disease and stroke. That's why it's so important to learn how to effectively handle anger in a healthy way.

If you view an unhealthy experience of anger as an opportunity to look deeper, then you will have the power to change it and become all the wiser for it, lowering your stress levels and helping you avoid burnout. But if you don't seize the chance to become *more aware of* and *heal the source of* your anger, then it will merely reroute and express itself in your body (unexplained back pain, headaches, etc.), your relationships, your job, or other seemingly unrelated aspects of your life—which will rob you of emotional energy.

For me, my anger rerouted itself into a *fish fight*.

I was staying with my dear friends Tom and Amy in Eugene, Oregon. Tom had just revived his saltwater fish tank, transforming it into a much less labor-intensive but equally beautiful freshwater tank. I stared into the 6-by-2-by-2-foot tank at 10 brightly colored Malawi fish as they adjusted to their new home—and to each other.

One fish in particular caught my attention. He was yellow with patches of gray and slightly larger than the rest. Periodically, he would whirl around the tank, and whenever he moved, all the other fish would rearrange themselves to maintain their distance from him, making him the isolated center of the performance. He would come to a stop, pause for 10 seconds, and resume his laps around the tank. It was like an ever-changing abstract painting of cobalt blue, tangerine yellow, and pearly white in motion.

As I kept watching, I began to see things differently. This wasn't a well-orchestrated performance for my viewing pleasure. It was survival of the fittest. These fish were swimming for their lives, fleeing in panic from the yellow and gray bully. As the power and hierarchy of the tank came into focus, my stomach sank and my heart began racing.

What made this bully think he could get away with such obnoxious behavior? I leaned right up to the glass. He immediately ceased swimming and turned to face me. He knew I was examining his bad behavior. I began speaking out loud (not paying any attention to how it might seem to the people around me), yelling: "Who do you think you are? There's no bullying allowed in this tank!"

The first two fingers of my right hand formed a V, and I pointed toward my own eyes and then toward his. "I've got my eyes on you, buddy."

He got the point. He didn't blink. (I don't know whether fish blink—but he didn't.)

"I'll have Tom take you out of the tank if you don't shape up! Watch it, or you're history, buddy."

Every muscle in my body was tense, as if I was in the middle of a fraught argument. As I walked away, it occurred to me. *Had I really just had a showdown with a fish?*

YOUR BRAIN AND STRONG EMOTIONS

Have you ever been surprised by the intensity of your own response? Or perhaps by the intensity of someone else's response to a seemingly innocent question or comment? It's biological. No, I'm serious, it is. And scientifically, it's referred to as an *amygdala hijack*.

The amygdala is a small but powerful part of the brain that serves as the seat of your emotions. Ordinarily, the brain works like this: the thalamus (the central processing system) takes in data, and then sends it on its way, first to the frontal cortex (the center of your logic and reason) and finally to the amygdala.

Yep, most of the time, we're supposed to *think* before we *feel*.

Your amygdala also stores some of your long-term memory, including emotional trauma. And when it receives data from the frontal cortex, it compares your present experience with your past experiences, looking for patterns. Biologically, it's a good idea to avoid repeating painful experiences. But sometimes it gets a little out of hand. In the amygdala's search for patterns, it tends to peek over the thalamus' shoulder to see if it thinks something matches an old and alarming pattern. If so, the amygdala can yank that data straight from the thalamus, bypassing the frontal cortex—and now you've been hijacked!

The amygdala doesn't *let* you think before you feel. It acts immediately to protect you from danger. And your emotions go haywire.

Just because a situation is similar to a stressful or traumatic experience in your past doesn't mean it is necessarily going to be traumatic this time around. Your frontal cortex could have told your amygdala that, *if it had stopped to listen.* Sadly, your amygdala thinks you're in imminent danger, and so your response to what is happening is out of proportion to the experience.

So when I lost my temper at a fish and accused him of bullying when, as far as I knew for sure, he was just swimming—my amygdala had taken control. I had flashed back to my experience of being bullied as both a child and as an adult and projected it onto that poor fish.

Around the same time that I was nearing the edge of burnout, a colleague had been intimidating me into giving him an easier patient load—but that wasn't my first experience being bullied. My older sister had bullied me throughout elementary and middle school. She had a habit of making me the butt of her jokes. And anytime something went wrong, I was the easy one to blame, even if I was asleep or not present for what was happening. Most traumatic to me was when she bullied me into drinking alcohol at the age of 13. I'd probably buried my anger about these experiences for years, but enduring it at work brought everything back to the surface. And when I saw it play out in the fish tank, something inside me came rushing out.

When this out-of-proportion reaction happens to you—and because you're human, it will—there is a simple way to soothe this (sometimes overly) protective part of your brain called the amygdala:

Step 1: Just stop. Pause. Even though your body and brain are screaming, notice what's happening and pause by taking a slow, deep breath engaging your abdomen. Notice your body's physical signals and manage yourself before engaging with anyone else. I'm not talking about stuffing or stopping the anger but just pausing and naming it so you can express it effectively, which might mean walking away for a while. Don't underestimate the power of three soft, deep belly breaths in the moment you're ready to react. Soft belly breathing will help the intensity subside, and once that happens, you'll have space and time to get curious about the underlying emotions.

Step 2: Get curious. Open up the pathway between your amygdala and your frontal cortex, and allow yourself to think, as well as feel. Pausing and getting curious gives you the space you need to move through your anger in a more healthy and productive way.

As we grew older, my sister and I had many honest conversations about what had happened. She shared how jarring it was for her to meet me as a two-year-old and how hard it was to adjust to sharing our parents' attention. It led her to feeling threatened and wishing I wasn't there, hence her bullying behavior. I expressed the pain it had caused me, and her apology helped me take the necessary steps to heal.

Once you understand what's driving your anger—for example, not being seen when you were a child—you have an opportunity to meet yourself with kindness and compassion. Use the following questions to get curious about whatever is upsetting you.

Rooting Out Anger Exercise

Begin by asking yourself:

1. What emotion(s) are driving my anger? (Hurt? Fear? Both?)

2. What am I protecting?

3. What boundaries are not being honored? Have I articulated them clearly?

4. What values am I defending?

5. When have I felt this way before?

Once you answer these questions, you'll discover the cause of what's upsetting you, such as past formative experiences. However, even if you simply address the current source of your anger, you'll be better off just by knowing and understanding *why* you're feeling the way you are. The most important part of this awareness is that you're kind and compassionate to yourself as you explore what emerges and develop a plan to heal it. It might be as simple as realizing you didn't draw a much-needed boundary, lacked a clear agreement, or felt taken for granted. Whatever it is, being able to articulate what happened and what you need to ask for in order to move forward will bring clarity and resolution, allowing the energy of anger to move through you, so that it no longer drains you.

SELF-DIRECTED ANGER

We all know anger when we see it—in others. Let's say you're engaged in an interpersonal conflict where you've just politely declined a request to cover a colleague's or partner's responsibilities and have been met with pushback and anger. You might take the other person's reaction personally, reverse your original decision, and agree to take over, sacrificing your own much-needed downtime.

And then you dread it. Your body's physiology starts speaking loudly: brain fog, generalized fatigue, and a pounding headache. The thoughts in your head are on repeat saying, *There's no one but me that he can ask, so I have to do this. I have no choice.* Resentment builds as you make your way through the task you felt trapped into saying yes to.

To gain clarity on how you got here, *get curious, not furious.* What if the anger you feel toward your colleague or partner is a way to avoid feeling a deeper and very real anger—toward yourself? After all, you're the one who got intimidated, doubted yourself, and caved. You are the one who didn't stand up for what your body, mind, and soul were begging for. Though saying yes may not have felt like a choice at the time—you chose it. Your utter exhaustion has, once again, taken a back seat to the needs of others. Did you fail to reinforce a personal (self-care) boundary? If so, why? Is it possible that you're angry with yourself for not taking a stand and saying "yes" to what you needed? (Stay tuned because in the social energy section, you'll become a boundary master!)

This more covert dynamic with anger is a silent conversation happening between you and yourself. Don't be fooled—the quality of your self-talk matters. Self-directed anger can quickly undermine your self-trust and ability to heal. It's a lot easier to blame and criticize other people's behavior (projection). It might be easier to focus on how inappropriate it was for the other person to have asked for the favor at all. (Self-talk might sound something like: *I think it's pretty obvious how overworked and tired I am. The nerve! He knows I worked last weekend because we were short-staffed.*) However, there are two equally responsible parties here. And let's face it, it's harder to take accountability and see your own part in a situation (healthy personalization). However, when you slow down and look within, it's almost like looking at your reflection in the water. Our external interactions often mirror how we relate to ourselves.

At moments like these, ask yourself, *How might my reaction have contributed to what happened? Am I really angry at the other person, or at myself?* Perhaps a desire to *stay safe* or *preserve harmony* drove your behavior. Maybe your natural instinct is to please others, and it's a pattern for you to self-sacrifice rather than communicate healthy boundaries. Whatever the reason, the most important piece is that you recognize the patterns that are often subconsciously resulting in critical self-talk.

The antidote to self-directed anger is compassion, grace, and forgiveness. Use the following three questions to guide you.

Healing Anger Exercise

Start by asking yourself:

1. Imagine your best friend coming to you with a similar dilemma. What would you advise them?

2. Do you naturally extend that compassion to yourself? If not, think about how you would talk to and comfort your best friend. And try using those words with yourself.

3. Now imagine a younger version of you, perhaps at an age when anger may have felt scary or unsafe. Using compassion, kindness, and grace, how would you comfort that version of you?

USING ANGER TO BECOME WISER

How you treat yourself reveals how you will treat others. If you are highly self-critical, you will find yourself critical of others. If you are compassionate with yourself when you make mistakes, you'll be more likely to be kind to others when they falter.

When you reflect, it may become clearer that the source of your anger (fear or pain) comes from within. Once you understand this, you can move from being a victim (stuck in a situation, at the mercy of another, and helpless to change your circumstances) into a *me-powered* creator who chooses a different response.

After you have a better understanding of your self-directed anger, give yourself permission to feel and experience the emotion fully. Vent in a journal. Scream in your pillow. Go ax-throwing. Call a trusted friend. Whatever ways you choose to express your feelings, the anger needs to have a pathway to move through you, so it does not get stuck inside you and express itself in unexpected or passive-aggressive ways.

If you recognize your anger as a clue that you need to set a boundary with someone who has crossed a line, it becomes a useful tool. Or if your anger tells you that you're not in a frame of mind to make an important decision, you can ask for time.

Newsflash: You can do a Take 2.

You might be wondering what I mean. Bring to mind your favorite movie. What was it? No matter which one you picked, I'm pretty sure it wasn't filmed in one take. The reason you love it so much is because after many, many takes, they got it just right. So why don't you allow yourself a do-over? Many people haven't even thought of the possibility of going back and asking for a second chance. Well, you've officially been granted the power of doing Take 2s. Notice how much better it feels when you realize you would have done it differently and then you get to do it that way! Making mistakes and owning them shouldn't separate you from others; it should connect you more deeply. It opens authentic conversation and allows you and them to be human. It also relieves the pressure of always needing to be right. Phew! Glad we got that cleared up.

MOVING BEYOND ANGER

At times, you may feel righteous in your anger. Perhaps your values have been thwarted or you've been wronged in some way. Or a situation may be spiraling out of your control, and your fear causes you to react with anger. When this happens, you're faced with a challenge: how to find forgiveness.

No one is perfect. Sometimes people are rigid. Sometimes they make mistakes. They can lose their cool when they feel like they've lost control. The most important question to understand is: After a mistake has been made, what happens next?

Years ago, I received an invaluable lesson on the importance of forgiveness, after a falling out with my friend Norm. He and I had known one another for a few years when we decided to buy property together. We were close and always had an easy time communicating—until his girlfriend became his fiancée. While he and I initially agreed, she had a different opinion on how to handle the major home repairs that we needed. It became clear to me that he was between a rock and a hard place. The difference of opinion quickly escalated into an intractable conflict—which was especially hard because we were living in separate units within a joint property. After a few particularly hurtful exchanges, Norm and I stopped speaking to each other. This went on for two years, living in the same place, which had become a toxic environment. Talk about an emotional and social energy drain!

Then one day I noticed that Norm had taken my recycling out, which was a thoughtful gesture. A couple days later, I noticed that he was about to get a parking ticket, so I texted to let him know. Thinking that these small acts of kindness reflected a softening between us, I invited him for tea at a local café. My then-boyfriend said, "After all that's happened, why would you invite him for tea?" The answer for me was simple: I wanted to stop carrying my resentment and hoped enough time had passed for us to reconnect in a more positive way. I missed my friend. And I was ready to forgive and let go.

When I met with Norm, it didn't take long for me to realize that my hopes of a truce would not come to fruition. Shortly after we'd started talking, he was livid that I mentioned our fight and stormed out. When I told my boyfriend about what had happened, he responded with some version of "I told you so."

Grace, compassion, and forgiveness are the way out and through anger. It can be difficult because sometimes forgiveness can feel like you're endorsing what someone else did or giving up control of a situation. However, forgiveness is really for *you*—and requires you to *give up the hope of having a better past*. Let that sink in for a moment. When you are not ready to give up the hope of having a better past, your blame can quickly turn into resentment, which, as the saying goes, is as effective as *drinking poison and hoping that the other person dies*.

Or you could think about the toll of resentment like this: Every time you see a person whom you're holding resentment toward, you're putting another invisible brick into a backpack you're carrying. And carrying that heavy load will eventually wear you down. When you decide to forgive another, you're saying, *I'm ready to put down this backpack of bricks and allow myself to be free from this experience.* Learning to let go is a powerful tool to lighten your emotional load. It won't change what happened to you, but it does change how you relate to your pain—and it frees up so much emotional energy.

Upon further reflection on the exchange with Norm, I was still glad that I had made the effort. Inviting Norm to tea with an open and curious heart was the equivalent of successfully putting down my backpack full of bricks. And when he stormed off, he not only left with *his* resentment backpack, he also picked up *mine*. The part that was in my control was the act of letting go. In this case, my forgiveness was powered by me—and that was enough.

Combining self-forgiveness with self-compassion is a potent recipe for combating anger. Unraveling the layers of resentment can take time, so give yourself grace and patience as you learn to accept the situation and all the players (including you) *as they are*, not as you *wish they would be*.

Forgiveness is an ongoing practice. You may need to forgive the same person (or yourself) for the same injury more than once. You can honor the experience that you've had—the relationship that dissolved, the colleague who misunderstood, the leader who didn't acknowledge your hard work, or the parent or sibling who didn't truly see and appreciate you. Whatever the experience, it played an important role in your growth and you becoming who you are today. That perspective can lighten your load, making it easier to move forward, without that heavy backpack full of bricks.

Forgiving Another Exercise

Here's one way to forgive others. Ask yourself: Are you ready to give up all hope of a better past? If yes, continue with the following steps. If no, you're not ready.

1. Become aware of your body's signals telling you something needs to be healed.

2. Take a deep breath in, and thank your body for communicating with you.

3. Complete these statements. Writing them down may help:

   • The impact of this relationship has been . . .

   • What I wanted from you that I didn't get was . . .

   • What I've always wanted to tell you is . . .

   • The ways I've held back are . . .

   • If I believed you did the best you could with what you knew at the time and treated you with compassion and forgiveness, I would . . .

4. Express what you need to say to the person directly, or have a friend stand in for this person and listen deeply.

5. Take a deep breath in, and notice how your body feels. Pay attention to anywhere that relaxes, lightens, or opens as you heal this energy drain. If you feel constriction or tightening, get curious about what else might be left unsaid.

Self-Forgiveness Exercise

Here's how to forgive yourself. Ask yourself: Are you ready to give up all hope of a better past? If yes, continue with the following steps. If no, you're not ready.

1. Acknowledge the physical sensations telling you something needs to be healed.

2. Take a deep breath in, and thank your body for communicating with you.

3. Complete these statements. Writing them down may help.

   - The impact of getting angry with myself has been . . .

   - What I wanted for myself that I didn't get was . . .

   - I've wrongly blamed myself for . . .

   - If I apologized to myself, I would say . . .

   - If I acknowledged that I did the best I knew how with what I knew at the time and treated myself with compassion and forgiveness, I would . . .

   - If I didn't do the best I knew how, I can always do a Take 2 or make amends by . . .

4. Express:

   - What do you want to say to yourself or apologize for?

   - What will be different moving forward because of this apology?

5. Take a deep breath in, noticing how your body feels after acknowledging and expressing what needs to be said. Pay attention to anywhere that relaxes, lightens, or opens as you heal this energy drain. If you feel constriction or tightening, ask yourself what else might need to be expressed.

RELEASE ANXIETY AND ANGER

When you find yourself angry or anxious, practices that connect your body and heart can help unwind and disentangle these challenging emotions. These include:

- **Physical movement / exercise.** Though sometimes exercise feels like the last thing you want to do when you're struggling, it can also be the fastest emotional reset. Stretch, go for a walk or a run—whatever you need to get your energy and blood flowing.

- **Shaking and dancing.** Dr. Jim Gordon at the Center for Mind Body Medicine taught me the power of shaking and dancing. This improvisational movement can be an excellent way to express pent-up emotion. Shaking is a movement-based technique in which you briefly shake your entire body to lighten your emotional energetic load. As famed choreographer Martha Graham once said, "The body says what words cannot."

- **EMDR (Eye Movement Desensitization and Reprocessing).** This evidence-based therapy helps lessen the stress associated with specific traumatic events and memories. Done with a trained practitioner, EMDR relies on bilateral stimulation, with eye movement or tapping, to regain emotional balance. The goal of EMDR therapy is that painful events and memories lose their emotional charge. If you are interested in experiencing EMDR, seek a trained provider, therapist, or trauma specialist with whom to partner.

- **Tapping.** Also known as Emotional Freedom Technique or EFT, this is similar to acupuncture in that it focuses on activating specific energy points in your body, reducing stress and grounding you in the present moment. If you are interested in experiencing tapping, seek a trained provider, therapist, or healer. Also, you may enjoy *The Tapping Solution* by Nick Ortner.

GRATITUDE FOR ANXIETY AND ANGER

It may be a little challenging to feel grateful for heavy, burdensome emotions like anger or anxiety. They can feel overwhelming—as if they are passengers trying to take control of the steering wheel. They can drain you of large amounts of energy and leave you feeling wrecked on the side of the road.

Please remember what they are trying to do: protect you. Anger and anxiety are clues providing important information about what is currently happening for you. And if you listen right away (so that they don't need to grab onto that steering wheel to get your attention), you can address the underlying concerns without expending unnecessary energy.

Because here's the thing about anger and anxiety: if you don't address them, everything just gets worse. They'll drain you of what little energy you have left—which can be next to none if you're on the burnout bandwagon. And now that you have a powerful emotional toolkit to navigate them, you're back on the road to being *me-powered*!

CHAPTER 15

STUCK IN SADNESS, DEPRESSION, OR GRIEF

y colleague Amy, an anesthesiologist from Chicago, was exhausted halfway through the first day of her weekend call, when she received her next emergent case: a four-week-old baby with pyloric stenosis. As Amy entered the ER, she looked over to see the mom, a disheveled, rough-looking woman with tattoos on her face and arms, standing next to her sick baby in a crib. Amy thought, *I can give this one to my resident. After all, it's part of the resident's training curriculum to learn to assess the patient, discuss anesthesia plans, and connect with the family.*

A few seconds later, her maternal instincts kicked in. *Even though she doesn't look like someone I'd connect with, we're both moms*, she thought. Her head was telling her not to get involved, but in the silence, her motherly heart spoke otherwise. And Amy listened. She approached the mother and inquired about her baby's unusual name, Prae (pronounced "pray").

The mother replied, "Last year, my teenage son took his last breath at this hospital. I never thought I'd have another baby, and Prae was the answer to my prayers." Amy was moved by this woman's story and assured the mother that she would care for Prae as if he was her own child.

As Amy was signing out to the pediatric nurses, she suddenly felt protective of the mother and worried that the nurses might see Prae's mother in the same light that she had originally—someone they couldn't relate to. So she made a point of introducing them directly to Prae's mother and explained the horrifying loss she had experienced the year prior and the meaningful origin of Prae's name.

As Amy started to walk away, one of the nurses approached her. "Dr. Murray, I thought you might want to know that we know Prae's older brother," she said. "He died of a gunshot wound in the ER."

Surprised and attempting to recall the names of recent trauma patients, Amy asked, "What was his name?"

"Clayton Harris," the nurse replied.

Amy was stunned. "Oh, my goodness. I remember him. I was there. It was an emergency case, so we temporarily called him John Doe."

She began to recall more details—watching skilled surgeons try unsuccessfully to repair the transected aorta and how she had desperately helped the team transfuse gallons of blood into him—to no avail.

"I prayed for Clay when he took his last breath," she told the nurse. "I remember standing helplessly in that OR when I realized we couldn't save him, thinking, *He has a mother*. I even said a spontaneous prayer out loud: 'May God bless her and help her through this terrible loss.'"

Amy was struck by this uncanny coincidence. She said to the pediatric nurse, "Please don't tell Prae's mom. It might stir up too many emotions for her and leave her with questions she doesn't have the bandwidth or capacity to handle right now."

Following this conversation, Amy recalled that the day after Clay died, she sought out John Doe's real name and proceeded to call every member of the anesthesia team. "Clayton Harris, not John Doe," she said to each colleague. "I just wanted you to know the real name of the patient you fought so hard to save."

The next morning, Amy sat at her kitchen table and shared the surprising coincidence with her 14-year-old daughter. While washing dishes, her daughter responded, "So what did Prae's mom say when you told her that you were with Clayton when he died?"

"Oh, I didn't say a word," Amy replied, explaining that it would be too emotional and the mother had too much on her plate with another sick child.

Amy's daughter exclaimed, "Mom, you have to go back and tell her!"

Amy could feel her entire body resisting that suggestion. Instead, she followed her Sunday schedule and proceeded to church. On the way there, in silence, she kept hearing the tone in her daughter's voice as she spoke with conviction that Prae's mother must know the truth. Amy began bargaining with herself and God. *OK, if for some reason, I get called back to the hospital this weekend, I'll swing by the pediatric floor and see if Prae's mom is still there, and maybe I'll consider saying something—that is, if the timing works out.*

The moment her beeper went off in church, calling her back to the hospital for another patient, she knew what she had to do.

Following the emergency case, she walked into Prae's room to find both his mother and grandmother next to the crib. She took a deep breath and said, "I knew Clayton. I want you to know that the best doctors worked tirelessly to save him. He wasn't in pain. And he was never alone. I was there when he took his last breath. In fact, I'm the one who gave him his last breath. I didn't know his name at the time. But I prayed for you and your family."

Prae's mother and grandmother wept. Prae's mother then began, "I had always wondered what Clayton's final moments were like. My worst fear was that he was alone and in pain. You're an angel. Now, thanks to you, I know he wasn't."

Choked up, Prae's mother continued, "Thank you for this gift," she said. "Now we have closure." They spent many more tearful moments together. In sharp contrast to her previous helplessness, Amy was humbled to experience the healing power of this sacred exchange with Prae's mom and grandmother.

Amy was dumbfounded, scanning her memory for all the times she may have missed opportunities such as this one—to connect because she was too fearful of losing control. *What if I can't handle the emotions that arise? What if other people have too strong a reaction? What if it takes too much time?*

In retrospect, Amy realized how many times she had actually felt drained whenever she attempted to avoid expressing her emotional energy. Yet contrary to her original resistance, the sacred exchange Amy experienced with Prae's family was positive and life-giving. In this act, which didn't change the outcome of Clay's destiny, she was able to dramatically alter his mother and grandmother's relationship to the final moments of his life. Clearly, Prae had given Amy a gift too—the lesson of what it means to care deeply *about* her patients instead of simply caring *for* them. This exchange brought profound meaning and purpose to Amy's work. By being willing to lean into the sadness of what had happened and speak truth to Prae's mother, everyone was able to *reveal*, *feel*, and *heal* what had happened. Tears are not something to avoid, but instead a pathway to connection and healing. They lead to significant emotional and social energy gains—and to becoming *me-powered*.

SHUTTING DOWN YOUR JOY

If you are not just going to survive, but actually thrive in today's fast-paced environment, you must invest in building your resilience and increasing your capacity to process challenging emotions. As author and grief expert David Kessler says, "To feel too much is dangerous, and to feel too little is tragic." Together, let's find that sweet spot, where your heart is open, you're connected to your colleagues, your family, and your purpose, but you're not overwhelmed by emotion.

In Chapter 12, I mentioned how trying to minimize feeling the challenging emotions, without realizing it, limits your experience of pleasurable emotions as well. If you've been wondering where all your joy has gone, it may well have disappeared because you've been shielding yourself from sadness and grief. Without joy, you lose the ability to feel connection, pleasure, and fun. Joy is an internal energy source that lights you up. When you feel joy, you are in alignment with your values—and that alignment will guide you toward overcoming the stress and burnout that would otherwise drain you of energy.

We all experience forms of sadness. Think of sadness as another emotion that can vary in intensity along a spectrum:

Disappointment → Sadness → Grief → Depression → Apathy

In your personal life, you might experience disappointment due to betrayal in a friendship or relationship. There's grief in losing a loved one or pet. Or loneliness may arise when people are separated during a move or breakup. At work, disappointment, sadness, and grief often surface during times of downsizing, organizational restructuring, or a leadership transition. Disappointment can surface at the conclusion of an inspiring project or time with a mentor. On a global scale, disappointment, sadness, anger, and anxiety all come together as people witness violence, poverty, injustice, and a sense of impending doom as the climate crisis continues unabated.

It's natural to attempt to dull these emotions because they can consume us if we're not careful. The problem is that when we do this, we also snuff out our joy. As you learned in the last few chapters, emotions provide critical data about what's happening, and their energy can get stuck within you if you don't acknowledge and face them. These emotions can show up in your relationship dynamics and your physical health, which only adds to your stress load. Disappointment, sadness, grief, and depression are no different. A study published in the *Journal of Occupational and Environmental Medicine* found that individuals with burnout are at a significantly higher risk of depression, anxiety, and suicide.[1]

So don't allow these emotions to get stuck within you and weigh you down. Instead, *reveal*, *feel*, and *heal* them so they become an internal energy source that honors your connection to others and teaches you valuable lessons.

BUILDING EMOTIONAL RESILIENCE

While you may think that you're more resilient without these challenging emotions, the truth is that true resilience doesn't come from an emotion-free life. It comes from gleaning the valuable data that emotions provide, experiencing them, and then letting them gracefully move through you. Here is a higher intensity version of the Body Map (see Figure 15.1) that shows how more intense emotions can have even stronger physical sensations associated with them. On the left side, you'll see the emotions. On the right are some examples of more intense physical sensations.

FIGURE 15.1 **Higher Intensity Body Map**

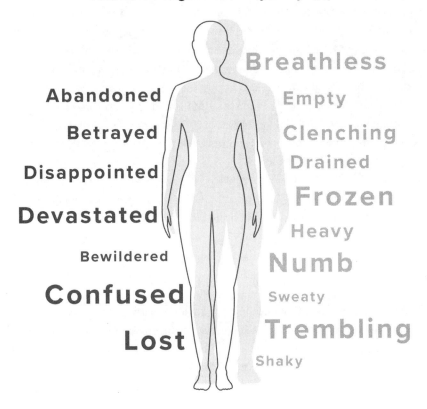

Disappointment

You may feel taken aback by a turn of events that runs counter to what you had hoped for. Maybe your request for an additional day off was denied. Maybe you learned that the colleague you confided in about a private matter betrayed your confidence. Or maybe you were rooting for your daughter's softball team, and they didn't clinch a place in the playoffs.

Disappointment is often situational. Whether you decide to swallow it—gulp—or put forth the energy to say something will often determine whether it dissipates or grows in intensity. If you decide to address it, maybe all you need to do is breathe and allow yourself the time and space for it to clear. You may want to vent and share it with someone else. But if left unaddressed, it will likely grow or show up as a recurring pattern at work or at home, depleting you of even more emotional energy.

Sadness

From disappointment, you can move into a deeper sense of melancholy. Sadness carries a slower, heavier vibration than disappointment and often lasts longer. In our interconnected world, where we get news from across the globe in an instant, it's a rare day there isn't something to be sad about. That's not all. Sometimes you're disappointed in your work or home life—with a missed expectation, the conclusion of a relationship or a mistake that cost you money or an opportunity. Sometimes sadness is the result of more than one experience of disappointment. Like a moat around a castle, sadness can make you feel alone and deplete your energy. Then, even if given the opportunity to connect, you may choose to remain alone, thinking, *I won't be any fun at dinner anyway.* That decision only reinforces the sadness and creates a cycle. Over time, if sadness is how you relate to your life, situations, or relationships, you may expect very little out of them. Unchecked, you can even slip into resignation and think, *Well, I guess this is just the way it's going to be.*

In your younger years, if you wept, you may have been made fun of or called names. So you may have gotten extremely good at shutting down tears. This is tragic because it means that to protect yourself and appear tough, you may have shut down your true self-expression.

The problem is that society has many judgments about tears, viewing them as unprofessional or a sign of weakness. Nothing could be further from the truth. The most tangible step to address sadness may surprise you: *let it out.* There are many ways to free yourself of sadness: journal about your emotions, share them with others, and yes, allow yourself to cry. Tears are a powerful way to release trapped energy.

Did you know that expressing tears is a biological healing necessity? Yep! Tears are beneficial to your body in both physical and emotional ways because they literally release your stress. There are three types of tears:

1. **Continuous tears** keep your eyes moist and functional throughout the day. They have an antibacterial agent called lysozyme that prevents infections and dryness in your eyes (and your nose!).

2. **Reflexive tears** are a response to a foreign object, such as dust, contact lenses, or the chemical released by a cut onion. These tears help the eye flush out irritants.

3. **Emotional tears** actually have stress hormones in them! William Frey, a biochemist, discovered this. Who knew the body uses tears as a physical mechanism to rid itself of stress and toxic chemicals in order to heal? After a good, emotional cry, the body also releases endorphins (the same feel-good hormones you experience after exercising), your heart rate and breathing slow down, and you'll get a great night's sleep.

Here's what I can tell you after decades of caring for patients and healing dysfunctional organizational cultures along with my own personal traumas—I've dramatically changed how I view tears. Rather than running from them and thinking their presence reveals my greatest flaws, I now share my tears with another person as an act of trust and courage.

Let's redefine tears. What if crying wasn't something to be ashamed of, but instead indicated that you *trust yourself enough and the other person enough to reveal what's closest to your heart*? That would be a sacred and meaningful exchange. In fact, tears can mean a variety of emotions—not just sadness or disappointment. There are tears of joy, relief, surprise, and anger. It's important to get curious, rather than assume you know what emotions are represented by someone's tears.

Express Your Tears Exercise

When experiencing emotional tears, here's how you can get to the root of why they're occurring:

1. Identify the emotion(s) beneath your tears.

2. Name what triggered the emotion(s).

3. Say what you need (time, space, talk to a friend, your favorite beverage, a hug, etc.).

4. If you find yourself having trouble with steps 1 and 2, ask yourself, "If my tears could talk, what would they say?"

When you put these components together, it can sound something like:

- I'm sad. I can't believe he said no to our offer. I could use a cup of chai and some quality time watching our favorite show tonight.

- I can't believe my vacation time was denied. I'm so disappointed that I'm missing the reunion. Right now, I just need to be alone.

- I can't believe I got passed over for the promotion. I'm the only one who took on mentoring the new hires. I need to be in nature. Let's go on a hike.

See how easy that was? It didn't even take much time. Expressing your emotions allows you to *reveal*, *feel*, and *heal* them by asking for what you want and transforming an uncomfortable experience into emotional energy gains—if you're in the mood for it—a social boost too!

Responding to Tears Exercise

That trust needs to go both ways. How can you be present for the sometimes awkward experience of someone else's tears? Here's a quick and easy way to remain empathic:

1. Hit your pause button, and take a deep breath.
2. Acknowledge the other person's emotion(s).
3. Get curious about what they need.
4. If they do not know what's causing their tears, you can ask, "If your tears could speak, what would they say?"

Here are some examples of ways you can respond:

- Wow. You've been through a lot. How can I support you?

- I'm sorry for your loss. What would be most helpful?

- I hear how deeply this has touched you. Is there any way I can be of assistance?

It's important to view others who are experiencing a tough time as resourceful, strong, and capable. This is dramatically different energy than *trying to save someone*. When you trust that another person can handle whatever life throws at them, you engage with them in a supportive and confident manner that catalyzes their growth and learning—without taking it on as your weight to carry.

WHEN SADNESS BECOMES YOUR ROOMMATE

When sadness goes on for too long—for six months or more—it's classified as depression. This is a sign that you've gone into fixed patterns of thinking, feeling, and being. When sadness and a loss of hope overtake your capacity for joy, you may feel lethargy or even paralysis. If you're depressed, you may feel stuck in body and mind, unable to take constructive action. Depression is associated with a weakened immune system. Our physical and emotional energies are very much intertwined.

The stuckness of depression, taken even further, can feel like being trapped, which may lead to feeling suicidal. If you or someone you care about is experiencing the sensation of sinking in quicksand, feeling trapped or heavy, or expressing hopelessness, it's time to get help right away. Those who are suicidal often cannot see a way forward. Most often, they disconnect from their loved ones and lives. They commonly describe feeling completely out of control, not feeling seen or heard, or feeling they've lost a sense of personal dignity and there's no reason to live.

. . . .

How to Approach Suicidal Thoughts

Suicidal thoughts are at the most extreme end of this spectrum. There is an urgent need to identify and deal with emotions *before* they lead to loss of life. As with most suicides, untreated depression is a common preceding factor.

You might be wondering how to know if this is the case? If you feel or express some version of:

- *There's no way forward.*

- *I don't see a way out.*

- *I feel helpless.*

- *Life isn't worth living.*

Ask the following questions:

Question 1: Have you considered harming yourself?

If yes, move to Question 2.

If no, get support as soon as possible:

- Find a reputable mental health professional.

- Call a mental health hotline or join a support group.

- Ask a friend to check in with you daily.

Question 2: Do you know how you would do it?

If the answer is yes, this is an emergency! Immediately call for help. In the United States, call the National Suicide Prevention Lifeline at (800) 273-8255 or the Suicide and Crisis Lifeline at 988.

If the answer is no, find a professional to speak to as soon as possible.

. . . .

Grief

Grief is a deep and profound sense of loss that doesn't only follow death. It can come with the loss of a treasured hope or dream, transition from single-hood to married life, from college to employment, or from "normal life" to a global pandemic. As you move from one chapter to another—happy or sad—grief can reveal itself and lead to your heart carrying a heavy load that adds stress and restricts you from enjoying your life.

Research expert Dr. Elizabeth Kübler-Ross created a framework in her book *On Death and Dying*, describing the grieving process in five steps: denial, anger, bargaining, depression, and acceptance. It's important to know that the process doesn't have to be linear, so you may experience these steps out of sequence or even simultaneously. Recognizing where you are in the grieving process can help you identify why you feel the way you do so you can navigate those emotions more effectively. Grief and loss expert David Kessler added a sixth step: *meaning*, which can help people find a sense of purpose to their suffering.

Kessler describes three distinct phases of grief. Suppose someone's partner was diagnosed with a terminal health condition. Three phases they will likely go through include:

1. **Anticipatory grief.** The fear of knowing grief or loss is coming. This is when the event hasn't happened yet, but someone is experiencing fear of what will happen next.

2. **Acute grief.** Often experienced in the first year after loss. This is when there is a vacuum in a partnership or relationship. Everyone handles major loss differently, but this phase requires adjusting to a dramatically new situation.

3. **Chronic grief.** Grief that persists after the first year. There is no right way to grieve or a time frame that is "too long" or "not long enough."

Grief can be an unexpected visitor. You may anticipate struggling on the first anniversary of a loved one's death, but be completely taken by surprise when instead it happens on a regular day when you hear their favorite song playing on the radio. There's no handbook that can definitively tell anyone *how* to grieve. There is only *your way of grieving*. The best handbook comes from your own heart, which requires that you are tuned into your emotions and allow them to guide you.

Socially, we may be encouraged to compartmentalize grief as a badge of honor. In fact, in medicine, Dr. Murray (the anesthesiologist who was taking care of Prae) and I discussed how profound it is to be health providers who face this type of grief daily, yet we are given no time and have no formal way to process our emotions. While it could seem noble to adopt a "keep calm and carry on" approach to grieving, how does that same approach feel on the inside? When was the last time you made space to grieve, even a small loss?

My grief education began early. My mother's brother, Mukesh, lived with us off and on, and I adored him. In Hindi, you call your mother's brother "Mama," so I affectionately called him Mukku Mama. He was present, engaged, and loving. I thought he was the coolest uncle ever. He would take me to the carnival and the latest movies, and not only did he ride motorcycles and fly airplanes, he snuck me ice cream *after* I had brushed my teeth. It almost felt like Mukku Mama was a big kid who didn't want to abide by my parents' rules either.

He was studying engineering at Michigan State University. After getting into a car accident and developing chronic hip pain that stopped him from sitting for long periods, he dropped out of college and started his own auto body repair business out of my parents' garage. He'd fix up wrecked cars and resell them.

After dinner one night, I remember him asking my older sister, "Ritu, do you want to help me work in the garage?"

"Not really, Mukku Mama. That sounds boring."

Slightly disappointed, he turned to me and inquired, "What about you, Neha? Will you help your Mukku Mama by holding the light, so I can work on the new car I just got?" Ritu was right. It didn't sound that fun, but I felt obligated to say yes.

Our nightly habit began. On his back, Mukku Mama would slide under the engine as I would dutifully stand above him holding an industrial shop light with a thick plastic orange casing. Much to my surprise, it wasn't boring at all. We talked and laughed for hours. My arm would get tired, but I barely noticed because Mukku Mama taught me about the makes and models of the cars. He told interesting stories about what made them unique and exactly how to restore each to brand new.

Most of all, Mukku Mama was curious about me. He asked about my skinned knee after roller skating. He was excited to hear of my latest high score on Atari's Space Invaders. He wanted to know what Mrs. White was teaching us in math class. We collaborated on what fun adventure we should plan as our next outing. It was the first time in my life that I remember feeling deeply seen and heard by an adult.

On the morning of Sunday, November 2, 1980, Mukku Mama and I officially became business partners. He began, "Neha, when you answer the phone, those customers wind up coming to look at the cars. They're so surprised that a 10-year-old girl has so much knowledge about used automobiles. You're charming and polite. I'm pretty sure they come to meet *you*, not me or the cars. But once they're here, it's easy for me to make the sale! Ever since we've been working together, I've sold three times as many cars as before. What do you say, for every call you answer that leads to a sale, I'll give you $25 of the profit?"

"Yes! Yes! Yes! I'd love to be your business partner, Mukku Mama," I exclaimed with sheer delight. All I could think to myself was, *Do you know how much candy, ice cream, and video games $25 buys? I'll buy my friends whatever they want. And we won't even have to ask our parents for permission anymore!* I was on cloud nine.

We had also planned that, later that afternoon, he would take me for my inaugural ride in the four-seater plane he had recently invested in with nine other buddies. Thirty minutes before we were supposed to leave, he got a call. In anticipation of our adventure, I began putting my shoes on. As soon as he hung up, he put his hand on my shoulder and began, "Neha, there's a change of plans. My buddy and I are going flying today instead of you and me."

"What do you mean, Mukku Mama? I'm ready to go! I get to be your copilot," I pleaded. "OK. I guess if you bring your friend, then he can be your copilot, and I'll just sit in the back, not the front," I begged.

"No, Neha. He just called and wants to bring both of his kids. And there's only four seat belts in the plane. So I'll have to take you next time."

I was devastated. I began jumping up and down and pulling on his arm, exclaiming, "That's not fair! You don't even know them. I'm your niece *and* now we're business partners. You can't do that, Mukku Mama!"

I felt betrayed and angry. As I watched him leave, it made no sense to me. *Why was Mukku Mama letting these random kids go on my adventure?*

Mukku Mama never came home that day. A hot air balloon unexpectedly drifted over the runway. As he was landing, while attempting to dodge the balloon, another small plane didn't see him below and descended on top of him. Apparently, the black box of his plane revealed Mukku Mama desperately trying to warn the pilot that he was there, only to find out that the other pilot had his radio off. He lost control and his plane crashed. Mukku Mama, one of his friend's children, and the other pilot died instantly.

My grief over losing someone I loved so dearly was so overwhelming that I barely mentioned it for decades. I imagine that the early grief of being separated from my parents and then my grandparents somehow figured into the mix. Because I couldn't express how deeply my pain ran, I felt very alone. I made up stories about why he died, and since I used personalization, they sounded like: *maybe Mukku Mama died because I was so angry at him.* A part of me wished that I had died with him. I definitely felt guilty for being spared. Mostly, though, my 10-year-old heart vowed to never love that deeply again. Love was too risky. I felt certain that if I ever loved someone so completely again, they would leave me. And further abandonment was not an option.

A few years ago, I went into my parents' garage and found that orange light that I used to hold by hand so my beloved uncle could work. The moment I noticed the light had a hook at the top, it hit me like a ton of bricks—he never actually *needed* me to hold the light up. It could have hung from the hood. His request for my help was an excuse to spend time together and bond. I broke down sobbing.

The tears I shed when I figured out that the orange light had a hook were incredibly cathartic. I remember going through a complete box of Kleenex and then sleeping like a baby that night. It was as if I had been carrying a heavy weight for decades. I never realized that I could let it go. I wish I had known years ago that tears are the body's way of expelling pain and stress.

My grief that day helped me understand my mother better as well. I fully grasped something that I had known but not quite understood: she had lost *both of her brothers*, one in a car crash and the other in a plane crash. No wonder she had anxiety. No wonder she was so protective of my sisters and me. No wonder she didn't want us all on one airplane together. Her grief had shown up in a different way than mine. And it can last a lifetime. That's why it's so important to acknowledge grief whenever it appears. That way you don't add more emotional stress to the stress you're trying to heal in your everyday life.

Grief Can Show Up Any Time

Ever since Mukku Mama's plane crashed, flying has become a somewhat spiritual experience that connects me to him. Rather than being afraid when the plane takes off or when there's turbulence, I actually feel a deep sense of calm—almost like his presence is in the cockpit protecting me. Just like he did that cool November Sunday in 1980.

As far as encounters go, somehow it seems like I'm always seated next to just the right person for deep and meaningful conversations to unfold. Once, there was a 29-year-old girl heading to her bachelorette party in Cancun who had been struggling to figure out why she had so many gastrointestinal issues her entire life. She was so afraid of what her skin would look like on her wedding day, later that year. When I told her she could heal if she saw a functional medicine physician or a naturopath, she hugged me so hard I could barely breathe. Another time, on a flight to Houston, I met a newlywed couple who were in a pickle with the husband's ex-wife, so we did a coaching session to help him draw healthy boundaries around his ex-wife stopping by unexpectedly. And there's the 33-year-old CEO Alex at the beginning of Chapter 4. I'm telling you that it's not just by chance that these experiences happen. I'm convinced there's a little bit of Mukku Mama healing magic happening in the air.

I began to notice a curious pattern at the end of these encounters. After only knowing these people for a few short hours and having wonderful exchanges with them, I would get all choked up when it was time to go our separate ways. I knew this was an out-of-proportion reaction to what was happening in the moment, so I started to pay more attention to it.

Eventually, I realized that it wasn't just on planes—it happened whenever it was time to leave after a meaningful exchange with a friend, a colleague, or a group of people. Come to think of it, I often became tearful after going through intense experiences with my patients and their families. Talk about an emotional energy drain! I had no idea how tired I was making myself because I didn't understand the grief I was carrying.

It wasn't until my forties that an amazing healer pointed out that I was having mini-amygdala hijacks. She said, "Well, of course you get tearful anytime it's time to go. In an instant, subconsciously, you become that two-year-old who had to unwillingly leave your grandparents or the ten-year-old whose uncle unexpectedly passed away. When your unhealed abandonment gets retriggered, you feel the unresolved pain."

"What do you mean?" I said. "I don't even think about that anymore. It was so long ago."

"Neha, you may have forgotten about it, but your amygdala hasn't. It's trying to protect you from any similar patterns of sadness, devastation, and abandonment."

When you become aware of loss, sadness, or grief, look deeper to the worries or fears that may be tied to it. This is how you can heal your past and accept the emotions in a healthy way without adding more burden to your day-to-day workload and relationships.

. . . .

Unresolved Trauma

If you find that you are on the more extreme end of stuckness—experiencing chronic grief, depression, or even suicidal ideation—it's worth considering how trauma could be playing a role. Unhealed trauma is often at the root of underlying sadness and pain, and if we continue to run from that pain, we'll never solve the problem. And most likely, loneliness and alienation will only continue to grow. For help, check out the documentary *The Wisdom of Trauma* by Gabor Maté, MD, or the book

The Myth of Normal: Trauma, Healing and Illness in a Toxic Culture by Gabor Maté with Daniel Maté.

RECOVERY AND HEALING

I promise you, there is a way forward. When we're able to move emotional energy, we regain our sense of possibility. This is vital. When we are hopeful and optimistic about our ability to come up with creative solutions to problems and take constructive actions, our joy returns in full, living color.

No matter how far you are from your peaceful heart, there are ways to come back to what I call "home."

FIGURE 15.2 **Coming Back Home Diagram**

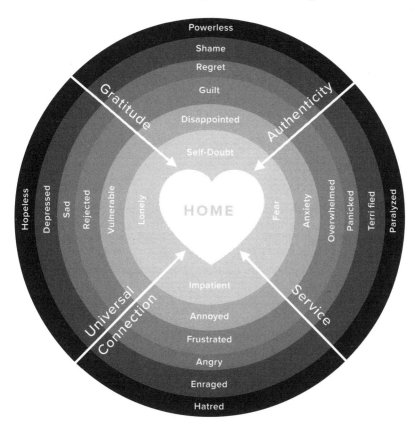

How you choose to move emotional energy from any level of stuckness may depend on your personal preferences. Some people prefer physical outlets, like dancing or boxing. Others are drawn to exercises that engage their intellect, such as reading, journaling, or working with affirmations. Still others would rather do less conventional therapies, like equine or art therapy, or maybe even a virtual-reality-based treatment. And if you're someone who thrives in community, you may prefer to find healing and gratitude in group activities.

The particular modality you choose is not the most important part of moving energy. What matters most is that you are taking steps to move this energy and that it's a way that feels safe to you.

Your options are infinite when it comes to healing your emotional energy. You may find that some of the body-heart connections mentioned for anxiety also help with processing disappointment, sadness, or grief (exercise, shaking and dancing, or tapping). You may want to experiment with what works best for you. The following are some suggestions that will get you started.

Water

Being close to water, even just gazing at ocean waves, can be a powerful reminder of life's ebbs and flows and that you, too, can be in your emotional flow. If you don't live near water or can't get to the beach, a lake, or a river, jumping in a pool or a hot bath (preferably with Epsom salts) can also serve as an emotional cleanse.

Holding an Object

If you notice stress in your body, find something to hold. Picking up a smooth stone or weight can be a simple but powerful reminder to stay present in your body. Even squeezing a stress cushion may help. Remember how the green fabric heart helped Stan?

Tapping into Your Senses

Engaging your five senses is a wonderful way to regain a sense of balance and well-being. When you feel at ease, it is always easier to process hard emotions.

- **See.** Some people feel a sense of healing as they gaze at beauty, whether in a museum or out in nature. You might also light a candle and focus your eyes on the flame, as a form of meditation. Laying eyes on a loved one (even when they're sleeping) can also be immensely relaxing.

- **Hear.** Music and chanting can be very healing. Put on your favorite songs or audio and allow your body to relax more fully. If you're particularly wound up, sound is a low-stress way to bring yourself back to center.

- **Taste.** Practice mindful eating. Stay fully present to what your body craves and take time to savor each bite.

- **Touch.** Locate your favorite fabric or piece of clothing that feels most soothing to wrap yourself in or put on. Cuddle up to a human or pet whose affection provides a calming experience.

- **Smell.** Use some lavender oil on your temples or your sternum. Lavender promotes calmness. You may also want to experiment with other scented oils, such as eucalyptus, frankincense, jasmine, or sandalwood. Or simply buy some fragrant flowers and enjoy how their scent fills your home.

A Body-Heart-Mind Connection: Guided Imagery

Engaging the power of your mind through visualization is so powerful. Super Bowl and Olympic athletes have been known to achieve victory by practicing visualization, imagining themselves performing at top levels. I have some guided imageries for you to try at *intuitiveintelligenceinc.com/pbmresources*.

A Mind-Heart Connection: Therapeutic Journaling— Psychoneuroimmunology

Author and researcher Dr. James Pennebaker found that when patients who had asthma or chronic disease therapeutically journaled 15 to 20 minutes per day expressing their feelings, they had a measurable increase in their immune function after only four days.[2] Journaling can have a powerful effect on processing trauma and grief.

Mantras

Think positive thoughts anytime you feel like you need a boost. Examples of mantras include: *I am safe. I am loved. I am whole, healthy, and well. I can handle whatever comes my way.* Some prefer to recite their mantras in the mirror. Others keep certain mantras easily accessible for moments they feel their mood dipping.

Get creative! What matters most is that the phrase resonates with you.

Gratitude

The power of gratitude can help get the more pleasant emotions flowing again. The trick is to find things you are genuinely grateful for. When you're in turmoil, it can be hard to reach for a "big" gratitude, but the good news is that small gratitudes work just as well. You might be thankful for the smile you received from a stranger, getting to work without hassle, or a funny text message from a best friend. Or you might initiate a moment of gratitude before dinner to hear what other people are experiencing.

Spiritual Connection: Prayer

Whatever your religious background, prayer can be a powerful way to connect with someone or something larger than yourself. This could mean visiting a place of formal worship—like a church, temple, synagogue, or mosque—or finding communion in nature. The specific way that you pray can strengthen your sense of trust and faith, and provide a deep sense of healing. Praying and intention-setting together with others can also be very powerful. Having a spiritual community can increase feelings of support and overall nourishment.

Interpersonal Connection

Here are a few ways to forge interpersonal healing:

- **Community.** Connect with friends and allow for mutual sharing and support. Dance around a living room or a fire pit together. Attend a healing retreat with others.

- **Professional support group.** There are many support groups, such as *grief.com* with David Kessler, where you can heal with a community that has experienced something similar to you. This can happen in person or remotely.

- **Being present together.** Sometimes just knowing you're not alone is enough. If you're working remotely, joining a working space in your neighborhood (such as WeWork) can provide a shared sense of community. This can also take place online, where you can be on video together, silently working on your own projects.

- **Being of service.** When we're at our lowest, doing acts of service for others can reorient our perspective. We take the focus off our particular pain and feel the benefit of spiritual connection. You may volunteer formally at a soup kitchen or mentoring program. You could also do ad hoc good deeds, like buying water, food, and supplies to create and deliver gift bags for the homeless in your area. Or you could make some food for a friend who's taking care of an elderly or dying loved one.

When we love someone and we lose them, it's important to create a place for all that love to go. A good example of this is the mother who lost her son to drunk driving and started the organization Mothers Against Drunk Driving (MADD). One constructive outlet for grief is to transform your painful experience into preventing similar losses for others.

Only lately have I realized that I channeled my love for Mukku Mama into empowering the next generation of leaders in their communication. Over the last few years, I've become a mentor to more than 70 teens and young adults, teaching them how to master communication with their parents, partners and peers. I absolutely adore them, and they express how helpful it is to learn how to navigate their anger, anxiety, and tears. Every time I get to be present for them, it heals me too. How lucky am I to get to play the role for them that Mukku Mama played for me?

If you are feeling a little weighed down after reading about sadness and grief, that's OK. In fact, it's normal. We've had a heavy couple of chapters, so I just want to check in. How are you feeling? What emotions have been surfacing? Are you feeling any sensations in your body? Yep, I am asking you to use your Body Map again. If you need to do some deep belly breathing, now is a good time.

CHAPTER 16

JUMP-STARTING JOY

I was a pretty serious child. Due to challenges early in life, I wasn't particularly playful or carefree. But I was able to find joy and play with Mukku Mama before he passed away. At the carnival, he would win big stuffed animals for me, and we would go on the upside-down roller coaster together. When he was babysitting, I got to stay up way past my bedtime. The irony is that despite the seriousness of my own childhood, I've come to realize that kids psychologically give me permission to play.

As I was struggling with the aftermath of my burnout, I decided to volunteer at a local community center. I set up a class where I taught kids about how the food they ate dramatically impacted how they felt. To be honest, I was a little nervous because at the time, I didn't have much experience teaching kids. But I quickly saw how much they loved to *play*, even through the simplest, most ordinary activities. For instance, I was dumbfounded that all of them somehow pronounced my name perfectly (*Nay*-hah) when most people, seeing how it's spelled—N-E-H-A—say *Nee*-hah. I asked the kids why they all remembered my name so easily, and they started giggling. "It's because Peter said your name sounds like a laughing horse—*Neigh-ha*."

Humor helps us learn, remember, and connect. To keep them engaged and help them retain information, all I had to do was make learning clever and fun! Since I wanted them to learn about food, I taught them about how the food industry was trying to trick them. In no time at all, they transformed themselves into unofficial food detectives—interested in reading nutritional labels, calling out which ones had trans fats and high fructose corn syrup when the packaging claimed they didn't. It took no time at all for them to catch the bad guys and begin policing their parents, explaining why they no longer wanted to eat "frankenfoods."

Now, so many years later, I still find that same joy and sense of play with my boyfriend's son Alok. He is so loving, present, and excited to chat about the latest video games or how far he's driven on Google Maps. He's memorized all the major highways across the United States and loves rap and hip-hop. When he spends the night, I give myself permission to be a kid with him. We catch up on the children's classics I missed while I was busy studying, like *The Lion King* and *Finding Nemo*. Sometimes we have dance parties—preferably to the non-explicit versions of his favorite songs. Other times we even have rap battles, if you can imagine! And Alok's presence heals me by reminding me of the value of fun and play. Being with him makes my heart smile.

The younger generation can keep you feeling vibrant. If you have kids in your life, whether you're a parent, an aunt, uncle, or mentor, consider using that as an excuse to play as well. Ask them what makes them belly laugh. They know! They're in touch with their silly, carefree, and playful selves.

How conscious are you about infusing joy into your days? My guess: not very. Many of us aren't—especially when we're feeling burned out. We can get too caught up in our to-do lists, and then after crossing off the day's items, we need time to *recover* from everything we've done.

In the previous chapter, we discussed that when you protect yourself from challenging emotions, you also limit your ability to feel joy. Now that you know how to *reveal*, *feel*, and *heal* your challenging emotions, guess what? The bonus is that you've expanded your ability to also experience pleasurable emotions, an essential component to healing burnout.

If you've been out of practice for a while, experiencing joy may not come easily to you. That's OK. Start slowly. If you've been depressed or depleted, you can't expect suddenly to start running across the hills like Julie Andrews in *The Sound of Music*. But if you tune in and focus your attention on moments of joy in your day, you'll notice yourself smiling more, even laughing—a natural boost to your emotional energy.

The following are some gentle suggestions to help you jump-start your joy.

- Listen to your favorite music

- Join an improv group

- Explore a new comedy club, dance class, restaurant, or museum

- Participate in a book club

- Take that cooking class you've been putting off

- Say yes to a social engagement

- Volunteer at a pet rescue shelter

- Take part in a collaborative art project, like a community mural

- Sports, whether it's joining a fantasy football league, regularly getting together with friends to watch games, or even playing on a local team

- Really, anything that lights you up!

Above all, one of the most universal ways to invite more joy into your life is to get out in nature. Whether it's a stroll through a garden, reading a book on the beach, or a backpacking trip, whatever your preference, I have never heard anyone say they didn't gain energy from being in nature. So enjoy the forests, the desert, the mountains, or the ocean—whatever healing form of Mother Nature you choose.

THE IMPORTANCE OF HUMOR

Comedian Bob Hope said, "I have seen what a laugh can do. It can transform almost unbearable tears into something bearable, even hopeful." Humor may be the single most powerful path toward developing resilience, gaining energy, and increasing joy in your life. It's a crucial aspect of relationships[1] and leadership,[2] reducing stress and improving your overall health.[3]

I learned this from my sister Ritu. One of the important roles she plays in our family is making us laugh. She has a great sense of humor. When life gets hard or stressful, Ritu helps bring us out of the heaviness by using her colorful imagination to catch us off guard. I remember when someone asked her what she was most looking forward to about moving into her 400-square-foot apartment on the Upper West Side of Manhattan, she casually replied, "I can't wait to get twin pot-bellied pigs, name them Chumpa and Juhi, put them on matching leashes, and take them for walks every day in Central Park."

My niece Simrin, who's now a teenager, has a natural wit. Last summer, the family was enjoying the Buffalo Zoo, and she was walking ahead of us. As she went by the bald eagle exhibit, she casually turned around, pointed, and said, "Hey guys, don't miss *the American symbol of freedom . . . in captivity*." And, she just kept walking. Her delivery was impeccable! We couldn't stop laughing.

My nephew Taj is another one who makes me giggle. From the age of two (while still in diapers) he could swing a golf club, hitting the ball 40 to 60 yards straight. By four years old, he'd participated in his first parent / child golf tournament and placed sixth out of fifteen teams. The funniest part is the reason he placed sixth (and not much higher) is because his emotional development wasn't quite up to par with his physical abilities. Once his ball was on the green, he was so worried that the game might be over, he would hit it back onto the fairway or in the sand trap—rather than "risk" putting it in the hole. Our nickname for my golf-watching, YouTube-obsessed nephew is Tajer Woods.

My friend Kathy, who worked as a nursing leader for years, has been on a similar self-awareness journey as mine. She recently shared one of the funniest exchanges she's had with her mom. As background, her mother, Nancy, spent most of her life in Southern California and worked in a plastic surgeon's office for 30 years. In her mid-eighties, Nancy's favorite pastimes are updating her wardrobe, happy hour on Fridays, and scrolling Tinder to find a date. One day, she noticed that her single daughter was headed off to work wearing scrubs, without her hair and makeup done properly. When she stated her disapproval, Kathy responded, "Mom, I'm just going to work!"

Her mother replied, "The problem with you, Kathy, is that all you care about is *what's on the inside*."

Dumbfounded, Kathy continued out the door. When she told me this story, the two of us could barely talk because we were laughing so hard. Often, an experience that has the potential to be hurtful can heal through shared laughter.

Of course, everyone has a different sense of humor. Whether you're delighted by burping, pooping, and fart jokes (as a doctor, the humor of those wore out a long time ago) or *New Yorker* cartoons, laughter will improve your quality of life. That is, if you use humor in a constructive way.

NOT ALL HUMOR IS CREATED EQUAL

As anyone who has been the butt of a joke can attest, sometimes humor can sting—and studies have shown that this kind of harmful humor hurts both parties.[4] There are four main types of humor:

1. **Affiliative humor** strengthens your relationships through a shared experience, such as watching funny cat videos together, playing games (as long as they don't get too competitive!), or having a shared experience.

2. **Self-enhancing humor** is finding humor in difficult situations and being able to laugh at yourself.

3. **Self-defeating humor** includes self-deprecation, jokingly seeing yourself as the victim.

4. **Aggressive humor** is a type of mocking humor, making fun at the expense of someone else—whether a stranger or someone you know.

You can see how the first two types will contribute to your overall well-being, as well as build connection with those around you. The last two types can detract from your energy (and that of others), leaving everyone feeling alone and depleted.

Humor *is* a powerful tool for healing and gaining energy. Consider for a moment what shared humor does: it exponentially magnifies each person's enjoyment of an experience. The feeling that someone finds the same circumstances funny, *gets* your jokes, and shares your sense of humor means that *they understand you*. It's a way of bonding because they're just like you in important ways, including how they perceive the world and what they value. This requires, of course, that the humor be relational, meaning, that it is cocreated and enjoyed by both people. Friends, partners, and teams who enjoy the same sense of humor often describe it as the joy that gets them through difficult times and enriches their lives with laughter. All positive forms of humor are associated with higher relationship satisfaction.

In closer relationships—such as romantic partnerships or close friendships, including between colleagues—you might develop private jokes. This creates a sense of a shared, safe space—somewhere risks can be taken.[5] That's what we all want in relationships—to feel safe, seen, and connected.

On your journey out of burnout, please take joy and fun seriously. Elevating your ability to feel joy is the result of living authentically. As you surround yourself with others who encourage lightheartedness in your life, notice the impact on your emotional energy. And as you learn to navigate your emotions better, your social relationships will benefit too.

EMOTIONAL ENERGY REASSESSMENT

Emotions indicate how you're relating to the experience of your life in this moment. If you're moved enough to experience emotions about a topic, an event, or exchange with someone else, then whatever it is—it's important to you.

1. Circle the areas in your life in which you feel joy, play, and satisfaction:

    Health   Social

    Money   Romance

    Family   Work

    Other _____

2. With whom and in what environments do you find yourself belly laughing?

    _____

3. Circle the areas in which you feel disappointment, sadness, or grief:

    Health   Social

    Money   Romance

    Family   Work

    Other _____

4. Circle the areas of your life where you are avoiding conflict or difficult emotions:

    Health   Social

    Money   Romance

    Family   Work

    Other _____

5. Overall, on an emotional level, are you experiencing a net gain (+) or a net drain (−) of energy?

    ☐ net gain (+)   ☐ net drain (−)

Once again, the way you determine this is by looking at your preceding answers and also by checking in with your Body Map. If you feel a constriction or tightness in your body as you answer these questions, you likely have a net drain in this area. If you have a feeling of openness, ease, or lightness in your body as you answer these questions, this energy level is likely a net gain for you.

Now that you better understand emotions, were there any patterns you noticed? Was there anything you learned that surprised you? Be gentle with yourself. This is the gateway of awareness that will lead you to removing any emotional blocks so you can jump-start your joy!

Emotional connections build strong relationships. And research shows that a shared sense of humor is an important factor that contributes to friendships and relationships enduring the test of time.

Now that you have a better understanding of how to navigate your physical, mental, and emotional energies, let's explore your social energy.

PART IV

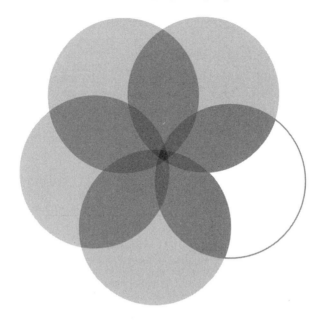

SOCIAL ENERGY

CHAPTER 17

NAVIGATING WE

There is no doubt that the quality of our relationships determines the quality of our lives. Equally important to your relationship with yourself is who you choose to forge relationships with. We are born into our families, but we get to choose our friends, partners, and work environment.

We've talked about physical, mental, and emotional energy, which are primarily generated from within. Social energy, on the other hand, focuses on the exchange between you and others. Does that mean you don't have influence or control over social energy? Absolutely not. You are still 100 percent in charge of your own energy levels. The reality is that whether you are an introvert (someone whose energy is increased by being alone) or an extrovert (someone whose energy is increased by being with others), you are always interacting with other humans. It's simply a part of life. From the clerk at the grocery store or your neighbor walking their dog to that detail-oriented client or your child's teacher, your relational energy fluctuates throughout the day with every interaction or exchange that you have.

Our relationships have a large influence on our health and can even help us heal and lengthen our lives. Don't underestimate the power of your social energy, especially its role in burnout.

We often think of our stress as coming from heavy workloads, and relationship dynamics are often a part of that. We can't escape people. But we *can* ease the stress that comes from misunderstandings, assumptions, expectations, and conflict.

I'm going to walk you through a few of the most common relational dynamics that play a role in burnout: your work style, a lack of healthy boundaries, how you make decisions, drama triangles, and conflict. Learning how to navigate social interactions is part of the journey toward stress relief and burnout prevention.

WHY OTHERS CAN CAUSE SO MUCH STRESS

Whether it's the coworker who is always in a panic or the family member who can't stop asking you to share their latest social media post, it's easy to be irritated by people who don't think like you do. And it can be one of your biggest stressors. There will likely be people who see a situation in the same way you do—and plenty who have a different approach. But here's the thing: *everyone* has reasons for thinking and behaving the way that they do. Everyone has a unique inner GPS and experience that has brought them to this point. The kicker is: *every one of them is valid.*

By that I mean, everyone has a unique perspective based on their experiences and approach to living in the world. Now, I'm not arguing that every single person *uses* that perspective and approach wisely; we're all at different levels of growth. Instead of letting your differences cause more stress, considering how someone else's approach can *actually help you* will alleviate stress and foster better relationships. Here's a simple way to better understand and value yourself and those around you at work and home—for your own sake.

There are four main work styles: Doers, Thinkers, Seers, and Feelers. Most people exhibit some combination of these four styles. The truth is that we have varying levels of proficiency with each, but one is usually our strongest cornerstone—the one we naturally default to under stress.

1. Doers

The currency of Doers is accomplishment, tasks, and to-dos. It's no surprise that their favorite activity is getting things ta-done! They tend to be busy bees. **A Doer's pace** is fast, and this constant activity gives them a boost of adrenaline and a sense of control, which keeps them far away from *having to feel* much of anything. They move at a quicker pace, driven by deadlines. Doers are often physically oriented, meaning they enjoy moving their bodies and engaging in hands-on work.

How would you know **a Doer at the gym**? They love efficiency. They're the ones on the elliptical machine, listening to a podcast *and* reading the paper. Accomplishing provides Doers with a sense of purpose, which energizes them and leaves them wanting to do even more.

If Doers had a motto, it would be "Just do it!"

If a Doer were a vehicle, they would be a Hummer, a bulldozer, or a tank, which would best describe their strong commitment to forward momentum. Because no matter what might get in their way, they're going to roll right over it and arrive at their destination. They love being the boss. And you know what? If they're not the boss, they prefer that the boss lives at least 3,000 miles away. Control and efficiency are the Doers' top priorities.

On the flip side, what do you think the **Doer's greatest fear** is? Well, vulnerability, of course. They dislike unpredictability and the mess that comes with feeling challenging emotions.

The gift of the Doer is that they are focused, get a lot done in a short amount of time, are able to meet tight deadlines, and come in *on or under budget.*

2. Thinkers

The currency of the Thinker is details, data, and knowledge. They're analytical. They like numbers. They love solving complex problems. **Their pace** is slower to give them time to think. They are great at doing research, but because they are so thorough, they can also miss deadlines.

How do you spot a **Thinker at the gym**? They'll have a way to document the weights and number of reps on each machine and a particular order in which they do their exercises. Suppose somebody is using the machine that the Thinker wants to use next. They'll wait. Thinkers value being sequential and methodical. *What* the Thinker is doing and *the order in which they are doing it* matter equally.

If Thinkers had a motto, it would be: "Do it once, and do it right!"

If they were a car, they'd be a Prius, of course! Because they would have thought through the best price, fuel efficiency, the environmental impact, the hybrid carpool lane advantage, and the practicality and ease of parking in compact spots. Thinkers are thoughtful and consider all factors in making a decision—they prefer no surprises.

The Thinker's biggest fear is looking foolish. They hate making mistakes. It's very important for a Thinker to get it right. This work style can easily lend itself to perfectionism.

The gift of the Thinker is their ability to solve complex problems in a linear, detailed, well-thought-out fashion.

3. Seers

The currency of Seers is ideas, innovation, and novelty. They like to brainstorm and talk through all possibilities. They love exploring, being nonlinear, and going in any direction their creativity takes them. **A Seer's pace** is often fast, switching from one idea to the next. They also love aesthetics. They will often sport a splash of color, cool socks, or an accent piece of jewelry, like a nice watch.

How do you recognize a **Seer at the gym**? Oh, you won't find them at a conventional gym! They'll be out in nature on the latest carbon fiber bike, blazing new trails for others to follow.

The motto of Seers is: "If you can dream it, you can be it!" (Walt Disney). It's all about reaching for the stars.

If Seers were a car, they would be a *red* convertible Cyber Truck (these trucks only come in silver and black) because red is a custom paint job!

What do you think **Seers' greatest fear** is? Because they love possibility and freedom, their greatest fear is feeling trapped. Keeping their commitments is a challenge for them because they are easily distracted and suffer from FOMO (fear of missing out). While they can be loads of fun to have at your party, they might not even show up. The problem is that there are many good options in life, and if they get distracted by a better option, they might choose that instead.

The gift of Seers is that they can see the future. Their innovation will keep them on the cutting edge so as to be different from the crowd.

4. Feelers

The currency of Feelers is relationships. They love people. They're happy to move at a slower **pace**—whatever it takes to build strong and meaningful connections. Empathy comes naturally. Feelers seek harmony and are in tune with other people's moods and emotions.

How do you know a **Feeler at the gym**? They're easy to spot because they're more about *socializing* than *sweating*.

The Feeler's motto would be an African proverb: "If you want to go fast, go alone. If you want to go far, go together."

If Feelers were a car, which one would they be? A minivan of course! It doesn't matter how everyone gets there, as long as we get to journey together.

What do you suppose a **Feeler's greatest fear** is? Rejection. They work hard to make sure other people like them. To ensure their approval from others, they can easily become people-pleasers. They tend to give so much that they are depleted themselves. The danger of this imbalanced outward focus is they can end up feeling resentful.

The gift of the Feeler is that they are the glue—of a team, a family, or a community. They ensure that everybody is participating and moves forward as one cohesive group.

See Figure 17.1 below for a quick summary of the four main work styles.

FIGURE 17.1 **Four Work Styles Summary**

DOER	THINKER
CURRENCY: Accomplishment	**CURRENCY:** Knowledge, data, numbers, sequential thought
PACE: Faster	**PACE:** Slower
SUPERPOWER: On time & under budget	**SUPERPOWER:** Complex problem-solvers
CAR: Hummer, bulldozer, tank	**CAR:** Prius
GREATEST FEAR: Vulnerability / losing control	**GREATEST FEAR:** Looking foolish
SEER	**FEELER**
CURRENCY: Innovation, possibilities	**CURRENCY:** Relationships, people, connection
PACE: Faster	**PACE:** Slower
SUPERPOWER: Visual, aesthetic & spontaneous	**SUPERPOWER:** Glue of the team
CAR: Red Tesla Cybertruck	**CAR:** Minivan
GREATEST FEAR: Feeling trapped	**GREATEST FEAR:** Being rejected

No one is consistent all the time. Some people behave one way in a work situation and another in their personal lives. And most aren't even aware of how various behavioral styles clash in everyday scenarios like lunch or dinner conversations, colleague exchanges, and yes, every team meeting. For example, when a **Seer** is happily brainstorming ideas ("We could do this or this . . ."), here's what else is happening:

- The Seers' world of possibilities serves to irritate the **Doers** who are thinking, "Which of these ideas are we *actually committed to doing*, and when can we get started? You're all talk and no action. Meetings like this are a waste of time."

- The **Thinkers** are frantically writing down *potential complications* that could arise from each of these "crazy" ideas, piping up with reasons why each idea isn't even humanly possible. They want to know, "How would we turn those ideas into reality? What about supply chain issues? Have you even given a thought to the mechanism of accomplishing this moonshot idea?"

- Meanwhile, the **Feelers** are tuned in to the energy of the group, checking in to make sure everyone feels heard and valued. "Anita isn't participating anymore. I bet she's upset because Bob interrupted her earlier."

- All the while, the **Seers**, preferring to keep all options open, continue to lob new ideas so that they don't get trapped into committing to a single approach.

When we don't appreciate diverse perspectives, it can work against us, creating stress for everyone involved. But when we value approaches different from our own, we can harness the gifts and vulnerabilities of each of us to get more done and in the best way possible. This may feel like it would take a lot of extra time or energy, but in truth, you're most likely already expending energy fighting against, complaining about, or resisting collaboration. Why not redirect that energy in a way that benefits you?

Certain roles tend to attract more **Doers** because they're more task-oriented. In a general sense, acknowledging there are exceptions, when I think of people whose primary behavior style is a Doer, organizational leaders, executive assistants, firefighters, financial analysts, athletes, surgeons, and parents come to mind. These are people who get a lot accomplished in a brief period of time. In keeping with their highest value of maximizing efficiency, you might notice they often cut a few corners in the process. And they can seem less interested in addressing the emotional aspects of relationships.

These unaddressed emotions are often an opportunity for the **Feelers** in the workplace or the household. What type of person am I talking about specifically? The sensitive child, the counselor, teacher, therapist, coach, nurse, and family physician, to name a few—those who find great satisfaction in deep and meaningful conversations. Feelers are curious about and enjoy meeting their students, patients, and colleague's families. They are also in tune with how they're feeling, and ask about any current challenges. Feelers are also the ones who sense the fatigue of an exhausted colleague and offer up a stash of sugar and caffeine to carry them over the finish line.

Thinkers are often more drawn to jobs that require complex problem-solving, such as lawyers, engineers, researchers, academics, accountants, and policymakers. They tend to be methodical, analytical, and thorough—especially interested in solving the most intriguing challenges. They are the ones unafraid of tackling a snarled accounting ledger or unraveling a complex chain of events to get to the root of a problem. Thinkers enjoy data and research. Unless they have outside pressure, they might not make a decision. There's always one more time they can go through a project to make sure they didn't miss anything.

To boldly move into the future, we need people who see the bigger picture. That's where **Seers** come in. They're the risk-takers and innovators. They often seek to improve processes and systems. They understand the importance of team dynamics and how family and organizational cultures impact productivity. They know how to motivate, engage, and inspire. Seers solve problems at the intersection of disciplines most people don't even think go together—health, business, leadership, technology, and legislative policy, for example. Seers transcend silos.

So which behavioral style is *your* greatest strength? And where do you experience friction with others?

LEVERAGING OTHERS

When our default is to project our problems, mistakes, or inefficiencies on one another by making the other person's behavioral style wrong, it only exacerbates tension and stress. This is how projection divides us and leads to unnecessary conflict and tension. When you're divided, it's hard to function as a team—at work or at home.

The truth is that the best teams, families, and communities are composed of all four work styles who value each other for their strengths and leverage their differences to solve complex problems and create ideal outcomes. For example, if a Doer and Thinker value each other, the Thinker will slow the Doer down enough to prevent mistakes, while the Doer speeds the Thinker up so they don't get caught in indecision. For example, together, they can produce a weekly concise but impactful podcast that is meticulously edited and produced. Win-win! To complete the team, they could use a Feeler to engage with the audience on social media and a Seer to plan next season's blockbuster theme—keeping the podcast relevant and cutting edge.

If you can see the value in others' work styles rather than draining your precious energy by focusing on how they are wrong or different from your own, you have the possibility to create an even better outcome.

What ways can you adjust how you interact with others to leverage their behavioral styles? Here are a few ideas:

- When working with a **Doer**, speak in headlines and bullet points, rather than in details. Trust that they will ask you if they need more information.

- If you're interacting with a **Thinker**, give them context, research, details, sources, and possibly even the latest article on a subject to give them the most information possible.

- If you're interacting with a **Seer**, it's important to let them know where you need their creative input and how what you're sharing is different, novel, or unique from the mainstream.

- If you're interacting with a **Feeler**, speak to them about how whatever you're suggesting will strengthen relationships, improve team dynamics, and create better connections.

When you illuminate other people's innate gifts and skill sets, you'll know how to make slight adjustments in your own communication in order to partner effectively with other work styles. And by all means, please articulate to others *how you work best*. This will reduce stress, improve collaboration, and create a net gain of mental, emotional, and social energy for everyone.

SOCIAL ENERGY ASSESSMENT

Circle your answers to the following questions:

1. Which work style(s) did you resonate with most?

   Doer   Seer

   Thinker   Feeler

2. Which work styles give you energy?

   Doer   Seer

   Thinker   Feeler

3. Which work styles drain you of energy?

   Doer   Seer

   Thinker   Feeler

CHAPTER 18

WHY BOUNDARIES MATTER

n this age of *faster is better*, "boundaries" can seem like a swear word. You might be thinking, *Setting limits at work or at home? That's not realistic. My life is changing constantly. I just have to do what needs to be done. Period.*

You may be reading this book because you've realized that the way you've been working is *not working*. Chances are your default is to put your own needs on the back burner—but you've been learning to undo that pattern. It seems obvious, but it requires a mindset shift from what your education, training, and cultural norms may have taught you.

A lot of the time, burnout is about boundaries (or lack thereof). You might be wondering where intentional boundary-setting might be most valuable to you. The answer is *wherever you're losing energy*.

It's a proven fact that humans physiologically influence one another, radiating an electromagnetic field (that can actually be measured!) that extends at least a few feet around us. When you say, "I picked up on his vibe," or "You're in my space," it's because you are being impacted by someone's electromagnetic field. Depending on the frequency of the field, it can feel synergistic to your own . . . or you may feel discord. And the way you navigate the intersection of your and other people's energy is through boundaries.

Healthy boundaries create safety and support; they often help an individual or group feel protected. These preferences, limits, or hard lines are important to speak out loud, rather than assuming people already know them. Boundaries may seem selfish at first, but in fact, they help you care for yourself *so that* you can consistently be there for others. Intact boundaries reflect self-awareness. Knowing and articulating specifically what you need is an important first step. This allows you to perform at your highest capacity without burning out. Healthy boundaries serve as a bridge in relationships. They allow you to effectively communicate to others what does and doesn't work for you. Knowing and setting boundaries takes courage. And if you aren't clear about what you need or want, you'll likely discover your boundaries *only after someone has crossed them.*

BOUNDARY VIOLATIONS

The value of knowing and drawing healthy boundaries has never been clearer to me than in the summer of 2013, when as a favor I agreed to let Maxine (the daughter of a dear friend) and her boyfriend, Rick, live downstairs in my San Francisco home. They were relocating for Maxine's summer internship. My hesitation had been that I was in the middle of upgrading my carpets, furniture, and decor, so I was more conscious about keeping it pristine. When they arrived, I called a house meeting to articulate my boundaries and asked, "Do you agree with these four rules of the house?"

1. Please take your shoes off before entering.

2. No smoking (cigarettes / marijuana) or drugs of any kind on my property.

3. Please notify me prior to having overnight guests.

4. If there is any ambiguity or conflict, anyone can request a house meeting.

"Sure," Maxine and Rick said, both nodding in agreement. "That sounds easy enough."

With these simple and clear boundaries, we began our summer of cohabitation. All went smoothly, until two weeks later, one afternoon following a nap, I exited my bedroom and was nearly knocked over by the smell of pot pouring through the house. I traced the source downstairs to the door of Rick and Maxine's room and knocked twice. No one answered. I knew Maxine was at work, so she likely wasn't involved. I entered to find the French doors to the back porch wide open, where two recently used bowls and a couple of lighters rested on the table.

Maybe my agreements with Maxine and Rick weren't as simple and clear as I had thought.

I'll revisit shortly how these boundaries unraveled, but first I'd like to discuss the importance of *knowing what you want* to successfully navigate a situation. When my friend initially made the request for his daughter and her boyfriend to stay with me, I needed to ask myself: given my home renovations and personal preferences, what would it take for me to say yes to them living downstairs for the summer?

Navigating shared territory requires knowing what you want *and getting agreement on those expectations up front*. This clarity builds not only self-trust but interpersonal trust in navigating the unknown together. While this experience with Maxine and Rick was a personal exchange, these principles apply both at home and at work. Even with clear boundaries, you may run into conflict—but at least you'll have a framework from which to begin the conversation.

TYPES OF BOUNDARIES

Boundaries give you guidelines that help you create the life you want. You may need to draw different boundaries depending on the situation, the person or people involved, and your particular desires and needs. But now that you're tuned in to your body, thoughts, and emotions, you have the data required to assess your needs and whether a situation, relationship, or environment is good for you or if it's draining your energy.

There are many types of boundaries. Let's explore some of them and pay attention to how you relate to each.

Physical Boundaries

What are you willing to *do* or *not do*—with yourself, with your material possessions, and how you physically engage with others? Some examples of physical boundary dilemmas include:

- **Your preferred wake-sleep schedule** (e.g., receiving or not receiving communication before / after certain times)

- **Your needs and rituals around physical self-care** (e.g., particular foods, frequency and type of movement, ways to center yourself)

- **Personal space preferences** with strangers, colleagues, friends, and family

- Knowing what **personal property** you are willing to share or not (clothes, car, home, to name a few)

Mental Boundaries

What are you willing or unwilling to *consider* or *discuss* regarding your beliefs—about politics, money, triumphs, or failures? Some examples of mental boundary dilemmas include:

- **Being clear about your own perspective** and deciding **in what settings** you feel comfortable sharing

- How to communicate if you're **uncomfortable discussing a certain topic** with particular people

- Deciding **how to address unethical or bullying behavior** in personal or professional situations

- Choosing how to engage in **conversations in which you are being manipulated** (e.g., when you have data that proves something, but you are being told it isn't true)

Emotional Boundaries

What are you willing to *feel* or *not feel*? Some examples of emotional boundary dilemmas include:

- **Choosing how to process your own emotions,** whether that means doing so internally, journaling, speaking with a professional or a friend, going for a run—or avoiding them altogether (not recommended)

- **In a challenging conversation,** when you feel overwhelmed, **do you ask for what you need** (time to think, space to reflect, support, an extension, etc.)? Do you override your emotions and power through? Or do you let someone else run right over you?

- **Engaging over and over with someone else's emotions,** hoping to soothe some of their emotional burden (i.e., trying to fix their problems or make them feel better)

Social Boundaries

In what ways are you willing or unwilling to *engage* with others? Some examples of relational boundary dilemmas include:

- **Splitting the bill:** When one person has had three adult beverages and you had none, how do you both handle the bill?

- **Discussing information about a third party:** For example,

  ○ "Billy told me that Jana didn't get promoted because she's too outspoken."

  ○ "Did you hear that Alan cheated on Alyse and now they're getting divorced?"

  ○ "I don't feel comfortable discussing Michael's personal life. I think you should probably ask him directly."

- **The degree to which you mix personal and professional relationships:** Are you friends with colleagues? Does your family know about work dilemmas?

- **Choosing when to say yes and when to say no:**

  ○ When you don't actually have the time, do you still take on another passion project?

  ○ Do you agree to cover someone else's workload when you're already stretched thin?

- **The types of people with whom you want to spend your free time**

BOUNDARY STYLES

What does it mean for you to have a good day at work? Think about it.

- For **Doers**, "a good day" means completing the most work in the least amount of time.

- For **Thinkers**, it means successfully tackling a thorny problem in the most methodical way.

- For **Seers**, it means brainstorming and coming up with novel ideas that can change the world.

- For **Feelers**, it means connecting deeply and sharing meaningful exchanges with colleagues, clients, and the larger community.

No matter which work style you prefer, to achieve fulfillment, you must determine *what you need to do your job well*, without sacrificing your energy.

Healthy, balanced boundaries are an important part of holding personal and interpersonal integrity. They provide structure. Nature knows this well. In fact, each human cell has its own clear boundary. If you recall from high school biology, each cell membrane is composed of a phospholipid bilayer that ensures the *good stuff gets in* and the *bad stuff stays out*. This structured but flexible boundary allows each cell to take in what will help it function optimally while simultaneously releasing what it no longer needs.

Problems arise when boundaries are drawn too tightly (rigid) or too loosely (porous). Recognizing your boundary-drawing tendencies based on your work style will not only help you gain clarity on what you want and need, but also strengthen your relationships and save you time. Be assured that no matter which work style you identify with, you can learn to draw the right level of boundaries for you.

Too Rigid

If your boundaries are too rigid, it's probably for good reason. This type of boundary may have been modeled by caretakers and family members in an effort to avoid vulnerability and maintain control. There are many explanations—conscious or subconscious—from not knowing how to handle strong emotions and coping with uncertainty to biologically protecting oneself in response to past or ongoing traumatic experiences.

Rigid boundaries can show up as physically distancing oneself, mental justifications for disengaging, or building emotional walls for self-protection. This is a natural human response to avoid pain and has helped people survive unimaginable circumstances. But long term, that level of self-protection may result in feelings of disconnection, isolation, and loneliness—blocking out love, connection, affection, humor, and soulful emotional exchanges.

Both **Doers** and **Thinkers**, listen up! Your boundary-drawing strategies may seem different, but that's only because of *whom you direct your boundaries toward*—yourself or others. Doers direct rigid boundaries at others, to keep moving, while Thinkers direct rigid boundaries toward themselves to get it just right. Common examples of "too rigid" boundaries for **Doers** include:

- Insisting on sticking to the original plan even when circumstances change

- Minimizing other people's emotions and telling them, "There's nothing you can do. You need to move on."

- Making statements rather than asking questions in interpersonal exchanges: "Yeah, well, this is how we've always handled that kind of situation, and it's worked out so far," versus "What about this situation do you think could use improvement? Do you have any ideas for how we could make the process more seamless?"

- Blowing up, becoming passive-aggressive, or taking an oath of silence in response to something unexpected happening

- Having a poker face, not revealing your true emotions

In general, Doers love crossing items off their to-do list. Ta-done! Their rigid boundaries often serve a higher purpose: meeting a deadline or staying on or under budget. To others, Doers' relentless focus on next steps can sometimes come across as dismissive and micromanaging. The danger is that if Doers hyperfixate on time and tasks, they often miss key emotional data that undermines their ability to collaborate and lead effectively. When Doers are perceived as lacking empathy, they lose connection in their relationships.

Dahlia was a high-performing executive partner focused on becoming the first woman leader at her firm. The path there would require her to overcome a big hurdle: getting the majority vote from 300 other partners. She approached this herculean task the way she approached any undertaking—with efficiency. She printed a comprehensive partner list and began calling them one-by-one, inquiring, "Hi John, this is Dahlia. I'm interested in leading the practice after Mark retires. Can I count on your vote?"

"You sure can, Dahlia. Good luck," John replied.

In addition to her already busy workday, in full-Doer-form, Dahlia was exhilarated as she checked off 25 partner calls per day. Proud to be making such steady progress, she calculated that by voting day, she would have spoken with every last one of them.

Next on her list was Sarah. Assuming that their 20-year collegial relationship would lead to a slam dunk, Dahlia was taken aback when Sarah responded, "I know how much this opportunity means to you, Dahlia, but unfortunately, I wanted to tell you—I won't be voting for you. I'm concerned that the firm's long-term success will require someone in this position who's not just focused on the bottom line—which by the way, you're *fantastic* at. I think we need someone with that ability who also has deep empathy and emotional awareness. I think you've been very successful in a world that values productivity above all else. But the next generation is looking for new ways of working—including flexibility, work-life balance, and a caring culture, not to mention higher purpose.

"That's why I'm voting for Aiden. My gut tells me he's the right one, not only to bridge generations, but he also has the forward-thinking vision to integrate the well-being of our teams alongside growth and profit.

"And I'm not the only one. There is a significant number of partners who have told me, in confidence, that they have similar concerns. If they haven't had the courage to tell you, I thought you should hear it from me."

Following an awkward silence, Dahlia began, "You're wrong, Sarah. Nobody works harder than I do. I've reviewed the partnership feedback data meticulously. I know exactly what people want. I care so much about this firm that I'm personally calling each partner one by one. My spreadsheet is more than half-done already. I don't have time for this. You're making a mistake and you'll be sorry," Dahlia said as she hung up the phone.

Later that day, Sarah was approached by her own leader, who disclosed that he had just left a meeting with Dahlia, who was livid and in disbelief after hearing Sarah's comments. He advised that if Dahlia won, despite Sarah's 20-year tenure, it would be in Sarah's best interest to look for another job.

Voting day came and went. As Sarah had predicted, Aiden won by a landslide. Much to Dahlia's dismay, she received a mere 17 percent of the vote. The following week, Dahlia dialed her old friend, "Sarah, I can't believe you were the only one who was willing to tell me the truth. Not only am I not ready to lead this firm, I've realized that my ex-husband was right. He told me I ruined our marriage because I was so focused on all that needed to be done, that I missed truly connecting with him and the kids. And now, I've missed the biggest opportunity of my career. I hope we can still be friends."

"Of course, Dahlia," Sarah replied. "Back when we started, all the firm cared about was that we were workhorses. The world's different now. Tuning into our own and other people's emotions is the only way to build a culture of trust, loyalty, and engagement. Without it, there's no collaboration or innovation."

"Yeah, I'm starting to understand that, Sarah. Maybe if I was willing to listen to your advice, I could have turned things around," Dahlia sighed.

Common examples of "too rigid" boundaries for **Thinkers** include:

- Leaving nothing to chance by dotting every "i" and crossing every "t"

- Having trouble making decisions when lacking empirical certainty

- Missing or delaying deadlines

- Intellectualizing one's own emotions while rationalizing those of others

Thinkers' boundary-drawing tendencies are driven by their affinity for solving complex intellectual challenges (in comparison to Doers, who are driven by their *need for speed*). Thinkers' intellect is their best defense mechanism against their greatest fear of *looking foolish*. While this strategy allows them to remain steady during a crisis and not get swept up in emotional swings, it also requires a level of detachment. So when challenged with emotional vulnerability, they tend to pivot toward statistics, research, or a more pragmatic approach to the topic at hand.

For example, after hearing about a colleague's daughter experimenting with drugs, a Thinker might respond with, "You might consider reading a parenting book." What seems pragmatic to the Thinker can come across to others as uncaring, judgmental, or disconnected.

Doers and Thinkers share the same goal when they have boundaries that are too rigid: avoiding certain emotions, like disappointment, anger, vulnerability, embarrassment, or humiliation. They seek to avoid an emotional quagmire that could either unpredictably delay their schedule (Doers) or cause unresolvable confusion (Thinkers). But when Doers and Thinkers can learn to be more flexible within themselves and with others, they will gain the power of authentic connection and deeply nourishing relationships.

How do you know if your boundaries are too rigid? You may feel isolated and lonely. Rigid boundaries protect you well and don't allow other people to cause you pain, but they also don't allow for connection, affection, or intimacy either. A good clue that this is happening to you is if you find yourself overreacting and guarding yourself when someone wants to form a personal connection with you.

Ask yourself:

- Which of these examples sound familiar?

- What are those boundaries protecting you from?

- What might happen if you loosened them?

Too Porous

Both **Seers** and **Feelers**, listen up! Seers, you typically have few boundaries around your own freedom and choice. Meanwhile, Feelers, your natural focus is on the needs of others. Common examples of "too porous" boundaries for **Seers** include:

- Missing your RSVP deadline to a private event

- Changing plans when a better opportunity arises

- Ignoring a notice to have all expense reports completed by a certain date

- Enjoying brainstorming, but not committing to the pragmatic steps needed to actualize those ideas

If you are a Seer, you probably know you're a unique breed. You can see the future. This sometimes makes it challenging for you to be in the present moment, here and now. As a result, you may not prioritize everyday situations such as routine tasks, catching up on emails, or relationship maintenance. You may not realize that wanting to leave all options on the table (unintentionally) can lead others to experience you as flaky or uncaring.

Your growth edge, Seers, is to learn how to set clear boundaries with yourself. It's true that making clear agreements means eliminating some options. That can bring up a primal fear of feeling trapped. In fact, you aren't trapped at all; you're making a choice and will grow from that experience. Know that if you procrastinate and *choose not to decide, you still have made a choice.* Inaction *is* a choice. Once you learn to make and keep clear agreements with yourself and others, not only will it *not* feel stifling or scary, you'll experience a whole new level of connection, collaboration, and higher vision!

Common examples of "too porous" boundaries for **Feelers** include:

- Saying yes when you really want to say no

- Taking on other people's pain and joy as if they are your own

- Prioritizing the needs and wants of others over your own well-being

- Not including yourself when making decisions

You may not have strong enough boundaries for a number of reasons. You may have had role models with loose boundaries. You may believe that the way to keep people in your life is by doing whatever is asked of you. You may be afraid of conflict and not want to lose something precious (e.g., a job, relationship, community, opportunity, or sense of belonging). Or your past experiences of drawing boundaries were painful or devastating, so you're not willing to make that mistake again.

In contrast to Doers, who often have overly strong emotional boundaries, Feelers tend to have weaker emotional and relational boundaries. When Feelers are with a distressed colleague or friend, they have the gift of empathy, feeling the other person's pain as if it were their own. This makes them popular with people who crave emotional connection and attention. The problem is that at the end of the day, people with this work style tend to internalize these intense experiences. Over time, this emotional weight they carry for others causes an ongoing emotional energy drain. Feelers run the risk of compassion fatigue. Fortunately, there is a cure: setting emotional boundaries.

We've all had the experience of feeling drained by someone else's emotions. It's part of being human and living among other humans. Contrary to what you may have experienced in your own family or been taught growing up, no one actually has the power to reach inside and stir up another person's emotions with their behavior. They can try, but your power comes from knowing that *you* have control over choosing how you respond. Following a conflict or tense exchange, while you may need time to process your emotions privately, *knowing where you end and another begins* will allow you to take care of yourself without unnecessarily blaming another. That's the next step in becoming *me-powered*.

One way to ground yourself in the face of intense emotion is by simply reconnecting to your body. If you are present when a friend or colleague receives painful news, like losing their job, you're witnessing a milestone moment in this person's life. Experiencing them digesting this news could easily feel overwhelming. Instead of closing your heart, get into your body. Put your hand on your abdomen, as a reminder to stay fully present. You may also adopt a mantra that helps you remain fully present. You might say to yourself: *I trust this person is strong and capable enough to handle their disappointment.*

Be compassionate to others who are in pain while simultaneously knowing *it is not your responsibility to change how they are feeling*. Listen deeply, and with each breath, imagine yourself radiating love and compassion their way. When you leave this person, wave or say good-bye to them physically, while also metaphorically waving good-bye to their disappointment—for the time being, at least. The key point is to not take on or take in their pain. Remember, you must know *where you end and they begin*. You can be compassionate and empathetic without taking on responsibility for changing someone else's emotional experience. You can support them without carrying their disappointment—it's not yours. You have your own life lessons to focus on and learn. Getting lost in other people's challenging emotions is a common way people avoid tending to their own.

A Special Note to Feelers

Deep down, your fear of being rejected is running the show. And you may be at risk of trying to *fit in* rather than *truly belong*. In this (often subconscious) quest to avoid feeling abandoned, you may overidentify with and get lost in other people's pain. This underlying pattern sets you up for high risk of codependency—where your boundaries blur and you take on responsibility for another person's behavior, emotions, or action. Their pain *is* your pain. Their stuckness *is* your stuckness. It's important to recognize and address any fears of rejection so that you can achieve greater clarity about your natural tendency and avoid the pitfalls of taking on other people's struggles, challenges, and emotions—at the expense of your own well-being.

While both Seers and Feelers can have porous boundaries, they are driven by different fears: Seers don't want to be trapped, and Feelers don't want to be rejected. Accordingly, the strategies to heal these imbalances are different. When drawing boundaries, Seers must take into account the needs of others, while Feelers need to include themselves in the equation.

How do you know if your boundaries are too porous? You may become easily overwhelmed. Loose boundaries allow other people's experiences to blur with your own, buckling you into an emotional roller coaster. A good clue that this is happening is if your mood fluctuates as your external environment changes.

Ask yourself:

- Which of these examples sound like boundary dilemmas you've experienced?

- What fear is driving these porous boundaries?

- What might happen if you strengthened these boundaries?

Just Right

If you have healthy boundaries that are neither too weak nor too strong (the Goldilocks zone), you can prevent energy drains while accumulating energy gains. You have a clear structure defined by what you value most, and you are simultaneously fluid and flexible to the situation at hand. With these boundaries, you feel grounded, no matter what environment you're in. You know who you are and what you value. You trust that you will speak up if you need to.

With healthy boundaries, you can allow yourself to feel and express a wide range of emotions. There's no need to fix or deflect other people's pain. You're comfortable with silence. You can handle a tearful outburst or a snarky comment because you have a clear sense of *where you end and another person begins*. You know that when someone else's issue isn't actually yours, you can still listen and process with them, trusting that they are strong, resourceful, and capable of handling their own experience. You're open to a variety of perspectives and effortlessly create the space for others to share their experiences.

You have control of the strength and integrity of your boundaries. How confident you are in drawing these boundaries in relation to others' behavior reflects your level of self-awareness, self-respect, self-trust, and self-compassion.

For example, in 2012, I delivered my first large-scale public talk at TEDx Berkeley. While on stage sharing personal stories, I surprised myself by becoming emotional twice, even to the point of tears. Following the event, the TEDx team invited all the speakers to mingle with the attendees. Each of us had a line of eager audience members waiting to interact with us. A Middle Eastern man in his early thirties approached me, "Dr. Sangwan, thank you for your most interesting talk. I very much enjoyed it. But I was curious, why did you have to fake-cry to get attention?"

If this had happened a decade earlier, when my emotional boundaries were not intact (meaning I allowed other people's opinions to dictate my experience and response), I would have been humiliated and devastated. My reaction would have been to defend, apologize, and explain why I had become emotional in an effort to (hopefully) change his opinion of me. I would have been trying to distance myself to avoid complete and utter shame.

To my own surprise, my efforts to repeatedly strengthen my mental and emotional boundaries paid off because in that moment I responded differently. I took a slow, deep breath and replied, "Thank you for your honesty. It sounds like you and I had a different experience of what happened on stage today. Is there anything else you wanted to share?"

"No. That's it." he responded, somewhat dumbfounded as he walked away.

Most people treat other people's opinions, comments, or perceptions as truth. If someone doesn't like them or criticizes them, the recipient assumes they must be the one in the wrong and reflexively moves into crisis repair mode. They desperately try to change someone else's opinion, justify their actions, or fix their "flawed self." I didn't feel the need to do that with this gentleman. I knew I had shared authentically; I knew my tears were real. Even though I didn't quite understand why I was so emotional—especially after having rehearsed the talk so many times—I was confident in my boundary of not justifying myself to a stranger.

When I went back and watched my TEDx Berkeley talk, I observed that I had become tearful the first time when I was sharing how my patient Brandon was recovering from a stroke and was explaining to me how important it was for *his father to be proud of him*, and a second time, when I was relaying that *my own father was proud of me* after a trip I had taken to Saudi Arabia. That day I learned that even if I've told a story countless times privately, the vulnerability of sharing that same story on a world stage can reveal what still needs healing.

You get to choose who you surround yourself with and which environments you are in. But once you're there, other people make choices to behave in certain ways. Their behavior is not in your control. Remember: only you have control over how well you know yourself and recognize your underlying intentions, what you choose to prioritize and value, and how you respond to a given situation. When someone questions you, it's an opportunity to check in to see if it rings true for you. If so, maybe you need to shift course. If not, thank them and move on.

THE ART OF SETTING BOUNDARIES

When preparing to draw healthy boundaries, reflect on the following.

1. Body Signals

How is your body physically letting you know something is off? Boundaries are often relayed through your body. Is there any constriction, heaviness, tightness, or discomfort? If you're held by someone you love, you may notice your muscles relax, your chest is open, and you take a few slow deep breaths. This likely indicates that you're comfortable with these boundaries.

On the other hand, if you're receiving a hug from someone you dislike, don't trust, or simply don't know, and your muscles tighten, your stomach turns, or you begin sweating, that tells you that you're outside your comfort zone. If you override your body's physical signals, you'll miss these valuable warning signs and perhaps even be surprised by the intensity of your reaction to what's happening.

2. Emotional Inventory

What emotions are you experiencing that tell you it's time to protect yourself or open up? Are you feeling content? Intimidated? Resistance? Anger? Anxiety? Or perhaps a sense of being trapped? Begin by using your body's data to name all the emotions that are arising (see Emotional Vocabulary List in Chapter 12).

3. Name That Boundary

What is the boundary you need to set? Use your body's wisdom and your emotional data to decipher the boundary that needs to be set or has been crossed. Sometimes you'll know what you need immediately. Other times you will need to put a short-term boundary in place as you figure out what you require. Here are a few short-term options:

- Ask for time, support, or space.

- End the encounter with some version of, "Now is not a good time. I'll reach out when it's a better time for me."

- Physically remove yourself from the situation.

4. Gain or Loss

What might you gain or lose by setting this boundary? Sometimes the other person may not even notice that you have set a boundary. Other times you may create conflict by drawing a boundary that puts an end to your job, opportunity, or relationship. Or it might be somewhere in between. What you know for sure is that the experience isn't working for you. What you gain is the opportunity to reset that experience in a way that matches your current needs.

5. Certainty

On a scale of 1 to 10, where 1 = no certainty and 10 = complete certainty, what level of certainty do you have about the importance of drawing this boundary? This is a quick check-in that allows you to get clear about what you value and why you're making this decision. It's OK if you aren't entirely certain, as long as you trust yourself to adjust as necessary.

6. Flexibility

On a scale of 1 to 10, where 1 = no flexibility and 10 = complete flexibility, how flexible are you with this boundary? It's important that you understand whether this is a rigid or fluid boundary. For example, given a choice, you might pick red wine over white, but in reality, either will do. This is a preference. Preferences are somewhat fluid. On the other hand, your boundary may be non-negotiable, such as if you have food allergies and wind up with an upset stomach, facial swelling, and itching when ingesting any of the foods on your sensitivity list. In that case, your boundary will be rigid.

7. Repeat Offenders

What are the consequences of violating this boundary? Consequences need to be realistic and match the boundary offense. The consequence of violating this boundary has to be something you can uphold and something that matters to the other person as well.

Knowing what you need and having the courage to articulate up front what will happen if this boundary is not respected are essential to setting clear expectations. If you're a parent, you've no doubt had practice enforcing consequences with your kids for crossing boundaries. For example, if you tell your teenager curfew is 11 p.m., you also need to let them know in advance that they will lose their car privileges next weekend if they are late. It's critical to the integrity of your word and the strength of your relationships that you follow through with your stated consequences. So take the time up front to think through consequences before you take any action.

How will you share your boundaries? And with whom? What do you want or need to be different? Set your intention to be courageous and kind. Stay calm, steady, and grounded in your body (using your breath and gravity). Practice drawing your boundary out loud with a trusted friend and get input on your body language, tone, and words.

How you choose to articulate boundaries and how you reinforce them is important. Don't be surprised if your level of boundary-drawing varies with different people in different situations.

HOUSE OF TRUTH

Now that you understand the difference between too porous, too rigid, and "just right" boundaries, I promised I would tell you how my summer house-mate saga unfolded. To recap, I had verbally requested that no one smoke in my place or on my property. No cigarettes and no weed. When I smelled the scent of pot generously flowing through my house and then found the lighters and used bowls downstairs, it was clear that my boundary hadn't been respected. I then called Rick, whom I suspected was the culprit and asked him, "What's going on downstairs?"

"Nothing," he responded. "My friend came to meet me earlier, and now we're out photographing in the park."

"Were you guys smoking pot in the house before you left?"

"Nope," Rick said. "Why?"

Annoyed that he was clearly lying, I replied, "Rick, I'm going to give you one more chance to give me a different answer. Were you two smoking weed downstairs earlier today at the house?"

He doubled down. "No way."

"OK, well, since we are all having dinner tomorrow at 6 p.m., it sounds like we need a house meeting then."

With similar incidents in the past, I had chosen to avoid conflict—and then lived with being upset because I hadn't spoken up for myself. I was aware that whatever choice I made eventually, I would have to look in the mirror and answer to the woman looking back at me. I brainstormed a few options.

1. I could ignore it and act like it never happened.

2. I could bypass the house meeting altogether, and text Rick that his actions were a deal-breaker and he needed to find alternate summer housing plans.

3. I could commit to having an authentic conversation with everyone involved prior to making my final decision about whether to allow my guests to remain in the house.

To decide, I had to ask myself: In this particular situation, what did I actually want? And what was the best way to proceed? The first option felt too porous for my comfort level, while the second felt too rigid. After some thought, I realized that the third was the "just right" boundary for me. This would give Rick a chance to explain himself, and if I stayed open and curious, maybe we could find a path forward.

My heightened level of emotion clued me in that there might be some healing to do *within me* as well. Considering no one got in trouble, hurt, or sick, I began to wonder, *Why am I having such a strong reaction? Did I just get amygdala hijacked? Had I experienced something similar in the past (where someone violated agreed-upon boundaries and then lied about doing so)?*

All of a sudden, several examples flooded my mind. Rick's disrespect and lies mirrored various dating experiences in my twenties and thirties—men who had run circles around me with their wit and charm as a way to cover up deceit. That wasn't all. Much to my surprise, with some additional reflection, I began to identify similar patterns with certain friends and family members, too.

Now I realized why this had upset me so much. I was carrying not only this experience but also a handful of others that had gone unaddressed and unhealed. With this expanded awareness, I was ready for the short-term discomfort (leaning into a potentially challenging conversation) that would hopefully lead to a long-term high (knowing that I had acted fairly, with my integrity intact, to potentially salvage my relationship with Maxine and Rick).

The next night, at the meeting, I began with, "I want to give you, Rick, the benefit of the doubt. It's looking like you thought you were above the rules that we all agreed to. I'm going to ask you one more time, were you and your friend smoking weed downstairs in my house yesterday afternoon?"

Rick confessed, "OK, we did. We smoked pot, but we weren't technically in your house. We were on the back porch."

"You were on my property, so please don't try to twist the truth. Either you smoked here or you didn't. Which is it?"

"OK, we did. I'm not making excuses, but this was because of my people-pleasing nature—to be a good host to my friend. I know you're a people-pleaser, too, Neha. I read it in your communication book, *TalkRx*. You and me, we're the same. I can tell that you would do the same thing by how hospitable you have been to me and Maxine over the past few weeks."

Before I could respond, Maxine chimed in. "Rick, then why have you been asking me to smoke with you downstairs and saying we can light incense and Neha will never know? You've asked me twice, and I said no."

Rick was not happy. "Whose side are you on, Maxine? I can't believe you don't have my back."

I was struck by Rick's mastery of avoiding personal responsibility. In addition to trying to guilt Maxine for telling the truth, he was also drawing an alignment between him and me (around people-pleasing) in an attempt to avoid the consequences of his actions.

"Rick, you're masterful—at being a con artist. But this time, I think you've even outsmarted yourself. The rest of us aren't fooled. Maybe Maxine actually *does* have your back. What if she cares so much about you that she's willing to get uncomfortable to speak the truth? You need to make a decision about whether you're ready to abide by the agreements you made with me or not."

With nowhere to hide, Rick responded, "I apologize and take ownership of my behavior. I'm embarrassed that I didn't tell the truth."

Maxine's face said it all. "Why would you violate agreements with Neha that you and I made as a team? You're ruining this experience for both of us."

Finally, we were getting on the same page. "Rick, I accept your apology, and I also want you to know that I feel taken advantage of."

Worried that I would ask them to leave, Rick reiterated, "I'm so sorry. Does it help that I told you the truth so soon after I lied?"

"No, not really," I said. "You didn't tell the truth because you value honesty. You did it because you got caught and were cornered into telling the truth. There's a big difference."

Rick pleaded, "But if you kick me out of the house, that means you didn't forgive me. As a coach, you teach forgiveness. How come you tell others to forgive, but when it's your turn, you don't do it yourself?"

I was stunned. He was projecting his own misalignment onto me. His words didn't match his actions, and he was attempting to find a way to discredit me.

"No, Rick. My ability to forgive you has nothing to do with whether you live in my house. It's my responsibility to choose who I allow into my sanctuary. This is a place where I cultivate peace and joy. My home is not a place that I want to be protecting and policing. I can forgive you and only see you at the park or the grocery store. Who I live with is independent from who I forgive. Do you understand the difference?"

He sheepishly nodded, looked at Maxine and then back at me. "Wow, I feel totally skewered—like I've been barbecued by you two."

My instinct was to comfort him and soothe his pain. Instead, I resisted the Feeler's urge in me to feel guilty for holding him accountable. As the meeting wrapped up, I concluded with, "I need some time to reflect on what just happened. Tomorrow evening, I'll give you my answer."

After the meeting, an epic integration occurred as I realized: the manipulations I had experienced with others in the past were not merely horrible events that had irreversibly scarred me. Each of those painful interactions had dutifully served to prepare me to recognize and articulate exactly what was out of alignment in this exchange with Rick. Each experience was a lesson that contributed to me finding the courage to stand up for myself.

With thoughtful reflection and awareness, each of us can identify painful past patterns and transform them into inspired actions that align with what we need and want.

The next evening, I met with Maxine and Rick and began, "You can both stay, on the condition that if there's a next time or even the slightest suspicion of you violating the boundaries we have agreed to, there won't be another meeting to discuss it. I'll simply ask you to leave. And Rick, I want you to know that Maxine's honesty is what tipped me into saying that you both can stay. I know that if you pull any shenanigans again, she'll tell me."

Rick couldn't contain himself, "Thank you so much, Neha! I told all my friends at dinner last night what I'd learned from our conversation: 'I totally got called out by this woman we're living with. She didn't fall for my BS. Who knew that moving to San Francisco for the summer meant I'd be living in the House of Truth?'"

I couldn't help but chuckle.

ADJUSTING YOUR BOUNDARIES

You might feel anxious, vulnerable, or upset as you practice drawing healthy boundaries. That's normal. Even once you know and understand your own boundaries, you may have difficulty maintaining them at first. Initially, when they are violated, you may do nothing or silently ruminate about the transgression. Sometimes you may get angry, hoping to instill fear in others when they cross your boundaries. Give yourself (and others) grace. You've just moved from being unaware of or ignoring your boundaries to knowing what they are and articulating them. And if you are someone who has boundaries that are too rigid—when you first let your guard down, beware. You may feel vulnerable or unsafe at first. Stick with it! Eventually, with practice, it will get easier. Be patient with yourself. Continue to communicate clearly. When necessary, take action. The goal is to become a boundary master who's clear, compassionate, and caring as you honor your boundaries and reinforce them as needed.

Keep in mind that other people might feel resistance or be upset when you communicate your boundaries—no matter how clearly, compassionately, or concisely you do so. This is where soft belly breathing and curiosity will serve you. If the other person is defensive and disrespectful, it doesn't mean that you shouldn't set a boundary; it's simply important information for you to consider. Pay attention to their feedback and make sure that how you drew your boundaries was fair and reasonable. The other person's reaction is out of your control. Remember, the success of your boundary-setting is not dependent on how the other person responds; it's about *you* and if *you were true to yourself* while also being compassionate and fair to them.

Know that just because you feel a certain way now doesn't mean that you will always feel that way. Keep examining the thoughts behind your willingness to set and maintain boundaries. Boundaries are a continuous conversation that we have with ourselves and the people we love and lead. You are changing. And over time, your boundaries will change, too.

We are communal beings that require connection and belonging to thrive. At first glance, social energy might appear as though it is more challenging to navigate than physical, mental, or emotional energy—but it's not, because so often, it comes down to *you knowing you*. Drawing healthy boundaries will take time and practice, but once you master this tool, you can navigate any arena of your life. Once you're clear on what your body's signals are telling you, how you formulate your thoughts, and what you feel and want, navigating issues with other people becomes, if not simple, then at least much more straightforward. Once you know how to integrate your human software, it will give you the energy boost you need to navigate almost any situation.

CHAPTER 19

CHOICES AND CONFLICTS

Y ou're making decisions all the time. Some are high stakes; others less so. These decisions shape your health, the strength of your relationships, and even how your day unfolds. Often, people don't even realize they have a choice in how to manage conflict. What you do when you encounter a challenge—within yourself or with others—will determine how long the conflict lasts and whether you deal with it temporarily or address the root cause.

Perhaps the following scenario sounds familiar: During the morning rush before leaving for work, your partner snaps at you, but you say nothing. Instead, the rest of the morning continues in silence. As you're heading to the car, you spill your coffee and notice a headache developing. Distracted and irritable, you impatiently cut someone off while turning into the parking structure—only to realize they were slowing down to allow an older woman with a walker to cross the street. When you get to work, the report you were supposed to receive isn't ready. You snap at your assistant (who happens to be a temp, filling in while your actual assistant is on his honeymoon).

What just happened is that the exchange with your partner rattled you and created discomfort. You discharged the frustration you had with your spouse onto *everyone else you encountered since*, but the original conflict remains unresolved. And now you've just created a few new ones all on your own!

You always have a choice in how to respond to a situation. In this case, responding to the actual cause of the stress (your and your partner's interaction), rather than other handy irritants (the car in front of you and the missing report), will *reduce* your stress instead of adding to it. And the better you become at addressing your discomfort early, the better you'll become at preventing unnecessary relational stress.

It takes bravery to lean into conflict. The reality is that you can't be courageous and comfortable at the same time. If there's conflict, you're going to experience discomfort. There's no way around that. But the choice you make determines whether you want the conflict (and therefore the discomfort) to be *short term* or *long term*. If you choose to lean into the discomfort now, you may feel uneasy initially, but after facing the reality of what's happening, you'll have the opportunity to create the best outcome for you. On the other hand, if you avoid it now, it will likely grow bigger, eventually reaching a point of crisis where you're forced to face the impact of your earlier choices.

Look, you didn't head down the path of burnout for no reason. You're at an inflection point in your life, and you have choice. The belief that you don't have options is an old, expired way of thinking. So if you are experiencing conflict, you have a few options:

1. Conceal your emotions by:

    - Keeping your feelings from the person with whom you're in conflict—and then either express those emotions to a friend or colleague

    - Changing the subject when things get awkward

    - Ignoring your feelings and minimizing your reactions and perspective

    - Saying nothing and avoiding them altogether

2. Reveal, feel, and heal your emotions by sharing your feelings with the person with whom you're in conflict

Each of these choice points are influenced by the stress you are feeling on physical, mental, emotional, and relational levels. You've spent a lot of time learning how to alleviate much of that stress. Now you can bring that together in how you handle conflict because, as we all know, conflict—whether direct or indirect—is a huge source of stress.

CHOICE POINT

Reflect on the choices you make on a daily basis, especially those that revolve around conflict. When you arrive at an emotional choice point, how do you consciously make that decision? Look at the Choice Point diagram in Figure 19.1 to help you better understand your decisions, including the ones you sometimes make unknowingly.

FIGURE 19.1 **Choice Point**

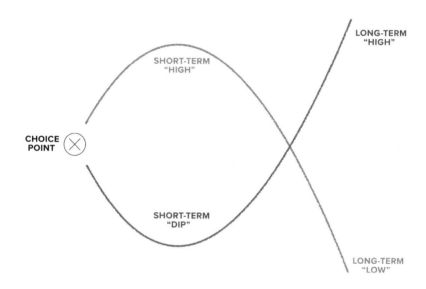

On the left, the X with a circle around it symbolizes a fork in the road, the choice point. There are likely an infinite number of options that you could choose, but for simplicity's sake, let's assume you are deciding between two options:

1. Conceal and avoid your discomfort in the present moment (short-term high) and end up with dissatisfaction in the long run (long-term low)

2. Reveal, feel, and heal the discomfort you are facing in the moment (short-term "dip" of discomfort) for a chance at creating an ideal outcome (long-term high). If you find yourself in a recurring pattern that you would like to change, understanding this Choice Point diagram will help you shift the dynamic more easily.

Years ago, I was taking care of critically ill patients being admitted from the emergency room when the ER physician, Dean, called me. "Neha, we have a 58-year-old with abdominal pain who needs to be admitted. How soon can you come and see him? We need the beds down here," he snapped.

Normally, I would receive a much more thorough history, including a summary of diagnostic tests, but clearly Dean was in triage mode and wanted this patient admitted—STAT. His tone annoyed me. I paused and asked, "What does the abdominal CT scan show? Has surgery been consulted?"

"I don't think it's necessary," he replied. "You can order an abdominal CT and call surgery if you want their input. I don't need any more data to know he's coming in." Then he abruptly hung up, which infuriated me even more.

That moment was a choice point. I had the opportunity to lean into discomfort right then and confront Dean, or I could lean away from discomfort and allow the conflict to continue.

Short-Term High

When you find yourself at a relational choice point, your protective underlying biology can be driving your decision-making. Often, you may hope that avoiding the conflict will make it go away, but you've already learned that it rarely does. In fact, avoiding conflict in the moment only makes it grow bigger. And then something very interesting happens. Not only does the conflict not go away, it *changes location*. It transforms from an interpersonal conflict (between the two of you) into an internal conflict (within you). Rather than a conversation between you and another person, it's now a battle with yourself as to *why you won't address it*. This is why choosing the short-term high may provide the immediate relief that you seek, but most often leads to you experiencing a long-term low (dissatisfaction) in an outcome, situation, or relationship.

For example, let's say you're upset with a policy at work, yet you choose to remain silent in meetings. You express your feelings by rolling your eyes and crossing your arms during the meeting and then later complaining to colleagues and family about how "ridiculous and damaging" the policies are.

While in the meeting, you opted for the short-term high (not speaking), which kept you comfortable in the moment (not risking vulnerability or judgment). In choosing safety, you have no hope of changing the outcome and are heading toward the long-term low, where your initial irritation most likely will grow into chronic frustration and helplessness. Not only did you silence your own voice, but you also cut yourself off from a more productive path: the possibility of changing your work environment. Then you discharged those pent-up emotions by blaming your leadership and place of work. This is a lose-lose energy drain—and it happens all the time.

When you repeatedly give into your biologically hardwired desire for safety (the short-term high), you are more likely to lose precious energy and weaken your overall day-to-day engagement. Choosing not to speak up in the moment will undermine your self-esteem and your true desires, and decrease your level of engagement and sense of purpose in a particular role or relationship. This is a common emotional and social energy drain.

Long-Term High

Another option is always available to you: you can choose the short-term dip of discomfort in order to create the long-term high (your ideal desired outcome). This choice requires self-trust, courage, and a willingness to move into the unknown—both within yourself and with others. You would have to take a deep breath and take the risk in the meeting to speak up and articulate why this policy may have been useful in the past but no longer is. Or you can advocate for why another policy would serve everyone in a better way. Yes, you risk feeling the pit in your stomach and your heart racing, but you must take the risk if you want change to happen. There could be judgment and backlash, should your idea not be popular or go against the grain. It's a risk worth taking because it allows you to actively navigate toward the long-term results you desire. You may also learn a lot from how your leadership, team, and others respond. You may learn that you've outgrown this team, this job, this company, and it's time to move on. Depending on how important this policy or decision is to you will determine the level of discomfort and risk you feel when you lean in. Another outcome may be that your team celebrates your bravery and leadership for speaking up. And you know exactly why this is the place for you to stay and grow in. You can't control other people's reactions, but you need to know what you value and whether you're committed to having authentic conversations in order to strengthen your relationships and create the long-term high in any situation.

Now that you understand the different aspects of choice point, take a look at Figure 19.2 to review what goes into choosing each of the different pathways.

FIGURE 19.2 **Choice Point Dynamics**

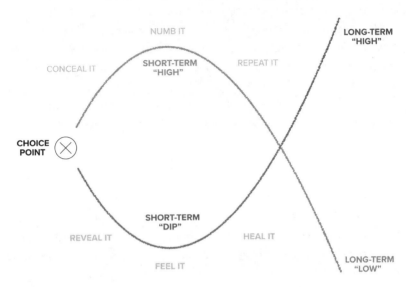

Now let's talk about one of the everyday ways this dynamic plays out in organizations, families, and communities—the Drama Triangle.

THE DRAMA TRIANGLE

First described by psychiatrist Stephen Karpman in 1955, the Drama Triangle is a theoretical framework of indirect communication, in which people talk *about* each other, not *to* each other. This dysfunctional dynamic provides an initially seductive (false, short-lived) powerplay that quickly transforms into a lasting and destructive force, undermining trust and draining relational energy. The Drama Triangle only serves to keep you—and everyone else involved—stuck in an unhealthy pattern of endless gossip. (In case you were wondering, yes, this also happens in families, communities, and many Bollywood movies.)

Unfortunately, at the choice point when I got angry with Dean, I leaned away from discomfort, choosing the short-term high. Rather than speaking to Dean directly, I tracked down Luke, a nurse and longtime confidant. "You are not going to believe what just happened! Dean is acting like he's the only busy doctor around here. As usual, he's trying to offload his share of the patient's workup on me!"

Luke replied, "Again? He does that all the time. And by the way, you're not the only one he does it to. Last weekend, when you were off, Dr. Sanders complained of the exact same dynamic. I don't know if Dr. Dean was the one Sanders was talking about, but that ER department, their MO (modus operandi) is to avoid work. They treat patients like hot potatoes. Their only goal is to offload work onto us, so that they can meet their department metrics and get a sweet bonus at the end of year. I bet Dean's got his feet up in the break room—stuffing his face with a gyro from Athena's House of Falafel. He probably made one of the already overworked interns go get it for him."

"Unbelievable," I said, shaking my head.

"Look, don't let Dean acting like a jerk stop you from taking amazing care of your patients," Luke said. "If I was sick, I'd want you to come rescue me from that hellhole of an ER."

Unbeknownst to me, something similar was happening downstairs. Once Dean hung up the phone, he turned to a colleague next to him and complained, "Why does Neha want the entire workup done in the ER? Docs like her are the bane of our existence. There's a reason I didn't do an internal medicine residency. It's not my job to do the whole workup! Once I know the patient is coming in, the workup can happen upstairs. What are we paying her for, anyway?"

Dean, speaking loudly at the nurses' station, might as well have had a megaphone, as three additional nurses overheard him carrying on. Armed with hearsay, when the nurses saw me coming to admit the patient, they immediately scattered. This only furthered my emotional buy-in to the drama Luke and I had just cocreated. *Luke was right*, I thought. *Where is everyone? What are they getting paid for?* As I headed into the patient's room, I muttered to myself, "Does anyone but me do any work around here?"

In offloading on Luke, I had lit a Drama Triangle wildfire, and thanks to Dean, another one was raging in the ER. This blaze was taking over multiple floors of the hospital, further fanning the flames of mistrust between all of us. (Keep in mind that this was all happening in the backdrop of us being in service to healing our patients.)

Ask yourself, who was the innocent one here?

Be careful. It's a trick question.

. . . .

Gossiping Versus Venting

There is an important distinction to make between gossiping and venting. Gossiping is a way to offload our emotions by talking about people behind their backs—without the intention of speaking with them directly. Venting to a trusted colleague or loved one—with the intention to gain clarity on your emotional response to a situation, so that you can then have a direct conversation with whomever was involved— is a common and potentially healthy way to process challenging interactions.

. . . .

The Drama Triangle is a destructive dynamic that undermines teams. It can result in an enormous, unquantified financial cost due to suboptimal performance and lack of employee engagement. As a consultant, when working with leaders and teams concerned about a dysfunctional culture and burnout, I ask questions to diagnose the role that the Drama Triangle might be playing in unraveling their mutual trust and relationships.

Before you can recognize yourself playing a starring role in this power dynamic, you must first be aware that it even exists and how it might be showing up in your life (see Figure 19.3 below for the Drama Triangle diagram).

FIGURE 19.3 **Drama Triangle**

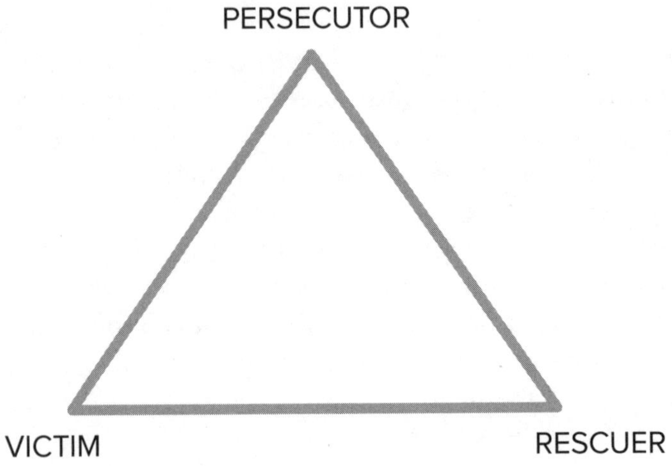

PERSECUTOR

VICTIM   RESCUER

As shown in Figure 19.3, there are three key players in the Drama Triangle: the Persecutor, the Victim, and the Rescuer.

1. The Persecutor

The Persecutor is the aggressor, the person who has done wrong or who appears to wield power unfairly over others. In a movie, this role is the evil adversary (e.g., Darth Vader in *Star Wars*). The wrongdoer might behave like a dictator, acting superior and attempting to control, shame, or blame others, with an attitude of "you're the problem, not me."

2. The Victim

The Victim is the person who feels wronged and acts helpless or feels powerless to change their circumstances (when in reality that may not be the case). In *Star Wars*, this role is the good-hearted protagonist who struggles to get a break (e.g., Princess Leia). In the comic strip *Peanuts*, it's Charlie Brown, whose poor-me attitude prevails in his language (verbal and nonverbal) and behavior, which might look like complaining or exasperation and feeling overwhelmed or helpless. In spite of their unhappiness, frustration, and resentment, they may be so accustomed to and comfortable in their role as a Victim that if a solution is offered, they might actually resist change.

3. The Rescuer

The Rescuer is the savior, the magical helper who shows up to save the day (e.g., Luke Skywalker / Han Solo) by comforting and consoling the Victim, affirming how egregiously the Victim has been wronged. They validate black-and-white thinking, such as the Persecutor is bad and the Victim is good. When the Rescuer is really on a roll, they might share additional stories of the Persecutor's outrageous behavior that they have heard or experienced—further solidifying the Victim's righteous stance in victimhood. The Rescuer often feels a sense of duty to fix the Victim's broken situation—as if, without the Rescuer, catastrophe looms for the Victim.

Whether consciously or subconsciously, each person participating in the Drama Triangle has a *self-interested payoff*. The Persecutor gets the temporary satisfaction of exerting a short-term act of power over the Victim—so as to put them in their place. The Victim gets to stay stuck and can make themselves *good* and the Persecutor *bad*. Victims don't actually want to confront the Persecutor, so they seek out an ally in the Rescuer to reinforce existing beliefs about how they are in a futile and unchangeable position. Don't you know? If two people believe something (instead of one), it must be true!

Initially, the Rescuer may seem well intentioned. On a conscious level, they feel as though they are in service to the Victim. They would tell you that their payoff is in being a good friend or being there for someone who needed them. What they are often unaware of is the underlying payoff: they get to feel needed and important. By jumping into the fray, the Rescuer sends a subtle message that they don't trust the Victim to handle the situation. Codependence is often a factor here, with the Rescuer ensuring that the Victim will stay dependent on them. On a deeper level, the Rescuer also experiences the side effect of being so consumed by helping another person that there's no time to focus on the *areas of their own life* that need attention. Subconsciously, the Rescuer may be avoiding their own problems and disguising that avoidance as concern for the Victim's needs.

There's an unexpected and indirect payoff between the Rescuer and Persecutor, too. While they may not even know each other, they have a relationship. Imagine if I hadn't said a word to Luke, but instead went home and complained about Dean to my friend Kathy. That would make Dean the Persecutor, me the Victim, and Kathy the Rescuer. Dean and Kathy don't have to know one another to still play out the dynamic of the Drama Triangle. What the Rescuer, Kathy, receives from Dean is a job that makes her feel important.

The end result harms everyone. The Persecutor has lost connection and respect, while their colleagues are gossiping about them. The Victim is wasting energy in an infinite loop of being stuck. And the Rescuer isn't growing and advancing in their own life but remains sidetracked in someone else's perpetual drama. (To see these dynamics in a diagram, see Figure 19.4.)

The question becomes how to recognize when the *price* of an experience exceeds the *payoff*—the moment when you're frustrated enough or have reached a tipping point to do whatever you need to transform a dysfunctional dynamic. Maybe you speak up, call a meeting, have honest conversations, or in more extreme situations, choose to leave a toxic environment.

FIGURE 19.4 **Drama Triangle Dynamics**

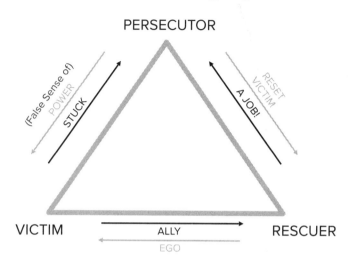

Luckily, in my case, soon after I learned about the Drama Triangle, the cost of participating in this unhealthy dynamic became clear. Even though in my story, I saw myself as the Victim, Dean as the Persecutor, and Luke as the Rescuer, I was humbled to realize that Dean's perspective was likely quite different. From his vantage point, he was the Victim, I was the Persecutor, and his ER colleagues were the Rescuers. How could we be mutually draining so much of our relational energy? I was stunned to learn that I might be contributing to discord with my colleagues and undermining trust between us when I blatantly spoke about Dean behind his back.

All of this could have been avoided if I had simply reached out to Dean immediately and worked to come to an understanding. Each of us involved in the Drama Triangle contributed to creating more conflict, rather than resolving it.

What about you? Do you recognize the Drama Triangle in your life—at work or at home? If so, which starring role do you most often play? And in what scenarios?

It's much easier for us to discharge our blame and disappointment onto other people than it is to experience and process it ourselves. It's intoxicating; many people feel drama and excitement in their lives by making other people bad or wrong. It takes a lot more courage and self-awareness to turn to someone and have an honest, curious, and compassionate conversation.

This is where reexamining your thought patterns (personalization, projection, generalization, and knowing the difference between fact versus fiction) can help you consider other possibilities.

STEPPING OUT OF THE DRAMA TRIANGLE

Here's the good news: the Drama Triangle is a house of cards. All it takes to collapse the entire dynamic is one person reaching a choice point and stepping out of this unhealthy pattern. Each role has a unique way to step out of the triangle.

The Persecutor

The Persecutor could acknowledge what happened, be compassionate, get curious about the other person's perspective, and be open to feedback to rebuild trust within the relationship.

In my example, Dean could have taken a deep breath (and vented to a colleague to gain clarity, if necessary) and then called me back to hash things out directly. He might have said, "Hey, Neha, I didn't like how our conversation ended. It's crazy busy down here, my fuse is short, and that's the reason I was curt with you. I know you guys are busy, too. It's important to me that we have a good working relationship. Do you have a few minutes to talk this out?"

Step 1: Shift from reacting to responding by hitting your pause button (taking a deep breath, going for a walk, or taking a break).

Step 2: Ask yourself, *What was my part in this? How did I contribute to the outcome?*

Step 3: Imagine that you were on the receiving end of your behavior. What could have made the other person be more receptive to your point of view?

Step 4: Reach out to ask for a good time to have a direct conversation.

Step 5: Be honest, compassionate, and take ownership for your part. Get curious, not furious about the other person's experience and how you might collaborate better next time (because there will likely be a next time!)

The Victim

The Victim could take ownership by speaking directly to the Persecutor (asking for leadership or additional support, if necessary).

With Dean, I felt unheard and dismissed, which triggered me. And if I had recognized that as it was happening, I could have been more resourceful (hitting the pause button, going outside for some fresh air, and slowing down my breathing). Instead of making a beeline to Luke, I could have asked myself, *What does this remind me of?* Dean's act of abruptly ending our conversation by hanging up the phone was a great parallel to that old and repeated experience of feeling unheard. The next step might have been picking up the phone and saying, "Hey, can we try our last conversation again? From past experience, I know tests and consults ordered in the emergency department get first priority, so I always try to make sure that they are ordered right away. Can you help me understand where you are coming from?"

Step 1: Pause to get curious about what old relationship pattern might be in play. Ask yourself: *What's familiar about this experience? When have I felt this way before? Do I try to reinforce being "right" by instinctually seeking out allies?*

Step 2: Resist the urge to speak to other people about the situation. Instead, turn to the person involved and ask for a good time to talk. If you do need to vent or get clarity, choose to speak with someone you trust who can listen without judging the offending party.

Step 3: Share what you heard, observed, or experienced, and ask for feedback on how the other person might have perceived what happened. Then ask for what you would like to be different moving forward. Last, get a clear agreement on what could work for both parties.

The Rescuer

The Rescuer could empathize with the Victim role and encourage them to have a conversation directly with the Persecutor.

Luke could have said, "Neha, I hear how upset you are by the lack of clarity on who's responsible for what part of the patient's workup. I know how much you value fairness and equity. Have you considered having a conversation with Dean to work this out?"

Step 1: To honor your relationship and connect with the other person, listen closely for the emotions and values behind the Victim's words.

Step 2: Gently offer an option for a new and practical path to the Victim by encouraging them to bring their concern directly to the Persecutor.

Step 3: If the Victim resists this suggestion, beware: they may not be ready to step out of the Drama Triangle. It's OK. You still have the choice to change your part in the dynamic. Don't be surprised if the person in the Victim role is unhappy with you or immediately seeks out another Rescuer. This means that you may feel the discomfort of *not being liked* or *not being wanted* while this transition is happening. The good news is that by choosing not to play the Rescuer role, *you like yourself more* and you've plugged a major drain in your social energy.

If you have often found yourself in the role of the Rescuer, be patient. You may experience some uncomfortable moments as the dynamics between you and the person in the Victim role begin to shift. You've taught other people that this is how you'll show up for them, so it's normal for them to feel annoyed or challenged when adjusting to your new way of being. Stay focused on being empathetic to what they are struggling with, how you can create healthier bonds, and elevate your relational energy by redirecting them to how they can solve the issue.

. . .

Next time you're faced with juicy gossip or a super-sized gripe, pay attention and identify the role you're playing. If you're in a power dynamic that's draining your energy, know that awareness is the first step to transformation.

The benefit to understanding how to step out of the Drama Triangle is that you have an opportunity to change your social dynamics for the better. If you're the Persecutor, taking personal responsibility and getting curious will result in greater rapport, mutual respect, and synergistic teamwork with those you love and lead. If you're a Victim, stepping out of this dynamic can break a debilitating cycle that may have been going on for years. This becomes an opportunity to develop confidence in your ability to create new outcomes. And if you're a Rescuer, you have the chance to dedicate your precious energy to bettering your *own* life. The more you take responsibility for stepping out of the Drama Triangle and other dysfunctional dynamics, the less stress, more trust and synergistic collaboration you will experience.

CONFLICT RESOLUTION

Sometimes conflict is all in our heads because we've interpreted data from another person without checking the truth; we've told a story and assigned meaning that wasn't actually there. Sometimes conflict occurs because our emotions have taken control. Many conflicts are just misunderstandings, or they happen simply because we haven't paused long enough to listen to ourselves or others. No matter the reason, if you avoid conflict or leave it unaddressed, it adds to your stress and accumulates in your body—which is exactly what you want to avoid.

As a general rule, when you are speaking up to identify a problem, it's best to come prepared with potential solutions. The uncertainty resides in not knowing how your thoughts will be received, what type of pushback will arise, and what potential conflict could result. To a certain extent, these factors are out of your control, but if you think carefully before the conversation, you may be able to prepare some potential responses.

Regardless of the outcome, what matters is that you have voiced your perspective to create positive change to shape the work or home environment of which you are an integral part. Often, this will encourage others to share (privately or publicly) that they agree with what you have said or to voice their perspective and emotions on a different topic. Choosing the dip of discomfort is an act of bravery. And you will learn and grow from the experience. At the very least, you will know that your ideas have been heard. In addition, if you stay open to hearing other people's reactions, you may create new connections—while gaining a broader perspective and a deeper understanding of the situation—and end up with an even more innovative solution for everyone. (For more practical guidance on conflict resolution and communicating clearly, listen to my audiobook, *TalkRx: Five Steps to Honest Conversations that Create Connection, Health and Happiness*, and visit my website *intuitiveintelligenceinc.com*.)

For now, remember: you always have a choice in how you respond to others. Your relational energy is *yours* to manage, not anyone else's—and you have the power to choose how you expend it.

SOCIAL ENERGY REASSESSMENT

Think about who you surround yourself with and use your Body Map to notice your *internal* experience when you engage *externally* with others.

1. Who are the top five people or groups you spend the most time with (in person or remotely)? List them below. Next to each name, circle the (+) = net gain of energy or the (−) = net drain of energy.

    1. _____ + / −

    2. _____ + / −

    3. _____ + / −

    4. _____ + / −

    5. _____ + / −

    Notice your internal experience as you see a summary of your social interactions. Does that overall picture inspire you? Or leave you feeling obligated?

2. Overall, on a relational level, are you experiencing a net gain (+) or net drain (-) of energy?

    ☐ net gain (+)   ☐ net drain (−)

    Once again, the way you determine this is by looking at your answers above and also by checking in with your body map. If you feel a constriction or tightness in your body as you answer these questions, you likely have a net drain in this area. If you have a feeling of openness, ease, or lightness in your body as you answer these questions, this energy level is likely a net gain for you.

Your coworkers, your significant other, your family, and your community can be an enormous source of energy gain or drain. Every day, you come to many choice points, where you decide whether you'll take the short-term high (to avoid what's happening in the moment) or take the short-term dip of discomfort (to create the life you want). Now you have some reliable frameworks to guide you toward becoming *me-powered*.

By cultivating solid social support, you'll have the synergistic strength that our hunter-gatherer ancestors knew was vital to survival. As you align yourself and your highest values with the *right others*—at home, at work, and socially—your community will become an undeniable superpower. A wonderful side effect of supportive relationships is that they improve your health, happiness, and performance, catapulting you on the journey from burned out to fully charged.

Congratulations! Now you know how to identify and embark on transforming your physical, mental, emotional, and social energy drains into energy gains. It's time to dive into the final and most important section of the book—spiritual energy.

PART V

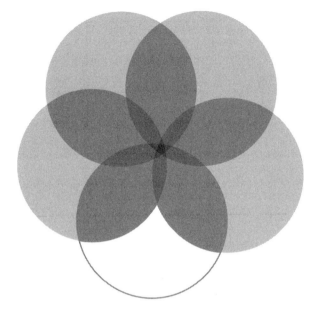

SPIRITUAL ENERGY

CHAPTER 20

WHAT YOU
VALUE MOST

You might be wondering, what does spiritual energy have to do with a book on burnout? Might its presence in a business book be by mistake? Perhaps you have preconceived ideas about what the word *spiritual* even means. Maybe you associate it with religion, the unknown, or something greater than yourself like galaxies, the Milky Way, or the universe. Maybe you think of spirituality as something used in times of uncertainty or crisis to find hope. Or you may have a different interpretation altogether of what spiritual energy is. In fact, you may not even associate yourself with being spiritual. These are all valid perspectives. In whatever way you relate to the word *spiritual*, know that this section will serve as an important catalyst and practical toolkit on your path to healing burnout.

After decades of healing patients, partnering with business leaders, and transforming toxic cultures into healing organizations, I have discovered that spiritual energy drives all other energy levels. Let me explain.

My definition of spiritual energy is my sense of and connection to deeper meaning and purpose in my life—both personally and professionally. Strengthening my spiritual energy comes down to the combination of identifying my highest values, believing in myself to take risks, and making complex decisions based on what matters most. My hope is that after reading this section, you'll have a broader definition of what spiritual energy means and a new relationship to it.

Although many people mistake burnout to be a sign of weakness or failure, it's not. Burnout is a *wake-up call*. It's often rooted in a breach that began on a spiritual level. Somewhere along the way—often for our own survival—we made a series of (what seemed like) small choices that gradually led us to deviate from what we value most. Perhaps we:

- Said yes when we really meant no

- Chose work over family—again

- Agreed to another late night rather than a good night's sleep

- Chose to stay silent rather than speak up

- Chose to comply, rather than stand up for our values

- Agreed to an ever-increasing workload to maintain our financial stability

- Began medicating our own symptoms of anxiety, insomnia, and depression rather than getting to the root causes of our stress

It is an unfortunate truth that the world in which we function doesn't always align with our idealistic goals and aspirations. Societal beliefs, including *do more with less, faster is better*, and *success requires struggle*, surround us. Operating according to them can lead us to compromise our own values as we try to keep up with the accelerating pace of life and organizational expectations.

As a clinical physician in the hospital, I experienced this type of disconnect, sometimes referred to as moral injury, even after achieving what I thought was my lifetime goal of becoming a physician partner. The rules and regulations dictating how I could treat my patients, what tests I could order, and what remedies I could prescribe (defined by what insurance would pay for), and how I sometimes had to cut corners (to align with hospital metrics) left me brokenhearted.

You may have experienced something similar when you became aware that a colleague was being underpaid because of their gender, disability, or age. Or you may have stood by as a skilled team member was harassed with no consequence. You may have found yourself silently observing as a client or vendor was taken advantage of or undercut to maximize profit. Or learned that another fabulous leader wasn't recognized for their achievements.

You may have ignored uncomfortable physical nudges, moments of mental discord, emotional unrest, and even relationship dysfunction in an effort to keep your head down and job safe. These seemingly small choices along the way may have led you astray from what mattered most—your highest values. You may have drifted so far that work has become more pain than pleasure. More endurance than joy. Surviving, not thriving. When your choices result in paying a higher price than what you're receiving in exchange, you're withdrawing from your spiritual bank account without replenishing it. This lack of alignment disconnects you from your true purpose and meaning, creating an enormous spiritual energy drain.

If this sounds like you, be kind to yourself. This happened because *you did the best you knew how with what you knew at the time*. Now that you know better, so you can do better. Even if you feel far away from what matters most, we'll bring all the data you've gathered so far together with your intuition to help you regain a sense of balance and find the best path forward. Your ability to gather and integrate data from both your inner and outer worlds is what allows you to make decisions in alignment with your own highest good—and for the greater good.

DISCOVERING YOUR VALUES

To get to the heart of what matters most, start paying attention to tasks, situations, and relationships that excite or energize you, and then get curious about *why* that might be. Whether you're an entrepreneur who has your own business or an employee of an organization, it's important to align your personal values, gifts, and skill sets with those around you.

One of the most inspiring examples of the ripple effect that can occur when your business effort, energy, and goals are aligned with your spiritual energy comes from a story about Jaipur Rugs that I read in the book titled *The Healing Organization* by Raj Sisodia and Michael Gelb. Producing artisanal handwoven rugs is labor-intensive and has traditionally been done by illiterate women who come from the weaver community, which many people of the Indian upper caste think of and treat as *untouchable*. Young girls in such families are barely educated, if at all. They start working at an early age, and then their parents marry them off in their early teens to another weaver family. These women are expected to bear children, cook, clean, and earn an income by making carpets. It is even customary for them to eat last, after their fathers, brothers, and husbands. In-laws, husbands, and the contractors who bring the carpet-weaving work to them routinely abuse these women.

N. K. Chaudhary founded Jaipur Rugs to change that industry. "These women are the innocents. They have never asked for anything from any-body. All they have done is serve others. I want to serve them," he said. So he created a company that makes handwoven rugs, employing and empow-ering these women directly, without middlemen. In addition to being paid well and treated with respect, these women are offered the opportunity to learn to read, write, and acquire basic accounting skills. Many of them have become successful entrepreneurs within the Jaipur Rugs system by expand-ing their own operations locally. In only one generation, these women gained the resources to send their children to college, an outcome that would have been unimaginable for an illiterate and *untouchable* woman.

When one of these women, Shanti, was asked, "How do you feel about the impact Mr. Chaudhary has had on your life?"

Welling up with tears, she replied, "To me, he is more than my mother and father. To me, he is God. He has given me life. Before him, I didn't have a life."

Ironically, as a young man, N. K. Chaudhary was told that he was too simple and innocent to survive in the world of business. Rather than feeling discouraged, he decided to use his highest values of education, hope, dig-nity, family, and innovation to serve and uplift innocent people through the power of a caring business. He has single-handedly transformed the trajec-tory of over 40,000 women, their children, and their communities. The power of using your highest values benefits not only your spiritual energy, it also has the potential to create profound healing in the world.

N. K. Chaudhary was so clear about what he valued, and he used these values to make decisions in his business, which meant he discarded the belief *profit over people*. Instead he believes in profit *and* people. Just imag-ine the world we could live in if we all knew what mattered most to us and took inspired action in alignment with those values!

Your Highest Values Exercise

Using the Jaipur Rug story as a guide, think about the way you run your business, your team, your daily work, your family, and for that matter, your free time and vacations. Jot down a few lines explaining how you operate and what values drive your decisions. Then ask yourself these clarifying questions to decipher your underlying motivations on three levels:

1. How do these actions benefit you (*me*)?

2. How do these actions serve others (*we*)?

3. What is their ripple effect outward (*world*)?

Scan the following list of common values in Figure 20.1, and circle each one that resonates with you.

FIGURE 20.1
Identifying Your Values

Abundance	Challenge	Decisiveness	Family
Acceptance	Change	Dedication	Friendship
Accountability	Collaboration	Democracy	Forgiveness
Achievement	Command	Determination	Hard work
Advancement	Commitment	Diplomacy	Harmony
Adventure	Communication	Discipline	Health
Aesthetics	Community	Diversity	Heart
Agility	Competence	Effectiveness	Helping others
Analysis	Competition	Efficiency	Honesty
Appearance	Connection	Effort	Honor
Appreciation	Continuous	Empowerment	Independence
Authenticity	improvement	Ethics	Individualism
Authority	Contribution	Excellence	Influence
Autonomy	Control	Experience	Innovation
Awareness	Cooperation	Expertise	Integration
Beauty	Cost	Fairness	Integrity
Belonging	consciousness	Faith	Intelligence
Caring	Courage	Fame	Intellectual
	Creativity		exchange

(continued)

(continued)

Intimacy	Passion	Satisfaction	Tradition
Involvement	Participation	Security	Trust
Joy	Peace	Self-acceptance	Truth
Justice	Performance	Self-control	Urgency
Knowledge	Perseverance	Self-respect	Vision
Leadership	Personal	Sensitivity	Wealth
Learning	development	Serenity	Wisdom
Logic	Physical	Service	
Love	challenge	Sophistication	**Additional**
Loyalty	Play	Spirit	**Values**
Meaningful work	Reputation	Spirituality	_____
Nature	Respect	Stability	
Objectivity	Responsibility	Status	_____
Openness	Responsiveness	Strategy	_____
Order	Risk-taking	Support	_____
Ownership	Safety	Tolerance	_____

Some values are easy to identify, such as family, health, or community. Others are deeper moral and spiritual values that you may have never articulated. Stay open and curious to see what you discover.

Another way to discern your values is to think of someone you appreciate, and describe three (or more) qualities you admire about them. I'll go first to show you what I mean.

In reference to N. K. Chaudhary, I admire that he didn't listen to other people's judgments, that he went against societal norms to work toward equality for women, and that he delivered on his belief that everyone matters and everybody can win. He exemplifies courage and what it means to embody a purpose-driven business that changes the world.

It's your turn. Who do you admire? And what values do you admire about them? Once you've taken inventory of which qualities you most admire about that person, guess what—you've just identified some of your own highest values. It's often easier to see these qualities in someone else, but if you can recognize them in others that means they're also present in *you*.

Are You in Alignment with Your Work?

Once you've identified your highest values, compare them with the values and purpose of your place of work. If you don't know your company's values, please request a copy of them. Then consider the following questions:

- Do you know *what* the higher purpose of your organization is? Do you believe in it?

- Do the actions of your organization *align* with their own stated higher purpose? If not, are they working toward that alignment?

- Do you know how *your individual contribution* impacts the higher purpose of your organization?

- Does what you do every day make a positive difference? If so, for whom?

- When someone asks you what you do for a living, does your answer inspire you?

- On a scale of 1 to 10, where 1 = no alignment and 10 = full alignment, please rate how well your core values align with those of the organization in which you work. If they are not aligned, this can be a key source of spiritual energy drain.

As you uncover where your values align with your workplace and where they may diverge, you will have more data to incorporate into the decisions you make about your work and self-care. This could mean that it's time to have a challenging conversation or potentially make a hard decision, or it may simply mean you get to be part of creating a better workplace, not just for yourself, but for those you work with and serve.

SPIRITUAL ENERGY ASSESSMENT

- What are the three most meaningful phrases someone could say about you?

  1. _____

  2. _____

  3. _____

- In a few sentences, describe a time you felt deeply valued and appreciated (at work or at home).

  _____

  _____

- What do you value most? Circle all that apply.

Love	Beauty
Trust	Play
Honesty	Efficiency
Service	Productivity

  Other (please specify) _____

- In what areas are you willing to take risks? Please circle all that apply.

  Physical (with my body: adventure sports, etc.)

  Mental (exploring new ideas / perspectives)

  Emotional (navigating emotions in myself and others)

  Social (meeting new people, forging new relationships)

  Spiritual (exploring the unknown, experiencing awe, seeking mystery)

  Other (please specify) _____

- In what areas are you less willing to take risks? Please circle all that apply.

    Physical (with my body: sports, etc.)

    Mental (prefer one right answer, black-and-white thinking, concrete data, etc.)

    Emotional (avoid emotions in myself and others)

    Social (interact only with familiar people in my community)

    Spiritual (hold fixed beliefs or have little interest in discussing the unknown)

    Other (please specify) _____

- What do you have faith in? Circle all that apply.

    Humanity   Community

    Science   Next generation

    Religion   Mother Nature

    Spirituality   Myself

    Family

    Other (please specify) _____

CHAPTER 21

STRENGTHENING SELF-TRUST

With your values clear, you can tap into your intuitive knowledge, which has been there all along, but too often ignored. The most obvious ways we gather information is externally—through books, articles, studies, what others teach us, numerical evidence, or data, to name a few. Internal data is often more elusive. I describe internal data as *your lived experience + your inner wisdom (including your intuition and highest values)*.

N. K. Chaudhary received external data from others that he was "too innocent to do well in business." He heard that input, saw what others were doing, and then used his own internal data (his lived experience + intuition + highest values) to align his choices to create a different external outcome. His experience told him that women were capable not only of doing the work but would also use the money they earned to invest in their families and their communities.

As you learn to integrate different forms of data (both external and internal) to make effective decisions, you'll build self-trust. You might even surprise yourself with what risks you're willing to take. The more self-trust you develop, the greater your spiritual energy.

Self-trust is a continuous process of self-reflection, self-analysis, and self-correction. It's about taking in, trusting, and integrating multiple levels of data to make good decisions in a rapidly changing, complex world. Trusting yourself includes a deep certainty that when circumstances, events, or opportunities change, you can rely on yourself—and collaborate with others—to figure out what to do next. It's a surefire way to becoming even more *me-powered*.

People often ask me, "How do I build more self-trust?" A simple and profound way to build self-trust is to make an agreement with yourself, however small, and keep it. Each time you show up for yourself, you will believe you're worth it and trust yourself even more. Bonus: by doing this you'll model how others should treat you as well. Expanding your awareness and learning from your mistakes will make you more confident to take risks and help you draw spiritual boundaries.

In Chapter 18, we discussed the importance of learning how to delineate healthy physical, mental, emotional, and social boundaries. It's also important to have spiritual boundaries. If you aren't aware of setting limits in this area, in the quest to please others and meet societal expectations you may compromise your own true fulfillment.

Spiritual boundary dilemmas include:

- Prioritizing a set time every week to honor your own self-care routine, spiritual practices, or religious rituals

- If taking soulless work is necessary to meet financial obligations, defining a clear set of criteria to weigh the physical, mental, emotional, social, and spiritual costs of saying yes

- Honoring another person's beliefs and values—even when they don't align with your own

Self-trust also means becoming aware of your blind spots, areas you have the hardest time seeing or listening to. Depending on your work style, you might be missing key information to build self-trust. Let's explore some common blind spots to give you an advantage right now. Pay attention to any examples that resonate or that bring up resistance. Both are important clues to what matters most to you.

Doers, Don't Mistake Busyness for Progress

If you're a Doer, self-reflection and self-analysis may seem like a waste of time. What you may not realize is that by focusing solely on speed, you're missing clues that are hindering your productivity, which may result in needing to repeat tasks. Sometimes the key to speeding up is slowing down (temporarily) to gather different types of vital data, enlist others in collaboration, and avoid unnecessary mistakes. Yes, Doers, it's entirely possible to honor your powerful drive for execution while also being flexible to accommodate real-time changes so you can accomplish even more.

Thinkers, Remember That Emotions Are Important Data, Too

As a Thinker, if you don't have proof (external data), you may dismiss your own or other's emotions (internal data). You may be missing out on the power of emotions to assist you in solving complex problems. Emotions are crucial data that can reveal hidden motivations and underlying intentions—factors that may be invisible but critical to consider as you analyze your latest dilemma. Taking into account both *external* data (numbers, knowledge, details) and *internal* data (body's physical signals, thoughts, emotions, desires, gut-knowing, memory, and past experiences) enables you to see a more comprehensive picture. This is about expanding the definition of data. Yes, Thinkers, by gathering more types of data, you will make better decisions and experience more joy—as you solve the most challenging problems.

Seers, It's Time to Trust Yourself to Commit

If you're a Seer, you'd rather be brainstorming and open to all possibilities. You're likely less comfortable deciding on which path to execute. Mastering this will empower you to transform your great ideas into reality. Yes, Seers, it is entirely possible to uphold the integrity and genius of your big ideas, while committing to making them real. And while you're often the life of the party, committing to actually *attending the party* will ground you and strengthen your relationships with others. You won't be missing something better, because your presence alone will make the party a huge hit!

Feelers, Including Yourself in the Equation Is Paramount

If you're a Feeler, you've learned to ignore the *internal* data coming from within you (physical sensations and emotions) and overridden those signals as unimportant in comparison to the external data you are picking up (the requests and needs of others). Nothing could be further from the truth. You may have struggled with self-trust, doubting your perceptions or feeling drained by your empathic nature. By tuning in to your body's wisdom and intuition to help you draw healthy boundaries, you will likely strengthen your connection to others while also getting your own needs met. The catch is that you must be careful to counterbalance your superpower of caring for others with an equal level of self-care and self-focus. Yes, Feelers, it is entirely possible to feel deeply connected by including N=1 (yourself) in the equation!

BUILDING SELF-CONFIDENCE

Just as your work style can expand, influence, or limit how much you trust yourself, so can your past experiences. It's very possible to have a lot of self-trust in certain areas of your life and less in others. How do you know? When you're in an arena where you have more self-trust, you'll naturally take risks, innovate, and adapt to change easily. Conversely, in the arenas where you have less self-trust, you may notice resistance to change and a desire to stay in your comfort zone. For example, if you've had an injury, you may be less self-confident in the physical arena. If you've experienced being mocked or shamed publicly and told you were stupid for sharing an idea, you may be more hesitant in the mental arena. A betrayal by a trusted friend or partner may leave you emotionally guarded, so you take few to no risks in love. Instead, you tell yourself you're satisfied with the unconditional love that comes from your pet. Often, immigrants or members of marginalized communities have had experiences of being treated poorly that would result in being guarded in social settings. Any of these experiences, including trauma, grief, or loss can either strengthen or weaken your self-trust—depending on whether or not you choose to reveal, feel, and heal the experience—and ultimately the meaning you make of that experience.

As a Seer and Feeler, I didn't have self-trust in the physical realm for years. In other words, you wouldn't have found me gardening or cooking dinner for myself or others. My eating habits were subpar. In fact, I joked that I was allergic to the kitchen. Takeout was a way of life. I often skipped meals, and grabbed a candy bar or chai to get my caffeine-sugar fix, rather than planning the week's healthy meals. Here's what's important to remember: just like building trust in your relationships is foundational, so too is self-trust critical to building your own confidence and spiritual energy.

In my case, it took getting sick to invest in and develop self-trust in the physical arena. In November 2016, while traveling abroad, I unknowingly ingested a parasite, likely from eating fruit or uncooked vegetables that had been washed in unfiltered water. Four months later, I noticed that the skin around my navel was so dry it was sloughing off. I put some cream on it and tried to minimize my concern. Then over the next two years, hypopigmented lesions spread all over my body—under my arms, on my chest, my abdomen, and my legs, as well as my face, moving down both sides of my nose. I'd been offered topical steroid creams, but they worked only temporarily. When I forgot to take them, the lesions returned.

Once again. I went down the functional medicine pathway we discussed in Chapter 6. My doctors biopsied my skin and found that the lesions were Lichen planus, a benign side effect resulting from an autoimmune breakdown of my gut. My stool sample revealed a parasite. Unfortunately, even after treating it with medication, the damage to my intestinal tract was extensive. The lining of my gut had been stripped, and my body had developed severe food sensitivities. I was now sensitive to hundreds of items, including gluten, dairy, sugar, coffee, corn, blueberries, broccoli—basically, everything I had been eating during those two years leading up to my diagnosis—including olive oil.

As anyone who has had to deal with life on a special diet knows, takeout wasn't really an option anymore. And here's the kicker: I spent my whole life taking care of other people's physical health but had spent little time investing in my own. I found myself feeling overwhelmed. I had already begun eating whole foods, but was resistant to the idea of focusing this much on what I was going to eat. This would be an entirely new way of relating to, prioritizing, and nourishing myself three times a day. The universe was sending me a strong signal—that it was time to value my own health as much as I valued helping others heal.

The Feeler in me knew that in the past, during times of pain and despair, I got through it by connecting with others who excelled in whatever arena I was struggling with. I had to become resourceful and develop these skills quickly. And so, at 48 years old, I asked for help—a lot of help—from everywhere I could get it.

As soon as I made the decision that my own health was my top priority, I remembered all the times my own mother had tried to interest me in her first love—gardening and cooking. Yet I wanted nothing to do with it. I was too busy with school, my friends, or athletics to be interested in the time and effort it took to shop, cook, and clean. I remembered how my aunt Beena, whom I affectionately refer to as *Beena Mausi*, often had me over to her place in Boston and nourished me with such delicious homemade food.

I called them both and told them I was finally ready to learn. The next day, Beena Mausi came over and began teaching me how to make simple Indian dishes—which thankfully included many unique foods that were foreign to my system, so I was able to eat them.

Four years later, the lesions healed and my energy returned, but something much more important happened: on a physical level, I began to trust myself more. When my old coping mechanisms no longer worked and I was faced with an enormous challenge, one that required a significant change in lifestyle, I showed up for myself. What if something like this happened in the future? What would I do then? It became clear that if I didn't know how to do something, I was resourceful enough to find people who did. And most important, I would *ask for help*.

The craziest part is that now that my taste buds have adapted, I crave the healing, wholesome foods that support my physical health. I'm officially *me-powered* in the kitchen, and I take joy in what once seemed like an impossible, overwhelming struggle to cook and plan meals three times a day. Sometimes, trusting yourself inspires you to take risks. Other times, life events force you to take a risk that you might not know how to handle—and greater self-trust emerges from there when you do!

One way I have built self-trust is noticing the moment I feel tired or under the weather. As soon as this happens, I don't allow my mind to blame or push my body any further. When I experience a sharp pain shooting into my neck from my right shoulder or my head feels a slight heaviness, rather than beating myself up for not being able to push through it, I take a nap or prioritize getting to bed early. Each time I do this, I wake up refreshed and feeling stronger. And I trust myself to take care of me when I say yes to opportunities. I also know that if it's too much, I'll listen to my body and adjust accordingly.

I've learned to trust myself, but there have also been periods when I lost faith in myself completely and didn't know what to do. One of those times was when I was deciding whether to stay in my physician partnership that provided job security for life, but it was simultaneously depleting my energy on every level. I remember the day I knew I couldn't do it anymore. But as the daughter of immigrants, I was so terrified of letting go of my financial security that I completely froze. It seemed like the idea of becoming an entrepreneur and paving a new path in medicine was such an enormous leap that I was destined to fail.

You see, no matter how much you work on yourself and build your self-trust, if you're considering taking a risk, you are likely to encounter your greatest fears that make you forget who you are and all that you are capable of. In those moments, it is critical to *surround yourself with others who believe in you*. That day, when I knew it was time to leave my medical partnership, but I didn't know where I would find the courage, I turned to my trusted colleagues Mark Hyman and Jim Gordon. I asked each of them if they thought it was realistic for me to build a new type of practice focused on healing the root causes of patients' stress by teaching them how to lean into healthy conflict, long before they ended up in an emergency department. When they both said, "Of course you can, Neha," I was beside myself. So I asked each of them, if I started a company called Intuitive Intelligence, would they be board members? They both, independently, without hesitation, said "Yes, absolutely." And just like that, I walked downstairs and submitted my resignation. Those two conversations were exactly what I needed to muster the bravery to take bold action in alignment with my spiritual energy and highest values.

Fast-forward to our first board meeting. I was trembling when I addressed them, "You both speak so eloquently, have written profound books that have paved a new path forward in medicine, and are such impressive trailblazers. How do I become like you?"

Slightly taken aback by my question, they were silent. They looked at me, then at each other, and back at me again. "We think you already are, Neha. That's why we're here. It looks like we're just waiting for *you* to believe it."

As tears streamed down my face, I felt more seen and valued than I ever had before. And I learned one of the most profound lessons on self-trust that day. There will be days when you can't locate your own self-trust—and that's OK. It's a sign that you're taking big leaps in the world. That's when it's important to look into the eyes of those who believe in you and allow them to reflect back their trust in you. That's an important way to remember that you are strong, resourceful, and capable of doing whatever you set your heart and mind to.

Your ability to trust yourself depends on how seriously you take N=1, meaning how much you weigh the importance of your own *lived experience and inner wisdom*. In a world that places the utmost importance on research data that has thousands of participants such as N=10,000 subjects, how much weight have you placed on N=1?

Honoring N=1 data prompts us to ask questions and believe in the possibility of creating solutions that serve others as well as ourselves. This is the root of win-win innovation—exactly what we need to adapt to the pace and scope of our ever-changing world.

Grounding yourself in your highest values empowers you to make decisions that align with who you truly are. This is how you build your connection to your true meaning and purpose (your spiritual energy). And remember, when all else fails, turn to those who have cheered you on and know what you are capable of. They will help you take the next brave step into the unknown.

You might be wondering how to align these principles with your current job. Let's begin by discovering what type of relationship you have with your current role and what type of meaning (if any) you derive from it.

SACRED EXCHANGE

I've learned a lot about whether someone is aligned on a spiritual level by asking, "Can you please describe your role and what you do?"

I posed this question to various members of a sales team. One person began with, "I'm a sales guy. I'm a cog in a wheel. Just a number around here—like the endless stream of clients coming through. If I don't make my numbers, I'm screwed. That's how I get paid. I clock in and clock out, counting the minutes until the day ends. I live for Friday happy hours."

Another responded, "I'm a customer care representative, listening deeply so I can serve the needs of my clients. If I keep my customer satisfaction scores high, I have job security. This stability has allowed me to raise my two children, take my wife on yearly vacations, build a comfortable home, and save for retirement. This job is the reason I've been able to give my family a good life."

I remember one in particular that surprised me when she replied, "My role? I'm a problem-solving specialist. I have the honor of working closely with clients as they grow their businesses. They trust me enough to share their greatest challenges, and together, we find innovative solutions that make the world better."

Her job was much more than a job. It was *a calling*.

Finding personal meaning in your work (or any role) can add dimensions of satisfaction, fulfillment, and even joy to the most routine tasks. Though we rarely speak about our work as spiritual, what we do on a daily basis *can be sacred*. Just reflect on how N. K. Chaudhary's work at Jaipur Rugs is about so much more than selling carpets.

Every interaction has the potential to reconnect you to why you said yes to this job or this company in the first place. What if a complaint was actually an opportunity for growth? What if feedback illuminating your blind spot was, in fact, a gift that made you more effective? What if disagreements or miscommunications between you and your colleagues were a chance to strengthen those relationships and develop a deeper understanding of one another? What if burning out and needing to seek support was the bridge to a higher, more aligned version of your life? Of course, there are days when you'll just go through the motions. But whenever you feel disconnected, exhausted, or overworked, remember: reconnecting to the meaning in your work is only one authentic sacred exchange away.

Rachel Remen, MD, a wise friend and mentor in healing, has said, "Perhaps the answer lies in learning to cultivate the meaning of our work in the same way that we have traditionally pursued its knowledge base. In times of difficulty, meaning strengthens us, not by *changing our lives* but by transforming *the experience of our lives*."

Sacred exchanges are alchemy—an experience where two or more beings come together and share themselves with one another, and once they part, they have each transformed and are no longer what they used to be. Sacred exchanges take place on more than a physical or intellectual level. They are multidimensional exchanges that move us because they bring meaning to whatever task we perform—such as being present to celebrate a milestone for a team member, listening deeply to a complaint from a customer, or offering a hand to a colleague who has a lot on their plate.

While it's much easier to look outward and comment on what others are doing or not doing, remember that the biggest impact comes from you aligning within. The most important sacred exchange is the one between *you and you*—the internal connection to your higher purpose. Without it, you cannot meaningfully collaborate with your colleagues, your partner, or your friends. With it, you build your spiritual energy, the foundation that can carry you through challenging dilemmas, devastating crises, long days, and hard nights. Your spiritual energy rests on what you're most passionate about and what truly engages you. Taking inventory of your spiritual energy can seem amorphous, but it's as simple as recalling experiences that inspire you, people who have greatly influenced you, and times when you felt fulfilled and most like yourself.

The Sacred Exchange Exercise

Sacred moments—what matters to you—reveal precious clues about your highest values. And your values will guide you toward your higher purpose (spiritual energy). These two questions are slight variations of what you did at the end of Chapter 20 in your spiritual assessment. So you can go back and read what you wrote there to get started.

1. Can you describe a time when you felt deeply appreciated or valued (truly seen and heard)? Describe what made it so unique or special.

2. When you're not in the room, what are the most meaningful words that could be spoken about you? Your answer to this question may provide guidance about where to prioritize your energy, efforts, and time.

The simple act of reflecting on each of these areas is the start of the most meaningful sacred exchange—the one with yourself. Cultivating a powerful and aligned relationship with yourself is critical for healing burnout and reconnecting to your passions and purpose.

When you engage in a sacred exchange with yourself, you strengthen your foundation of self-trust. And when you serve others from this grounded awareness—as a leader, colleague, neighbor, advocate, partner, parent, sibling, or child—you make integrated decisions that serve yourself *while* you consider others. Together, let's explore each of these topics and discover practical decision-making tools that will help you on the path to becoming *me-powered*.

CHAPTER 22

MAKING BETTER DECISIONS

Most people are on autopilot, completely unaware that external influences (rather than their inner guidance) are driving the important choices in their lives. There's a big difference between leading your life from the *inside-out* versus from the *outside-in*. When you're leading from the outside-in, your external environment dictates your choices. You may struggle to be consistent in your decision-making. This often stems from not reflecting inward. You may feel lost if you:

- **Have *not* gotten clear** on the invisible components of your inner GPS (body's signals, thoughts, emotions, desires, what you value in a particular situation) or

- **Have gotten clear, but are overriding** what you want in order to adapt to your external environment

Have you ever thought about *whose values* are guiding your choices? A desire for harmony, wanting to belong, or feeling pressure to conform to the dominant opinion in the room can leave you feeling like driftwood in the ocean (outside-in decision making). On the other hand, when leading from the inside-out, you feel more like a sailboat with a rudder. You have internal structure and guidance because you're making decisions based on what you value. You're able to pick up on and interpret your body's wisdom, understand how you form your thoughts, and identify how you feel. You know who you are, what you value, and what you want. This is what you've been learning to do—and it requires tuning in to your body's wisdom and intuition, so you gain the self-trust you need to make the right decisions for self-care and alignment. Let me give you an example (pay close attention to the choice points each person has along the way).

WHEN TWO AMYGDALA HIJACKS MEET

I'm a Seer / Feeler, so my creativity emerges when I'm connecting with people. Sometimes that connection comes through clients, and sometimes it comes through conversations with people I've hired. One such consultant was Jane. I'd hired her to help me craft the next level of my work, and we were going to be collaborating closely over many months. Since this was a longer-term project, she requested that I pay her 100 hours up front. I agreed, requesting that she provide me with a weekly declining balance of our time together.

We worked remotely for several months. Then in June, I had to travel to the West Coast for three weeks to speak and teach. The three-hour-earlier time shift meant our 8:30 to 11:30 a.m. Eastern time slots would not work while I was away. I asked Jane to please coordinate new times with my assistant, as I had a less predictable schedule while traveling. She agreed, and it seemed to go well.

Upon my return from California, we met for a two-week work retreat at my place in Boston. We created a daily routine where we would collaborate for a few hours in the morning and again in the afternoon. Typically, we would eat dinner together (unless she met up with a friend).

It all seemed like it was going well—in fact, dare I say, it was easy. We were both in a rhythm—at least I thought we were. Around 11 a.m., in the middle of our final morning session in Boston, Jane interrupted our workflow to let me know she had just completed her prepaid 100 hours. She requested that I wire her another hundred. "No problem," I answered. It struck me as odd at the time, but we were making good progress and there was more work to do. That was on a Thursday. I wired the money the next day.

The following Tuesday, when we resumed our virtual sessions, she opened the conversation by declaring a new policy for our work together: "I didn't want to say anything while I was staying at your place because it could have made things uncomfortable, but there were a lot of times when you were away on the West Coast that I had to shift my schedule to adjust to yours. Going forward, if you need a time change, you'll need to give me 48 hours advance notice, or I'll have to charge you and take it off the balance. I do it with all my clients. I haven't done it with you, but given what happened while you were in California, I need to."

As far as I had known, the scheduling in California had worked for both of us. If Jane had grievances about my time on the West Coast, she had given no indication of it to me or my assistant. She had just completed a two-week in-person work retreat with me but hadn't mentioned a word about this. On top of that, she requested a substantial amount of money be prepaid.

I took a deep breath and got curious. "What exactly wasn't working for you while I was out of town?" I asked.

"You're undermining my ability to make a living," she said, her voice sharp and cutting. "You would shift things around, and then when some of my other clients needed me, I was unavailable. And by the way, you're not treating me as an equal."

Over the years, I've learned that my amygdala gets triggered when someone assumes I have negative intentions toward them. My brain received this communication as her questioning my motives or assuming that I didn't have her best interests at heart. I zeroed in on her concern that I wasn't treating her as an equal because, as a Feeler, my goal was to be partners, and I didn't want her to feel otherwise.

"What have I done that's made you feel that you're not being treated as an equal?" I asked.

She explained that during our video sessions while I was in California, I had agreed that my "homework" in between sessions was that I would read two articles, but I hadn't been able to do it. In our next session, I had surrendered to the chaos of my life on the road and said, "Can we please just review the articles now?" I knew that meant I would have to *pay her time* to review the articles together, but given my travel commitments, I didn't see a better option.

She had replied, "I don't think that's a good use of our time."

I then responded with, "Probably not, but my schedule is booked solid, so I'm not going to be able to do it otherwise. I'm sorry. Now is my only available time frame. If my not having read this material is slowing us down, then I'd like to review it together now so that we can keep moving forward."

Jane had passed by her initial choice point, when she could have given feedback on the schedule changes while I was traveling. At choice point number two, she avoided telling me her concerns while we were in person for two weeks. Unfortunately, allowing that internal conflict to go unspoken caused it to erupt during a virtual work session. Although I didn't know exactly what was driving her unexpected and sudden rule change, my best guess was that she was trying to draw boundaries—although my interpretation was that she was making unilateral demands and accusations.

Now, I was at a choice point. At the time, my stomach was in knots. My inner GPS was on high alert. I was physically experiencing nausea and mentally running through scenarios of what might have happened. My emotions were a mix of anger, hurt, and confusion.

I felt stuck. The meeting we were in, as well as the eight hours of collaboration scheduled for the following two days, fell within Jane's new 48-hour cancellation policy. I panicked and thought, *I don't want to throw all this money away, so I better just keep going.* Ironically, after this tense exchange, we refocused on the work at hand, acting as if nothing was wrong.

THE IMPORTANCE OF ALIGNMENT

Later that day, I sat with all that data, sorting through it to identify if anything felt out of alignment with my values.

At first, in the conflict with Jane, I felt lost. I wondered whether I had in fact treated her unequally. I wondered whether I had imagined the fun and productive time we'd spent working together in Boston. I wondered what *I had done* to make Jane feel like I wasn't someone she could simply have an honest conversation with, someone who could hear and appreciate her side. I wondered what *I had done* to drive her to set such a hard and fast boundary.

As I journaled, I realized that nearly every question I was asking was about what *I had done or contributed* to this outcome. The only thought pattern I was using was personalization. While it's good for me to be curious about my part in a situation, I also needed to consider that other factors could be in play. What if this had something to do with Jane's need for control of her schedule and structure in her work (projection)? Or it may have been a way she protected herself due to past experiences that didn't go well. She may have had an amygdala hijack of her own. She may have lost money in the past or might be tight for money now. Or maybe there was a bigger factor than both of us (generalization) that I was not aware of. I wouldn't know which, if any, of these stories were true unless I asked her.

I paused and tuned into my inner GPS while also considering her concerns. I knew what was true for me: I had acted in good faith based on the information I had been given. I paid Jane up front because I wanted her to feel valued. I assumed generous intent and that if something was wrong, she would ask me about it—not tell me. I had said I would read the articles, and when I was unable to, I had been honest. I was even willing to pay for the time to do it (during our live session) to ensure our forward progress on the project.

When Jane changed our agreement, I had shut down and didn't ask if the 48-hour rule could start the following week. My amygdala hijack of being controlled and bullied in my younger years assumed that because she had the money and she made the rule, I had no power. This may or may not have been true, but it certainly limited what I thought was possible in the moment.

The next day, Jane and I spoke. I told her not only was I depleted, but I also felt trapped, without the ability to ask for time. I was emotional and upset. Following that conversation, Jane refused to engage in further dialogue. Which left the question: *What should we do now?*

What was clear was that even after nearly a year of partnering, Jane didn't feel comfortable giving me feedback, asking for what she needed (versus unilaterally telling me), or even having a challenging conversation to explore the explosive exchange we had. So how would I respond based on my values of clear communication and honest partnership?

Over email, Jane and I agreed that we would no longer work together. She returned most of the unused money, and I went on to create a new partnership (based on greater trust, honest communication, and shared values) with another consultant. I hope Jane did the same.

This is why it's so important to pick up your body's signals and trust them. Then allow yourself to pause, pay attention to your thoughts, express your emotions, clarify boundaries, and address conflict early. Ideally, you do all of this with kindness, while giving and receiving feedback. The decision to discontinue work with Jane was a relief, and that's how I know it was made from the inside-out. When you take action in alignment with your values—even when it means ending a relationship—you receive a net gain of energy. When you don't take your values into consideration or even know what they are, it's easy to experience a net drain of energy through delays, confusion, and mixed messages.

Some people assume that because I write books on communication, I'm immune to conflict or relationship challenges. That's not true. When these issues come up, I can react, get defensive, and feel emotional just like anybody else. The difference is that I have an array of tools and resources that help me get back on track. I am sharing these with you, so you're able to do the same.

. . . .

For more guidance on handling conflicts, making agreements, and speaking up for yourself, listen to my audiobook, *Talk Rx: Five Steps to Honest Conversations That Create Connection, Health, and Happiness*, which offers practical steps to use your inner GPS for clear, effective communication.

. . . .

FIVE-STEP DECISION-MAKING TOOL

Rather than making decisions solely from the outside-in, what if you had a quick and effective way to assess what matters most to you? This five-step decision-making tool uses one question from each of the five energy levels to expand your perspective and integrate your body map, thoughts, emotions, and values to determine:

- What you're willing to stand up for

- What you're willing to let go of

- What you say yes or no to

- What you're inspired by

- What makes you feel obligated

With every decision that comes your way—especially the big ones—ask yourself these five important questions to assess information—both externally and internally. (Note: if you are pressed for time, starting with questions 1 and 2 can be a good way to decide if this dilemma can be simplified into an easy yes or no.)

Question 1: Does this request, opportunity, or idea align with your highest values? (Spiritual Energy)

This is the most important question. If you have a request, an opportunity, or an idea that *doesn't align* with what you value, that's an easy NO.

Question 2: Does this idea, opportunity, or choice result in a net energy gain or drain? (Physical Energy)

Tune in: How is your body communicating with you about whether you want to do this? In other words, are you making this decision from a place of inspiration (energy-giving) or from a place of obligation (energy-draining)? Are there any resources or support you could ask for that would transform the opportunity from an energy drain to an energy gain?

Question 3: What's the primary emotional driver that you're experiencing—fear or excitement? (Emotional Energy)

Are you making this choice out of fear (e.g., fear of not having enough money, fear of losing security, or are you making a choice to escape a job, relationship, or situation), or are you making this choice from a place of joy, possibility, and excitement?

Question 4: On what timeline will this opportunity impact you—immediately, short term, or long term? (Mental Energy)

Will there be a period of discomfort worth enduring in order to reach your goal? What obstacles might you encounter as you strive toward your ultimate objective?

Question 5: What potential impact could this opportunity have on others in your world? (Social Energy)

How might this choice or opportunity meet your needs and synergistically meet the needs of everyone involved? Or how might making this decision adversely affect others?

It's a YES if your answers above to all five questions align, meaning that the request, opportunity, idea, or choice:

- Passes your values filter test (this is non-negotiable), on question 1

- Energizes you (and you have the support and resources to take care of yourself as you do it—otherwise, ask for what you need to help you make your decision), on question 2

- Moves you toward something you're passionate about with joy, excitement, and possibility, on question 3

- Will be a positive outcome in the long run, even if there are shorter-term challenges, on question 4

- Will positively impact your and others' lives, on question 5

It's a NO if your answers above to all five questions don't align, meaning the request, opportunity, or idea:

- Doesn't pass your values filter test, on question 1

- Drains you (and / or you do not have the support and resources to take care of yourself as you do it), on question 2

- Is motivated by fear, scarcity, or lack, on question 3

- May benefit you immediately or in the short term, but could potentially cause longer-term problems, on question 4

- Will negatively impact yours or others' lives, on question 5

It's a MAYBE if you:

- Answered that the request aligns with your highest values, on question 1

- Said it feels like an energy-draining obligation, on question 2

- Realize that fear is a driving factor, on question 3

- Are unclear about how the timeline will play out and whether or not there is a longer-term benefit, on question 4

- Are unsure how this will impact you, your community, and the larger world, on question 5

The "maybe" is the *somewhere-in-between* zone and requires a little more thought and effort. Many decisions fall in this "maybe" category, so next we'll do a deeper dive into questions 2 to 5 to guide you through decision-making uncertainty. (Note: you already know that if a decision doesn't pass your values filter test in question 1, then it's an easy no. There is no ambiguity there.)

Question 2: Physical Energy

If you experience a sinking feeling, heaviness in your body, or a sense of depletion when you answer question 2, pay attention! When you're acting out of obligation, your body sends clear messages.

The way this works for me is that physically, I experience throat and chest constriction, muscles tightening, and jaw clenching. My body literally contracts to protect me—and I feel an energy drain. On the other hand, when I feel passionate and inspired, my body often feels relaxed, open, and light. When I'm receiving an energy gain from an experience, I sometimes even get the chills.

So the question is: What's happening for you?

Note: I'm not saying that everything you do has to be inspiring and energy-giving (that's nearly impossible!), but what is most important is noticing how often you make decisions out of obligation that *deplete you of precious energy*. This helps you diagnose important misalignment such as people-pleasing, lack of healthy boundaries, or making choices that lead you down the path of burnout. If you are continuously out of alignment with your energy, you may find yourself paradoxically being really busy while simultaneously feeling empty, depleted, and often disconnected from the meaning in your work.

Question 3: Emotional Energy

If you suspect that fear is driving your decision, pay attention if you hear yourself use phrases like "have to" or "should." Get curious about your experience.

- What role is fear playing in your thinking and decision-making (e.g., fear of judgment, losing credibility or security, fear of failure, or scarcity mindset)?

- Where in your life did you hear about or experience a similar situation that didn't turn out well (for you or someone else)?

- If it was a past experience for you, ask yourself, what has changed that would allow you to take that risk now (even though it did not seem like a good idea previously)?

- Once you've worked through the fears, you'll know that excitement and anticipation have taken its place when you begin to think or say phrases such as "I want to," "I can't wait to," or "I'm excited to."

- Finally, if you allow yourself to come from inspiration, what possibilities could exist?

Question 4: Mental Energy

This is a good time to review the different short-term and long-term outcomes.

- Immediately, what do you anticipate the effect(s) of saying yes or no could be? For you? For the other person / people this decision impacts?

- What would you be gaining or giving up? In the short term? In the long run?

- If you were giving it your best guess, what level of risk or discomfort might arise on this timeline (high, medium, low)?

Question 5: Social Energy

If you are unsure how your decision may influence others, begin by making a list of stakeholders (any other people / groups who may be impacted). Then if you say yes or no to this decision, ask the following questions in relation to each stakeholder:

- What does this stakeholder desire or value with respect to the issue?

- How much are they impacted by this decision (high, medium, low)?

- What are your joint interests?

- Do you anticipate any conflicts arising from your decision?

- What are your best strategies for creating value for this stakeholder?

- If you make a particular decision, whose needs would be met?

- Over time if you view this decision as part of an ongoing relationship versus an isolated transaction, does this decision unlock additional opportunity to create value for this stakeholder?

Using the Five-Step Decision-Making Tool as a framework will expand your perspective and guide you to making clear and effective choices that serve you and those around you.

Realigning When You've Gone Astray

Sometimes life doesn't go the way you want it to. Sometimes you put in so much effort, give it your all, and still don't get the job, the relationship, the connection, or the creative project that you worked so hard for. And you find yourself wondering, *What did I do wrong? Was it simply not meant to be? Should I stop trying? Stop dreaming?*

Of course not. I've discovered that when I feel this way, it's most often because of a misalignment within myself. Maybe I was working hard for the wrong reasons or toward the wrong goal.

When you feel you're off track, take the time to *reconnect to your highest values* and you'll be heading back in the right direction.

Trust that whatever choices you've made were the right ones to provide you with information and give you the opportunity to learn. This hard-won wisdom will guide you in taking the next step. As you learn more, you may get reinforcement that the decision you made was the right one. If it's not, trust that you will figure out what to do next. This is about giving yourself grace and building self-trust through value-based decision-making. Allow yourself to do the best with what you know in the moment, make mistakes, and change course if necessary.

Congratulations! You now know the life-changing skill of making quick and effective decisions based on your highest values. This will give you a spiritual energy gain as you navigate our complex world with more ease. There are no guarantees. Sometimes the Five-Step Decision-Making Tool will lead you to an unexpected outcome, as in my work with Jane. Other times, it will lead you into a new world of possibility—better than you could have imagined. Regardless, when you trust yourself, you have the confidence of knowing that you can handle whatever comes next.

CHAPTER 23

NAVIGATING CONTROL AND CHANGE

n January 2012, I was invited as a last-minute speaker replacement at TEDx Berkeley. I had a mere eight days to prepare to give the highest-profile talk of my career thus far. I was as thrilled as I was petrified.

The "Ten Commandments of TED" suggested that I be well rehearsed and memorized—and at the same time, emotional and open. *No problem*, I thought. Emotional and open is my forte, and hard work is my middle name. I cleared my calendar and began working feverishly on my speech—writing, rewriting, and rehearsing it over and over again. I called in an entire team to support me, working with my best friend, Kathy, my parents, my speech coach, my graphic designer—practically everyone I knew was on call that week to help me prepare.

On the day prior to the event, I asked a healthcare leader and friend Linsey to give me honest feedback on the final script. I proudly delivered what I had been tirelessly creating, and then sat back and awaited the final stamp of approval I anticipated he would give.

Linsey was silent for a few moments. Then he began, as sincerely and gently as he could in his South African accent, "Neha, the reason I hire you for my teams is because you're real. Your authentic stories are transformative, your tools are practical, and the genuine emotion you express moves people. What you just read sounds formal and canned. My suggestion is to rewrite it, so it sounds more like you."

I was dumbfounded. Didn't he understand that my speech was tomorrow, at 4 p.m.? I skipped dress rehearsal and stayed up half the night rewriting it. At 6 a.m., when Kathy came to pick me up, I was still at it. I was dressed and ready, but I hadn't fully memorized the latest version. *I'll just use my note cards*, I thought. *They only gave me a week to prepare. I'm sure they'll understand.*

The curtains opened with the first speaker, Charles Holt. His 14-minute talk, "Finding Your Voice," was peppered with song and dance as he shared about his family, faith, and vulnerability. It was as if he was having an intimate conversation with 2,000 of his closest friends. To give you context, Charles played the lead in *The Lion King* on Broadway.

I was mesmerized by his performance, and simultaneously my panic elevated to an 11 (out of 10). I was nowhere near ready for this! Kathy saw the look on my face and said, "Ne, let's head to the green room. We've got five hours to get this done. You're not on until 4 p.m. And pink note cards clearly aren't an option."

I must have gone over my talk what felt like more than a hundred times, and each time I would get lost or stuck, Kathy would tell me with the deepest love, "Great job. You made it further than last time. Let's do it again. Repeat this section, and once you get it, we'll go back to the beginning. You've got this." Just like the day of my first board meeting with Jim and Mark, when I felt hope draining, I would just look in Kathy's eyes and be reminded of her faith in me, which helped me muster the courage to try again.

By 3:30 p.m., I had made it through 80 percent of my speech without looking at the note cards, but I still hadn't made it through the whole thing. Kathy placed her hands on both my shoulders and said, "Now, I'm going to go out and root you on from the audience. Ne, just trust yourself. You've got this."

I so did not have it yet. Suddenly, I felt so alone. My heart began pounding out of my chest, and all I could imagine was me under those bright lights drawing a blank, about to make a total fool of myself. I continued to recite what was written on the cards over and over again, faster and faster—hoping for a miracle.

Then, out of nowhere, I looked up and saw Charles Holt walking toward me. He must have seen the desperation on my face, as I paced back and forth, because he asked, "Are you up next? How can I support you?"

My mind was still racing. How could I be authentic and be prepared at the same time? How could I ever deliver a talk that came anywhere close to his? I felt panicked and out of control. The fact that we'd *never even met* simply didn't seem important in that moment. I blurted, "Would you please breathe with me?"

"Of course," he replied calmly, as if this was the most natural request in the world from a total stranger. "Sometimes, before we go on stage for a show, we breathe together to ground ourselves."

He enveloped me in a hug, and we began taking several slow deep breaths together. And then it hit me: *This wasn't about me. I couldn't control how my talk would be received.* I had certainly been trying; I was as prepared as was humanly possible in the time I had been given. But that white-knuckled grip of control that got me over the finish line of writing my talk was now about to undermine my performance. I said, "This isn't about me forgetting my lines, making a mistake, or being perfect, is it? It's about being in service to the audience and doing the best I know how to honor them. That's what you did, isn't it?"

"Exactly," he said with a knowing smile. "That's all you have to do. Trust yourself and let go. You're in service to the audience now."

A voice came from behind the curtain. "Neha, are you ready to mic? You're up next."

"Yep," I said. I set my stack of well-worn pink note cards on the table, smiled back at Charles, took a deep breath, and walked out on stage.

You can watch my TEDxBerkeley talk if you're curious. It's titled "The Communication Cure." The talk wasn't perfect. I flubbed some lines, and at times, my slides weren't in sync with what I was saying. But because I had relinquished my tight, clenched control, I was able to be present, authentically myself—so much so that I was moved to tears. (Yep, this is the same speech I gave when I was approached by the young Middle Eastern man who was so suspicious of my tears being an attempt to fake-cry to get attention. Perhaps it was because of my heroic effort and Charles' heartfelt kindness and wisdom that I was able to be so certain of my own authenticity. I knew that I hadn't forced anything, but instead had simply surrendered to the experience.)

RELEASING CONTROL: PERSONAL VERSUS POSITIONAL POWER

It feels good to be in control, doesn't it? We feel powerful, and more than that, the world feels predictable. Control may look like knowing who we're working with, knowing what our workload will be, or having the flexibility to manage our time, schedule, and energy.

When this happens, it's wonderful—but it isn't always possible. Life happens, and other people's decisions require us to adjust (just like when someone else's delayed work means you have to scramble to complete yours). Naturally, at times of uncertainty or involuntary change, we can feel vulnerable, even when we've made decisions and drawn boundaries in the name of our own self-care.

Powerlessness is one of the most challenging emotions to experience. But let me assure you that you do have power. The question is: Are you sourcing the right kind of power? **Positional power** is sourced *externally,* meaning that it is given to you by an outside authority: by a person, leader, team, organization, board, or government, for example. It may come through financial resources, a title, or decision-making control over an entity or community. While you may exercise your positional power, it can be taken away at any time due to any reason. Others' approval of your performance determines whether you get to keep the job or title.

Also, when that positional power is challenged, it can shake your self-esteem and sense of self-worth. You may find yourself making unilateral decisions and resorting to statements, like:

- "Because I said so!"

- "I'm in charge. Do what I say!"

- "If you don't like it, then leave."

Positional power is useful, but it has its limits. If you find yourself seeking positional power only, it may be helpful to explore what accomplishment or success means to you and how you might find deeper, more meaningful success through personal power.

Personal power is generated from within; it's *me-powered*. The foundation of personal power depends upon your level of clarity and conviction about your highest values and core beliefs. When personal power is solid, you're able to make quick, easy decisions and take inspired action. You have unlimited control—of yourself. Because your power is rooted in self-trust, you are a natural leader. Your self-confidence enables you to take risks and initiate change. Even without a designated title (positional power), you command respect and attention and have the ability to create a powerful ripple effect. You take into account not only yourself but others, as well as your collective impact on the world. When you make mistakes, you own them and self-correct. Examples of personal power include:

- When asked your opinion, even if it potentially could differ from others, you answer with compassion and authenticity.

- When invited to participate in a new or challenging experience—as long as it aligns with your highest values—you trust yourself to say yes!

- When unexpected events occur, you tune in to your inner GPS, get curious about what others are experiencing, and then take your next best step.

CONTROL VERSUS POWER

At its heart, control is an attempt to create safety. The conscious or unconscious drive for stability and power plays a major role in many people's careers and lives. Countless clients have said that they experience *positional power at work* but *no personal power at the dinner table*. Often, we get caught up in trying to have control over ourselves or others based on external factors (outside-in) without recognizing where our real power comes from (inside-out).

We must be careful, though, because the positive intent underlying control can quickly become corrosive. We hold ourselves to impossible standards, driven by our relentless inner critics spewing judgments about ourselves and our colleagues. When we rely too heavily on the need for control, we ensure an outcome opposite from our original intention—unattainable perfectionism that results in paralysis and a depletion of energy. We wind up with little to no personal power.

In our ever-changing world, when we feel vulnerable, trapped, or like we haven't been given enough time to do a good job, fear sometimes kicks in. I saw this firsthand in 2007–2008, when I was selected to mentor my colleagues through our transition from paper charts to electronic medical records. Every physician in our 6,000-person practice arrived at a choice point to either take:

- **The short-term high** by digging in their heels and resisting the change through a variety of tactics, including but not limited to decreasing their clinical time to 70 to 80 percent, changing their jobs, or retiring prematurely (long-term low)

- **The short-term dip** by learning the new computer program and working longer days for a few months, ultimately resulting in everyone having integrated patient data in real time, which sped up the process and decreased their documentation time (long-term high)

One of the physicians who was adamantly opposed to transitioning to electronic medical records promptly changed his mind when he realized he could pull up radiology films electronically in real time to explain to patients what he saw and why he was making a particular recommendation. He also began to marvel at the power of everybody making this concerted effort and the ease with which he could integrate enormous data in very little time.

Change often comes with discomfort. As difficult as it can be, it's easier if you feel that you have input or some ability to influence the outcome. Involuntary change can be the fast track to feeling helpless or powerless across all work styles. But here's where personal power matters. The only real control you have is over yourself and how you respond and make decisions in the face of change. In reality, embracing change does often mean *ceding control*—something most of us don't do naturally—but it doesn't mean giving up power.

VARYING REACTIONS TO CHANGE

The following are ways that the various work styles deal with change:

- **Doers** create an illusion of control with their endless to-do lists. Involuntary change often brings up vulnerability and discomfort with the unknown. Personal power for Doers comes from embracing their emotions and learning to let go—giving them greater adaptability to change.

- **Thinkers'** sense of control comes from having enough time and space to think through complex problems logically. Factors outside their control that make them feel rushed or flooded by emotion can leave them feeling overwhelmed and stuck in the decision-making process. Personal power for Thinkers comes from learning to trust themselves more, expressing their emotions, and speaking up or making a decision, even before they have all the data.

- **Seers** can feel like they've lost control and are trapped if involuntary changes occur (e.g., the addition of unexpected policies or restrictions) without their input or influence. Absent the process of creative brainstorming, Seers can feel powerless to shape their world. They do not respond favorably to being told, "This is the way we've always done it." Personal power for Seers comes from strengthening their ability to make clear agreements and commit to one path (perhaps with a built-in timeline for reflection and reevaluation).

- **Feelers'** illusion of control and purpose is based on the strength and closeness of their relationships. When time with clients is reduced, they feel disconnected from their team (remote work environments), or someone unexpectedly ends a relationship without the willingness to discuss it further (being ghosted). In these types of scenarios, they often feel discouraged and helpless. Personal power for Feelers comes from learning to trust themselves and drawing healthy boundaries when they aren't being treated with respect.

A common reaction to having our sense of control challenged is defaulting to an all-or-none mindset. Maybe your partner tells you that they don't really want to be bothered with the grocery list right then because they're in the middle of something. If you're in an all-or-none mindset, you might think, *OK, I'll never ask my partner about groceries again. This is just something I'll have to handle on my own.* This mindset is limiting, because it causes you to take on *more* than you have to, and all you get in exchange is a sense of momentary control, followed by resentment toward your partner.

You have options. Instead, do what seems counterintuitive—slow down and tap into your personal power to:

- Recognize your reflexive controlling tendencies

- Learn to pause and tune in to your inner GPS

- Get curious, not furious

- Open yourself to new possibilities

- Cocreate the future together

In this instance, you might notice your desire for a one-size-fits-all approach to grocery shopping, which comes from a desire for control. You might need to pause and notice how this impacts you: do you really want to do *all* the grocery shopping? Nobody asked you to. What else might be possible for you? Maybe you can adapt to how your partner is not ready to discuss this right that second but will be free in an hour or two. Maybe you can allow for the possibility of taking turns; there are more choices than simply (a) shopping as a couple or (b) having it always be your job.

Navigating Change Exercise

To skillfully evaluate challenging situations, begin by taking inventory of your own resistance to change.

- What have been the three most consequential changes that you've faced over the past few years?

  1. _____

  2. _____

  3. _____

- On a scale of 1 to 10, with 1 = no resistance to change and 10 = highest resistance to change, rate your resistance to those three changes initially and reassess what level of resistance you had after six months.

	Initially	*After Six Months*
1.	_____	_____
2.	_____	_____
3.	_____	_____

  How did your resistance evolve over time? What made it easier? What made it more difficult?

- Next, identify how much control and input you felt you had with each change.

  ○ How would you describe the level of change you experienced (small, medium, large)?

- ○ What was the timeline over which the change occurred? How much time was there to adjust?

- ○ In relation to the change, what were you most concerned about?

- ○ Was the change voluntary or involuntary? (Voluntary change can be difficult, but despite the discomfort, you may also experience a sense of personal control.)

- ○ Was there an opportunity to provide input to shape the change?

- ○ Did you have a chance to evaluate the impact of the change on your job, life, or relationship? If so, what were the short-term and long-term benefits / drawbacks?

There is great power in gaining awareness of what drives you, what you're afraid of, what you're excited about, and the price versus the payoff of any decision. No matter what the situation, it's important to understand what you would be letting go of. What part of letting go would bring relief? What part would bring grief? Do you feel agency in making this decision? What was your part in contributing to this outcome? In relation to what you don't have control over, how can you exercise personal power?

When you find yourself feeling like you have no control, pause and ask yourself, what is causing me to feel this way? Then consider what true personal power would give you in the situation. Sometimes when you feel stuck between a rock and a hard place, letting go of controlling the situation is your best option. Even that is a choice—and an act of personal power.

CHAPTER 24

THE POWER OF SURRENDER

How do you know when it's time to choose a different way forward? Usually, when you find yourself fighting a tide—so myopically focused on life working out in a particular way that you cannot see another path forward. That's a big clue that it's time to consider surrendering.

Think about the inner tension that arises from being attached to having life unfold in a specific manner. Maybe you experienced this when applying to university, certain that your top school was the only way forward—until you received the rejection letter. Perhaps you didn't get your dream job in your ideal city. Or in your personal life, maybe you spent years trying to make a broken relationship whole, even when all the signs pointed you toward separation . . . and then your partner announced that they're leaving. Who were you in these moments? Did you gracefully let go? Or did you resist change?

Realizing that you need to surrender is often the result of ongoing struggle. You've tried so hard, in so many ways! In these moments, surrender does not mean admitting defeat (even though it might feel that way initially). Surrender is opening your eyes to the reality that there is another way—and most likely, a better way. When you're able to truly let go, life will surprise you by filling the "empty" spaces with new gifts—people and experiences more suited to who you're becoming, what you need to learn, and insights into what you're supposed to do next.

When you give yourself the grace of surrender, you regain precious energy. This happens because you're not spending so much of your bandwidth trying to force a wild, messy life to unfold in a particular, manicured way.

Often, surrender happens when someone says no—management passes you over for a promotion, a key collaborator bows out, or a loved one stops communicating or decides to leave. Initially, that 'no' is probably going to sting. Yet this is also a moment for you to breathe and remember that as much as you love control and certainty, even you don't know how life will unfold. Maybe the employer that rejected your application folds under the weight of a scandal. What if your first marriage was not a failure, but instead an opportunity to learn to become more present, communicate more clearly, and ask questions to deepen your future relationships? What if getting fired wasn't a disaster but, instead, a chance to discover your true mission and passion? What if burning out isn't the end, but, instead, the new beginning of a fulfilled and purpose-driven life? I can assure you, it has been a powerful reset for me because it has led me here to you.

As the saying goes, "When one door closes, another opens." Take a minute to reflect on the deep truth in this statement. Can you think of any such example in your own life?

Despite initial disappointment, life does tend to work out. Doers, you may go on to achieve something even better than you've originally set out to do. Thinkers, you may apply your problem-solving process to a bigger, more relevant issue. Seers, you may learn to accept when you can't change the status quo and eventually realize your brilliance in other ways (because we know you have no shortage of genius ideas). Feelers, you *will* find your people—those who *get you* without condition or qualification—as soon as you are able to also value yourself!

RELIEF IN SURRENDER

Of course, there are other players: people, circumstances, unforeseen mishaps, weather, traffic, universal laws, births, deaths—you name it. That's what makes the journey of life fascinating, interesting, and yes, sometimes disappointing and devastating. The secret is staying curious and open to the possibility of life surprising and delighting you with the unexpected. Even if you can't imagine what a particular lesson might be, eventually, that new perspective will come, so long as you keep the doors to your heart and mind open.

I learned this lesson from my dear friend Jacqueline. Her and I were both physicians at the same hospital. In fact, the only reason I knew to call the psychiatrist Roger when I burned out that fateful day in 2004 is because he had helped Jacqueline navigate her burnout only six months earlier. She had used her burnout to transform her life by leaving our team, and instead, aligning with her highest values of family, faith, health, beauty, and entrepreneurship. She began spending more time with her twins, husband, and dog, and took out loans to start her own cosmetic spa business. I remember her choosing a butterfly as her business logo and saying that she hoped to be a catalyst for her patients to transform, not just on the outside but on the inside as well. She began walking every day, cooking, taking excellent care of everything in her life, including herself, like going to get regular mammograms. (Yes, even though we make those recommendations to you, it's common for health providers to be delinquent in our own self-care.)

One day, she called in a frenzied voice, "Neha, you're never going to believe this, but the radiologist missed a lump under my arm 10 months ago, and now I have stage four breast cancer."

Jacqueline began by embracing all the recommended Western medical treatments, and I watched as her beautiful black curly locks were replaced by colorful silk scarves. At times, she felt better, but her overall trajectory was on the decline.

At one point, while we were on a walk by the river, I saw her visibly get short of breath. We sat down on a bench overlooking the water and once she was feeling better, I said, "It sounds like we've exhausted all the oncologic treatment options, Jacqueline. Are you open to having an energy session with a healer who has had miraculous results for some of my friends and family? I'd love to gift you a session for your birthday!"

She paused and said in a low voice, "Not really, Neha. You've talked before about healers over the years. But you know, I'm Christian and my spiritual belief system doesn't allow me to explore that."

I was in so much pain after she spoke because it meant we were out of options. "But it's noninvasive!" I argued as tears ran down my face. "What if it could help? Shouldn't you at least try it?"

There are things you can control and others you can't. When you're feeling angst-ridden about something out of your control, that's your cue to ask, "Can I change or influence this?" And if the answer is that you've already exhausted the options that you know, ask yourself, "How can I surrender and trust that I can handle what comes next?"

I felt powerless to influence Jacqueline's decision, so I surrendered. And for the next six months she became increasingly distant as her prognosis worsened—until she was hospitalized. During that time, I tried to call her room and for the first time ever, even as a physician, I was instructed that the patient wasn't taking calls from anyone.

A few weeks later, I got a text from her, saying she had recovered from a bad case of pneumonia and wanted to talk. When we reconnected, she began, "Neha, remember that healer you told me about? I'm ready to try an energy healing session with him. But I'm too weak to drive, and I don't want to ask my family to come with me to something that might make them uncomfortable or cause conflict. Will you take me?"

My heart leapt out of my chest, "Of course, Jacqueline—I'll arrange it this week!"

We didn't say much on the ride there; both of us silently praying for a miracle. I was barely breathing as the healer helped her onto the massage table and positioned her on her side with her legs bent. He stood before her, with one hand on her shoulder and the other on her knee. I sat in complete silence for 45 minutes watching him work, with his eyes closed. After what seemed like an eternity, he opened them and looked at me.

"Bruce, can you help her?" I inquired.

And that's when he uttered the words I dreaded most, "I'm sorry, Jacqueline. It's too late. Your system is shutting down. This is part of your life path now. I don't know how to say this gently to you, but there's nothing I can do to change this process. I've spent our time together infusing you with the highest white light energy I can, and you're going to feel really good for about 10 days. So please use that time to take care of anything you need to."

Jacqueline and I were speechless as we stared silently at one another. I immediately felt guilt and regret for recommending an experience that couldn't heal her. About 30 minutes into our drive home, I mustered the courage to break the silence. "Jacqueline, are you mad at me for bringing you to see him today?"

"Gosh, no," she answered. "I'm not mad at all. He was right. In the last hour, something happened. I feel better than I have in years. In fact, ever since he spoke, I've been feeling massive *relief*. Because when I was in the hospital, I was just trying so hard to fight and not let go. I thought no mother would be so cowardly as to let go when she had two growing children who needed her. I thought I was selfish for wishing I could just die. But the truth is that I'm ready to let go and surrender. I didn't think it was moral or right for me to do it. And I guess the gift he gave me was to trust my body, my heart, and my intuition; trust my partner; and trust that these beautiful souls will grow up brave and strong. I have given them what I came here to give them. My job is complete."

I pulled over, and we held each other until we both stopped crying. We clasped hands in silence the rest of the way home.

About two months later, while I was out of town, Jacqueline passed away. Those who attended her funeral described a beautiful tribute to her. Together, they all released a kaleidoscope of live butterflies—to symbolize how she had transformed her family, her patients, and the world with her exquisite and unforgettable presence.

Are you starting to see how much personal power there is in surrender? It simply means that you are choosing to spend your energy elsewhere—focusing on the lesson you need to learn, rather than trying to force your journey to unfold the way you want it to. It also means you can surrender to what *other experiences life might have in store*. Often when you fully surrender, you open the door to a quicker and easier path. In the long run, surrender often leads to higher ground. The catch is that you have to cede control of needing to write that path in vivid detail before you ever travel it. Sometimes you have to surrender to the limits of what you are capable of doing. Sometimes you surrender to circumstances outside of your control, like a global pandemic or a hurricane. And there are times that you surrender to the people you lead and love, to honor their path and how it may be different from what you would have chosen. Is there anything that's been on your heart and mind that you know it's time to surrender to?

In those moments that life seems to be guiding you in a direction that you feel resistant to, the need for surrender can show up in smaller ways. These moments are no less potent than the louder circumstances that can lead us to surrender. Maybe you sense it's time to have a meaningful conversation. Or you have an everyday experience, like a car breaking down, that seems to carry a larger symbolic significance. As Eckhart Tolle says, "Always say 'yes' to the present moment. What could be more futile, more insane, than to create inner resistance to what already is? What could be more insane than to oppose life itself, which is *now* and *always now*? Surrender to what is. Say 'yes' to life—and see how life suddenly starts working *for you* rather than against you."

SPIRITUAL ENERGY REASSESSMENT

1. What are your top five values?

    a. _____

    b. _____

    c. _____

    d. _____

    e. _____

2. What percentage of the time do you use your highest values to guide you in decision-making? At home? At work?

3. Describe a time when you have trusted yourself to take a risk and it worked out.

4. In the future, if your self-trust is shaken, name one person who will remind you of what you are capable of. What would they say to you?

5. Describe a time when you experienced a sacred exchange, an interaction with someone else that deeply moved you.

6. Is there anything you have outgrown and are ready to surrender to now?

7. On a scale of 1 to 10, with 1 = not at all and 10 = deeply connected, please rate your alignment with meaning and purpose in these areas:

    Work

    Home

    Social circles

8. Overall, on a spiritual level, would you say that you're experiencing a net gain (+) or net drain (−) of energy on a spiritual level?

☐ net gain (+)   ☐ net drain (−)

Once again, the way you determine this is by looking at your answers above and also by checking in with your body map. If you feel a constriction or tightness in your body as you answer these questions, you likely have a net drain in this area. If you have a feeling of open-ness, ease, or lightness in your body as you answer these questions, this energy level is likely a net gain for you.

Congratulations! You've completed the physical, mental, emotional, social, and spiritual energy sections and are now equipped to integrate and embody being *me-powered*.

CHAPTER 25

BECOMING ME-POWERED

I t has been almost two decades since I burned out. And without hesitation, I can say that what I once thought was the biggest failure I could ever imagine was, in fact, one of the most pivotal and important milestones in my life. On June 17, 2004, the universe sent an unmistakable message: the lack of alignment *within me* was my biggest obstacle. To overcome it, I needed to shift from sourcing my energy and validation *from others* to being *powered by me*.

This life-altering experience revealed hidden patterns and my perspective began to shift and expand. Rather than viewing crises as something to avoid, a failure, or an adversity, I noticed that they served a much higher purpose. In fact, as a physician, I repeatedly witnessed the power of crises to crack open people's hearts and minds—and fast-track them to emotional and spiritual alignment. People in a crisis were able to immediately identify and prioritize their highest values. The clearest example of this came through physical breakdowns on individual, community, and global levels. In crises, people suddenly discovered the power of what they had faith in, found the courage to make much needed change, or shifted into selfless service to others.

On an individual level, I observed it in my patients. I remember a 63-year-old gentleman who, moments earlier, had declared "I'm not religious. So please don't have a chaplain or anyone like that visit me, OK?" I smiled and nodded, "Sure, no problem." A few moments later, he developed crushing chest pain. Without hesitation, he put his palms together above his chest and began crying out, "Am I going to die, Doc? Dear God, please save my life!"

On a community level, when divorce broke a family apart or a loved one was diagnosed with cancer or unexpectedly passed, I witnessed their community suddenly find time (in their otherwise busy lives) to deliver meals, babysit, and organize candlelight vigils. The invisible connections between them and being in service to one another became their highest priority.

On a global level, conflict or any natural disaster can mobilize millions of people to donate their money, time, and energy to those in need—often people they've never even met. These events initially cause shock and devastation, but often transform and awaken people to new ways of connecting to themselves and one another.

During burnout, my inner GPS began to speak louder than the voices around me, unraveling what I once held as truth. And new possibilities began to emerge.

What if *doing more with less* isn't the eternal goal? And, instead, it's about living *more aligned* with my highest values and *worrying less* about society's measures of success.

What if *faster isn't always better*? And, instead, sometimes the wisest decision is to *slow down in order to speed up*.

What if *success doesn't require struggle*? And instead, I know a choice is right because it's easy and results in a net gain of energy.

Burning out put me on the path to discover my true calling. In my private practice, I partner with clients to heal their stress and get them off medications, rather than on them. In my company, Intuitive Intelligence, I share these principles as an author, speaker, executive coach, and organizational consultant. It's been a joy to bridge the science of medicine with the art of communication to bring true health to patients and organizations— *awakening people to their power and then empowering them to live it*.

Now you, too, have the tools to reverse the crisis of burnout and make choices according to what matters most to you. Here is a guide to identify your progress.

FIVE LEVELS TO BECOMING ME-POWERED

Level 1: Other-Powered

One hundred percent of your focus is external. You react based on the opinions and emotions of those around you. You're tuned in to data from your colleagues, friends, family, and the outside world, and are disconnected from the data that comes from within you. You're unaware of your body's physical clues. You use familiar coping strategies, such as sugar, caffeine, alcohol, or taking on even more work to override any unpleasant signals. You use your thoughts to silence your body and emotions. You might even push through uncomfortable relationship dynamics by either avoiding conflict, stewing, or bullying to get what you want. You power through your day and are surprised when you collapse on your bed at night. You're running on fumes.

Bottom line: Your attention is other-focused, and you may find yourself experiencing a net energy drain across multiple levels. This is the danger zone and the fast track to burnout!

Level 2: Me-Conflicted

You're focused on external data, but you're beginning to notice your internal cues. You may receive your body's stress signals, but you may not be clear on what they mean or what to do about them. Even if you do know what you want *and* value, you might hold back for fear of repercussions or judgment. You continue to choose the short-term high (e.g., avoiding saying no, powering through alone) at the expense of your long-term well-being. You're most likely to take action only when you're forced to (e.g., you get sick; losing an opportunity, a job, or your partner). You endure and may even view soldiering on as a badge of honor.

Bottom line: You've become an internal observer—aware of when you're out of alignment with what you value. You still aren't prioritizing yourself, so internal conflict is likely your biggest source of energy drain.

Level 3: Me-Aware

You have an inspired practice of quieting your mind and listening to your body, heart, and spirit, and you may even tune in at a designated time (through running, cycling, yoga, meditation, prayer, journaling, reading, therapy, coaching, personal development groups, etc.). But when you're outside your regular practice, it's difficult to maintain this level of awareness. One of my clients described this as feeling zen on her yoga mat and experiencing road rage on the way home.

Bottom line: *You're on the right track as you embark on the journey of self-care and have moments of clarity and integration.*

Level 4: Me-Aligned

You're aware of when your body is talking and can recognize when something is off. You might even make an extra effort to recharge. You decipher your thoughts and emotions, giving yourself space to acknowledge them. You are open to feedback, take personal accountability of your part in a situation, and draw healthy boundaries. You are more consistent—in certain arenas of your life. However, your level of alignment may shift depending on the environment you're in (work, home, social, etc.) and the amount of perceived risk if you were to speak your truth.

Bottom line: *You're well on the path to healing burnout and living an aligned life.*

Level 5: Me-Powered

You know your highest values, make decisions based on them, and take action according to what you stand for. This is true in *all* your roles and relationships, including the one with yourself. You are not only in tune, you also adjust naturally and organically to both your emotional and physical signals. You're open to feedback, and you listen to your own heart slightly louder than you listen to the voices of others. Your physical, mental, emotional, social, and spiritual energies are aligned and serve as your *internal power source*.

Beyond your inner alignment, you are also able to hold an expanded perspective. You integrate both internal and external data within yourself, partnering with others, and honoring the interconnectedness of our world. You seek win-win-win outcomes.

You, my friend, have officially become *me-powered*.

Bottom line: *You're well equipped to navigate an ever-changing, sometimes tender, and aching world.*

· · ·

Depending on where you are, what's happening in your life, and what roles you play, you may fluctuate among these five levels. That's perfectly normal. Be kind to yourself.

It would be nice if we all continuously lived on level 5, but let's be honest, we're human. When you find yourself under pressure, it's more important that you recognize *what level you're on*, so that—with self-awareness and your *me-powered* toolkit—you can reroute and do a Take 2. This will enable you to integrate both external and internal data to realign with your highest values.

External Data + Internal Data = Integrated Decisions

WHAT REALLY MATTERS

Starting in my twenties, I was fortunate enough to get a front row seat to the end of life. What surprised me was that none of my critically ill patients spoke about what most of us spend a majority of our lives chasing: material items and professional titles. They never mentioned their houses, their cars, their position on the org chart, or how much money they made. None of it was going with them on the next leg of the journey. Instead, what mattered most was whether they had:

- Felt loved

- Loved others well

- Made an impact on the world

- Any unaddressed regrets

Their regrets were sometimes about mistakes they had made. But more often, they were about *missed opportunities*—when they couldn't muster the courage to take a risk and become vulnerable. They spoke about not saying "I love you," or "I'm sorry," when their pride stood in the way. And they spoke about the times they didn't believe in themselves and had underestimated what they were capable of achieving. What these regrets had in common was that their choices were out of alignment with their highest values.

Isn't it odd that we spend so much of our lives focused on what we can see and measure, when what's most important are the invisible connections within and among us?

When we're oblivious to the invisible aspects of life, we miss tuning in to our senses to appreciate the magnificence of our human body and the possibilities that emerge from a curious mind and open heart, such as:

- Getting goosebumps when truth is spoken
- The contagious laughter that arises from a well-delivered and perfectly timed remark
- The comfort and safety of a trusted friendship
- The surprise and delight of an unexpected gift
- The inner warmth of a tender, loving touch
- Heartfelt gratitude for help in a time of need
- Receiving a kind gesture from a stranger
- The deep inner peace that comes with being fully seen and acknowledged
- Exploring the awe and mystery of nature
- The passion that emerges from being connected to meaning and purpose
- The courage to be vulnerable when faced with a challenge
- The profound satisfaction that comes from a life well lived

Burnout leaves you with little to no energy and robs you of experiencing the joy and beauty in life. Will you tune in to the signals of your internal GPS? Will you choose to live fueled by inspiration? Will you become *me-powered*?

Trust your inner wisdom. It will guide you toward a purpose-filled life filled with love, joy, impact and meaning—the best destination of all.

ACKNOWLEDGMENTS

When I saw acknowledgements on my to-do list today, my heart smiled—because the day has finally come to shower love on everyone who has dedicated their careers to healing stress and burnout, and those who have walked beside me and selflessly given of themselves to make it possible for this book to be in your hands right now. *WE* made it over the finish line! Profound appreciation, heartfelt gratitude, and enormous love are radiating from my heart as I reflect on the journey of birthing *Powered by Me*. And I am forever grateful for your insight, wisdom, and support.

Let me start by thanking role models who *didn't just tell me but also showed me* that I could heal and that physician-entrepreneurship was a thing. **Jim Gordon**, from the first time I attended The Center for Mind-Body Medicine's training as a burned out, devastated physician, you took me under your wing, guided me, and believed in me. Who sends a single Indian woman in her late thirties to represent your work in Saudi Arabia? You do. You have always encouraged me to fly. Thank you for being committed to heal humanity through trauma and the wounds of war. Thank you, Lynda, Kathy, and my entire CMBM family for working tirelessly to heal trauma wherever it surfaces across the globe. **Mark Hyman**, you are a true master of the physical body. Thank you for our honest conversations and being willing to boldly go where few have gone to transform hearts and minds in order to empower health and healing across the globe. Thank you for being a trusted colleague and friend who has been there for me at some of the most challenging times of my life. I see, appreciate, and value you. **Susan Blum**, thank you for giving me your dermatology appointment and pointing me on the right autoimmune path. I respect and admire you as a physician, a mother, a colleague, and a healer. **Rachel Naomi Remen**, you are an icon in medicine and a healer who saw the epidemic of burnout decades before the world did. Thank you for our monthly physician burnout healing groups up in the mountains of Marin—where you so lovingly guided us back to our own truth. **Deanna Cherrone**, without your meticulous attention to detail, your mastery of functional medicine, along with our weekend writing extravaganzas, the physical section of this book would simply not exist! Thank you for being my doctor and mostly for being a true friend. **Param Dedhia**, each time I hear you speak, I learn. You are an articulate and inspiring colleague, and thank you for teaching me everything I know about sleep! **Shaheen** and **Rohit Khosla**, thank you for your incredible hospitality as I tirelessly worked on this project. You made me feel so at home. **Kamal Sran**, **John Hart**, **Lynn Dunham**, **Mei Wong**, **Joel Evans**, **Vamil Divan**, **Posh Parashurama**, **Bill Grief**, **Emily Thomas**, **Marjorie Dejoie**, and **Alisa Peet**, thank you for being study buddies and fellow healers who know what this path has asked us to sacrifice. **Vivek Mohan**, your brilliance, hard work, mentoring, and impeccable notes are the only reasons I aced our organic chemistry summer and got accepted into medical school in the first place. Thank you, **Bobby Mukkamala**, **Carol Bradford**, **Ken Yanagisawa** and **James Denneny**, for inviting me to address the National Academy of Head and Neck Surgeons. You are healthcare thought leaders who are changing the world. Thank you, **Drs. Tate Shanafelt**, **Jo Shapiro**, **Christine Sinskey**, **Kevin Hopkins**, **Liz Harry**, and **Paul Bernstein**. You are fellow innovators blazing the trail to healing this global epidemic. Your research and wisdom have laid the foundation for how I think about and address burnout. **Liz Harry**, you spent time answering my questions and clarifying the nuances about burnout research. Thank you for being so willing to collaborate, even when you had so much on your plate. **Sharon Mowat**, **Linsey Dicks**, **Alan Chan**, **Julie Sher**, **Louise Addision**, **Terry Stein**, and **David Sobel**, thank you for your unyielding support early on. **Diane Coppa** and **Sujata Easton**, you are the reason my first mind-body communication groups took off. **Abdul Wali**, thank you for giving me the best interview question: *Can you please describe a day in the life of your dream job?* I am so happy to share that nearly 20 years later, the vision I expressed to you that day has become my reality. Thank you for being a heart-centered and thoughtful leader.

Thank you, **Gabor Mate**, for your profound guidance on the difference between being lonely versus walking this MD entrepreneurial path alone. And a shout-out to my dear friend and Saudi travel buddy who passed away before I could finish this book, **Paul Rosch**, the head of the American Institute of Stress. Thank you for modeling a lifetime of servant leadership and continuously shining a light on the toxic effects of stress. Our Saudi adventures will always hold a special place in my heart. Thank you, **Dr. Bonnie Zimmerman**, for our one-on-one sessions that reignited my spirit. **Dr. Vignesh Devraj**, thank you for believing in the wisdom of the body and healing so many through the ancient science of Ayurveda.

Andrea Vinley Converse, you are my teacher, editor, and friend—and the one who urged me to pivot from *The Power Handbook for Women* to writing a book on burnout. Your surgical precision with words and organization in the virtual world astound me. With you walking beside me, we can do anything! Thank you, **Nikki Van der Carr**, for your agility and editorial gifts that beam from the middle of a rainforest in Hawaii. Thank you, **Annette Bourland**, for thoroughly and meticulously guiding me through the book proposal process. Thank you, **Jamie-Clare**, for your creative input and desire to learn and grow as a human. Thank you, **Casey Ebro** (and the McGraw Hill team), for being creative and flexible. Thank you for being a woman of your word, allowing me the freedom and agency I needed to make sure we were aligned parents before birthing this book into the world. Thank you, **Steve Straus** of THINK Book Works, for your attention to detail and for having a level of excellence in your work.

Thank you to my stylist, **Sara Pollan DiMedio**, **May Bagnell Photography**, **Gaston Safar**, **Amal**, **Dave Anders**, and **Belkys Ramirez**, for your artistic eye and making sure I look and feel my best. Thank you, **Joao Maria** and the OLO Creative Farm team, for capturing our most precious moments speaking in Lake Como and for making the emergency toolkit fabulous. **Alla Klymenko**, through Resilience 2.0, you are a bright light leading so many out of darkness and despair. **Rochelle Schieck**, your combination of groundedness in your body and spiritual clarity have elevated my energy across the board. Thank you for teaching so many how to drop inward.

Thank you, **Rimma Boshernitsan** and **Nico**, for joining us on a truly healing Costa Rican journey and for throwing The Energize and Awaken West Coast launch party. **Katie Hughes**, profound gratitude for your fishbowl feedback.

Michael Higgs, you are just rock solid. From your connection to the natural world to your love of family to your thoughtful input, you always show up with an attitude of service. I look forward to every encounter with you. **JC Lozano**, thank you for your animated presence, our 6 a.m. work sessions, and your willingness to banter and cocreate until we get it just right. Thanks for adding color and magic to my world. **Karin Hibma Cronan**, your home should literally be a museum! Thank you for your strategic identity expertise, life wisdom, and mastery of words, which are unparalleled. And gratitude to you, **Analisa Goodin**, for introducing us. Thank you, **Christina Lomeli-Anaya**, for your social media savvy, your clear structure, and your inspiration to show my more playful side. **Amber Villauer**, **Alexis**, and the entire NGNG team, you are organization and business strategy geniuses. Your loyalty, hard work, and enthusiasm are unparalleled. Thank you for training my team and honoring the emotional roller-coaster it takes to deliver something of value and excellence to the world. Amber, you put your whole heart into your craft and the way you show up in life. Your son is lucky to call you mom. **Mark Fortier**, **Allyssa**, **Chandler**, and **Emma**, I have high hopes that our partnership will help millions. Thank you for teaching me about the world of PR. Thank you, **Reza Ghobadian**, for being a dependable partner who keeps my numbering world in order. **Katie Ligouri**, thank you for your upbeat attitude as we spent our summer scheduling, interviewing, and editing 17 guest blogs for burnout. You taught me about Bumble and Snapchat and just made work fun. And thank you, **Jeannette Boudreau**, for being an attorney I enjoy speaking to. Your meticulous eye and strategic thinking have made a huge difference. **Patricia Fripp**, thank you for being my friend, consultant, and secret weapon for clever openings and closes. You are a role model for living a passionate life. **Michael Hague**, you taught me the elegance of storytelling. Thank you for our conversations and sharing your brilliance with me. Thank you, **Dan Pallazo**, for consulting on the book and for inspiring my joy in movement.

Sonia Madera**, **Amy Trezona**, and **Juliana Gelb**, thank you for being healers, teaching beside me as we experimented on how best to heal burnout over Zoom. Thank you **Tom Trezona**—you are the definition of excellence in healing.

Rajesh Vashist and the SiTime team, **Brad Brooks** and the Censys team, thanks for being so forward thinking in your team's growth and development. Thank you, **Wayne Berson**, **Bill Eisig**, and **Steve Ferrara**, for being leaders willing to invest in your people and for rocketing Conscious Business Leadership Academy (CBLA) into the greater world. **Cathy Moy**, you are a wise and courageous leader, with a generous spirit. So glad you are a hop, skip, and jump away. **Matt Becker**, you are a servant leader. Thank you for being interested in your own growth and naturally envisioning win-win-win outcomes. **Christopher Towers**, thank you for being a passionate communicator. Your wisdom, warmth, and courage shine brightly. **Jay Duke**, thank you for your commitment to your own growth and learning. **Stephanie**

Giammarco, thank you for your love of data and your genuine curiosity. Thank you, **Hitesh Shah**, for having the vision for CBLA and your unwavering perseverance. You are the reason CBLA became a reality. Thank you to our CBLA coaching team (**Joni**, **Roxane**, **Nick**, **Christopher**, **Ken**, **Steve**, **Gaurav**, **Gaizka**, and **Pablo**) for being willing to get on board early and figure out how to elevate leaders across the globe.

Thank you, **Christine Heckart** and **Uday Keshavdas** and the entire Xapa team, for being loving, dedicated pioneers who are scaling this work through digital gaming.Thank you, **Ullas Naik**, for being willing to do your own work to elevate to the next level of leadership, where I know you will create a better future for women and children across the globe. **Deepan Shah**, thank you for helping me translate ideas into the written word. Your sheer brilliance, hardworking nature and compassion give me hope for the future. Thank you, **Hitesh** and **Claudia Shah**, for being my West Coast family. I appreciate your love and encouragement every step of the way.

To my youth leadership groups **NextGenAreTheNewWorld** and **Conscious Community**, thank you for connecting me to my younger self and allowing me to be your Mukku Mama. Keep speaking your truth and showing up deeply connected to what matters most. You are our future.

Thank you, **Karen Guggenheim** and **Tal Ben-Shahar**, for pioneering the World Happiness Summit and being trailblazers who take action on your visions. Thank you, **Arun Sardana**, for sharing your story and transforming your pain into purpose to heal the next generation. Thank you, **Charles Holt**, for being at ease in who you are and being able to be there for others. Your extraordinary talent inspires me and touches the hearts of many. **Amy Murray**, thank you for sharing your heartbreaking and heartwarming story about Prae. You are so much more than a physician, friend, and colleague— you're a healer.

Thank you to my **Sunday book club**, for whom I had to get these chapters written. Each of you listened deeply, gave profound feedback, and shaped this book into what it has become today! **Tushara**, you are a lifelong learner, always working to be a better mother, friend, and human being. Keep shining your light brightly. The world needs your vision and unconditional love now more than ever. Thank you, **Daria Medvetske**, **Kateryna Biochenko**, **Anita Ward**, **Rosie Ward**, **Charu Manocha**, **Karin Hibma**, **Demetra Anagnostopoulos**, and **Niko Drakoulis**, for being leaders willing to do your own work and for being such passionate advocates. Thanks to my endorsers, **Jo Riley**, **Kip Tindell**, **Bob Chapman**, **Bob Anderson**, and **Gervase Warner**, you have lent your names, hearts, and kind words to support my dream that, together, we can heal this global epidemic. **Terri Cole**, you are a true boundary master. Thank you for being as witty as you are confident, playful, and wise.Thank you, **Christa Quarles**, for being an eternal student, a servant leader who leads with strategy, brilliance, compassion, and authenticity. Your personal power grows everyday. **Theresa Gattung**, thank you for going on your own journey in order to then bring this healing to the women of New Zealand, Australia, and beyond. **Jayne Millard**, you are a pillar of strength, integrity, and leadership. Your beauty radiates from the inside out. Thank you for sharing your heart so fully. **Sam** and **Georgia Perkins**, you two are already changing the world. Each of you are entrepreneurs who make planet Earth a better place.

Thank you to the profound humans I have met in flight, **Tushara Dilane**, **David Eagleman**, **Biniam Gebre**, and so many more. Our sacred exchanges were alchemy and have forever changed me.

Susan Sobbott, thank you for your friendship, your marketing and branding genius, and your powerful insight and encouragement every step of the way! **Kathy Trost**—my soul sister—I am grateful for your brilliance, your undeniable beauty (both inside and out!), your genuine compassion, and your energy healing. Your support has lifted me beyond words. **Mesina Sanders**, thank you for your intuition, wisdom, and open heart. I am stronger because you are in my life.

Ritu, **Sarika**, **Jeffrey**, **Simrin**, and **Taj**, our life adventures and lessons have made me a better human being. Thank you for making my heart light up. **Mom** . . . words can't express what it means to have shared this healing journey with you, as I now birth your second grandbook baby into the world. So fun to have you in the book club to challenge my thinking and expand my perspective. Thanks for being a guiding light in my life. **Dad**, as we read and reread the manuscript, it has been a pure delight to experience your curiosity and detailed feedback. It is an honor to have had your insight and sincere presence rooting me on. **Abilasha Singh**, it has been a gift to travel the various phases of life with you, become good Indian children, and get to know you better through this burnout book writing process. Thank you for sharing your whole heart and soul. **Beena Mausi**, thank you for our long talks, delicious meals, and for always being there for me, especially when it got hard. **Shruti** and **Albert**, **Nidhi** and **Brian**, what a delight it has been to deepen our connection. **Poonam Mausi**, thanks for being an entrepreneurial physician and healer and giving this life all you've got. I have always admired your strength. **Rashmi Mausi** and **Raghav**, I admire your tenacity and how, despite the stress life hands you, you get up and work to make each day better than the last. I love each and every one of you.

Phoebe M. Shaw, you are an old soul. Thank you for so generously supporting Raj and me—along with every heart we have the privilege of touching. Thank you for reminding me to take breaks, nourishing me, pulling cards, and being a bright light in my world. You take on any task with excellence and pride. On the days writing this book felt too hard, you lightened my spirit and reframed my thinking. You are an absolute gem—dependable, hardworking, loyal, generous, gorgeous, and kind.

A deep bow of gratitude to my partner, **Raj Sisodia**, for making fresh coconut milk chai with love each morning to transition me from my *world of dreaming* to my *world of doing*. Thank you for being the paradox of a powerful man who values vulnerability and wants to communicate. Thank you for loving me with your whole heart and being a kick-ass author yourself. We're so lucky to travel the world, share what we're so passionate about, collaborate and play together on this consciousness-elevating journey! I learn so much from you everyday.

To **all my clients**, my **patients**, and to you, **the reader**—your desire to learn and grow is what fuels a better tomorrow. Thank you for being willing to do your own work. Join the conversation online, and together, let's heal our world one heart, one family, one company, one community, one society, one country at a time.

P.S. If anyone runs into Alex, the 33-year old CEO I met at the beginning of Chapter 4, please gift him a copy of the book. It's here, and I hope it finds its way to him.

NOTES

Chapter 1

1. Ben Wigert, "Employee Burnout: The Biggest Myth," Gallup, March 13, 2020, *https://www
   .gallup.com/workplace/288539/employee-burnout-biggest-myth.aspx.*

Chapter 2

1. "QD85 Burnout," *International Classification of Diseases 11th Revision,* World Health
   Organization, January 2023, *http://id.who.int/icd/entity/129180281.*
2. Christina Maslach and Michael P. Leiter, *The Truth About Burnout* (Hoboken, NJ: Jossey-
   Bass, 1997) 17.
3. Christina Maslach and Michael P. Leiter, *The Truth About Burnout* (Hoboken, NJ: Jossey-
   Bass, 1997) 18.
4. Christina Maslach and Michael P. Leiter, *The Truth About Burnout* (Hoboken, NJ: Jossey-
   Bass, 1997) 20.
5. Christina Maslach, et al. "Maslach Burnout Inventory," Mind Garden, 2016, *https://www
   .mindgarden.com/117-maslach-burnout-inventory-mbi.*
6. "Self-Assessment: Evaluating Your Well-Being," Stanford Medicine, 2023, *https://wellmd
   .stanford.edu/self-assessment.html.*

Chapter 3

1. Linda V. Heinemann and Torsten Heinemann, "Burnout Research: Emergence and Scientific Investigation of a Contested Diagnosis," *SAGE Open* (Jan-Mar 2017): 2, *https://
   journals.sagepub.com/doi/pdf/10.1177/2158244017697154.*
2. Mark J. Doolittle, "Stress and Cancer: An Overview," *Stanford Medicine: Surviving Cancer,* 2023, *https://med.stanford.edu/survivingcancer/cancer-and-stress/stress-and
   -cancer.html*; Aditi Nerurkar, et al., "When Physicians Counsel About Stress: Results of a
   National Study," *JAMA Internal Medicine 1,* no. 173 (2013): 76–77, *https://jamanetwork.com
   /journals/jamainternalmedicine/fullarticle/1392494.*
3. Sheila A. Boamah, et al., "Striking a Balance Between Work and Play: The Effects of
   Work–Life Interference and Burnout on Faculty Turnover Intentions and Career Satisfaction," *International Journal of Environmental Research and Public Health* 2, no. 19 (Jan.
   12, 2022): 809, *https://www.ncbi.nlm.nih.gov/pmc/articles/PMC8775585/.*
4. Ben Wigert, "Employee Burnout: The Biggest Myth," Gallup, March 13, 2020, *https://www
   .gallup.com/workplace/288539/employee-burnout-biggest-myth.aspx.*

5. "Healthy Brains," Cleveland Clinic, 2022, *https://healthybrains.org/brain-facts/*.

6. "Workplace Stress," The American Institute of Stress, 2023, *https://www.stress.org/workplace-stress*.

Chapter 4

1. "NIOSH and APA Sponsored Conference Will Examine New Research on Work-Related Stress, March 10–13 in Baltimore, Maryland," *CDC.gov*, Feb. 23, 1999, *https://www.cdc.gov/niosh/updates/apaconf.html*.

2. Mohd Razali Salleh, "Life Event, Stress and Illness," *Malaysian Journal of Medical Sciences 4*, no.15 (Oct. 2008): 9–18, *https://www.ncbi.nlm.nih.gov/pmc/articles/PMC3341916/*; Yun-Zi Liu, Yun-Xia Wang and Chun-Lei Jiang, "Inflammation: The Common Pathway of Stress-Related Diseases," *Frontiers in Human Neuroscience 11*, (June 20, 2017): 316, *https://www.frontiersin.org/articles/10.3389/fnhum.2017.00316/full*; "Stress Management for the Health of It," National Ag Safety Database, *https://nasdonline.org/1445/d001245/stress-management-for-the-health-of-it.html*.

Chapter 5

1. Marc B. Stone and Robert B. Wallace, eds.,"Prevalence and Consequences of Thyroid Dysfunction," *Medicare Coverage of Routine Screening for Thyroid Dysfunction* (Washington, DC: National Academies Press, 2003), 21–27, *https://www.ncbi.nlm.nih.gov/books/NBK221535/*.

Chapter 6

1. "Diagnosis of Celiac Disease Increasing in Western World," *Beyond Celiac*, Feb. 21, 2020, *https://www.beyondceliac.org/research-news/diagnosis-increasing/*. Mark Hyman, "Three Hidden Ways Wheat Makes You Fat," UltraWellness Center, *https://www.ultrawellnesscenter.com/2012/02/13/three-hidden-ways-wheat-makes-you-fat/*; Mark Hyman, "Gluten: What You Don't Know Might Kill You," *drhyman.com*, *https://drhyman.com/blog/2011/03/17/gluten-what-you-dont-know-might-kill-you/*.

2. "Diagnosis of Celiac Disease Increasing in Western World," *Beyond Celiac*, Feb. 21, 2020, *https://www.beyondceliac.org/research-news/diagnosis-increasing/*.

3. Shweta Khanna, Kumar Sagar Jaiswal, and Bhawna Gupta, "Managing Rheumatoid Arthritis with Dietary Interventions," *Frontiers in Nutrition 4* (Nov. 8, 2017): 52, *https://www.ncbi.nlm.nih.gov/pmc/articles/PMC5682732/*.

4. G. A. Bray, S. J. Nielsen, and B. M. Popkin, "Consumption of High-Fructose Corn Syrup in Beverages May Play a Role in the Epidemic of Obesity," *American Journal of Clinical Nutrition*, 79, no. 4 (2004): 537–543. Review. *https://drhyman.com/blog/2011/05/13/5-reasons-high-fructose-corn-syrup-will-kill-you/*.

5. "The Truth About Fats: The Good, the Bad, and the In-Between," Harvard Health Publishing—Harvard Medical School, April 12, 2022; *https://www.health.harvard.edu/staying-healthy/the-truth-about-fats-bad-and-good*.

6. "Abdominal Fat and What to Do About It," Harvard Health Publishing—Harvard Medical School, June 25, 2019, *https://www.health.harvard.edu/staying-healthy/abdominal-fat-and-what-to-do-about-it.*
7. "Dietary Supplements: What You Need to Know," National Institutes of Health, Jan 4. 2023, *https://ods.od.nih.gov/factsheets/WYNTK-Consumer/.*

Chapter 7

1. "What Are Sleep Deprivation and Deficiency?" National Heart, Lung, and Blood Institute, March 24, 2022, *https://www.nhlbi.nih.gov/health/sleep-deprivation.*
2. Eric Suni, "Circadian Rhythm: What It Is, What Shapes It, and Why It's Fundamental to Getting Quality Sleep," Sleep Foundation, March 22, 2023, *https://www.sleepfoundation.org/circadian-rhythm.*

Chapter 8

1. Sachiko Chikahisa and Hiroyoshi Séi, "The Role of ATP in Sleep Regulation," *Frontiers in Neurology*, Dec. 27, 2011, *https://www.ncbi.nlm.nih.gov/pmc/articles/PMC3246291/.*
2. C. M. Hearing, et al., "Physical Exercise for treament of Mood Disorders: A Critical Review," *Current Behavioral Neuroscience Reports*, Dec. 2016, *https://www.ncbi.nlm.nih.gov/pmc/articles/PMC5423723/.*
3. Kazuya Suwabe, et al., "Rapid Stimulation of Human Dentate Gyrus Function with Acute Mild Exercise," Sep. 2018, *https://www.pnas.org/doi/10.1073/pnas.1805668115.*
4. "Physical Activity and Health: A Report of the Surgeon General," Centers for Disease Control and Prevention, Nov. 17, 1999, *https://www.cdc.gov/nccdphp/sgr/adults.htm#:~:text=More%20than%2060%20percent%20of,Women%20than%20men.*
5. "Target Heart Rate & Estimated Maximum Heart Rate," Centers for Disease Control and Prevention, Jun. 3, 2022, *https://www.cdc.gov/physicalactivity/basics/measuring/heartrate.htm.*
6. Elena Volpi, Reza Nazemi, and Satoshi Fujita, "Muscle Tissue Changes with Aging," *Current Opinion in Clinical Nutrition and Metabolic Care*, July 2004, *https://www.ncbi.nlm.nih.gov/pmc/articles/PMC2804956/.*

Chapter 15

1. Emer Ryan, et al., "The Relationship Between Physician Burnout and Depression, Anxiety, Suicidality and Substance Abuse: A Mixed Methods Systematic Review," *Frontiers in Public Health*, no. 11 (March 30, 2023): 1133484, *https://www.ncbi.nlm.nih.gov/pmc/articles/PMC10098100/.*
2. James W. Pennebaker and Joshua Smith, *Opening Up by Writing It Down* (New York: Guilford Publications, 2016); Karen Cangialosi, "Healing Through the Written Word," *The Permanente Journal*, no. 3, 2002: 68–70, *https://www.ncbi.nlm.nih.gov/pmc/articles/PMC6220635/#b4-permj-6-3-68.*

Chapter 16

1. Gil Greengross, "How Humor Can Change Your Relationship," Nov. 17, 2018, *Psychology Today, https://www.psychologytoday.com/us/blog/humor-sapiens/201811/how-humor-can-change-your-relationship*.

2. Leigh Buchanan, "Why Funny Leaders Are Better Leaders, According to 2 Stanford Professors," *Inc.com*, Feb. 1, 2018, *https://www.inc.com/leigh-buchanan/everyone-loves-a-funny-leader.html*.

3. Mayo Clinic Staff, "Stress Relief from Laughter? It's No Joke," *Mayoclinic.org* July 29, 2021, *https://www.mayoclinic.org/healthy-lifestyle/stress-management/in-depth/stress-relief/art-20044456*.

4. Rod A. Martin, et al., "Individual Differences in Uses of Humor and Their Relation to Psychological Well-Being: Development of the Humor Styles Questionnaire," *Journal of Research in Personality* 37, no. 1 (February 2003), 48–75, *https://www.sciencedirect.com/science/article/abs/pii/S0092656602005342?via%3Dihub*.

5. Jeffrey A. Hall, "Humor in Romantic Relationships: A Meta-Analysis: Humor Meta-Analysis," *Personal Relationships* 2, no. 24 (March 2017), *https://www.researchgate.net/publication/314634799_Humor_in_romantic_relationships_A_meta-analysis_Humor_meta-analysis*.

INDEX

ABOUT THE AUTHOR

NEHA SANGWAN, MD, founder and CEO of Intuitive Intelligence, Inc., is a mechanical and biomedical engineer, physician, and communication expert who empowers business leaders and organizational teams to excel under pressure. She's a *doctor of being human*, connecting people in power to their humanity and helping humanity discover its power.

Dr. Sangwan bridges the worlds between our physical, personal, and professional lives with Intuitive Intelligence—a combination of physical, mental, emotional, social, and behavioral knowledge that, when applied practically, improves communication and elevates decision-making to create win-win-win outcomes. Neha has pioneered comprehensive programs that combine the science of medicine with the art of communication to catalyze resilient and healing organizational cultures. She consults with a range of organizations from tech to iconic Fortune 100 companies. Some of her clients include American Express, Apple, Google, BDO, Stanford University, Harvard's Brigham and Women's Hospital, and University of Michigan.

A cofounder of the Conscious Business Leadership Academy (CBLA), a program for CEOs to learn and implement the principles of Conscious Capitalism in their organizations, she and her consulting team support executive team alignment for leaders globally.

Dr. Sangwan is a thought leader and international speaker on the topics of high performance, emotional agility, conflict resolution, and the unique communication struggles of teams in high-stress environments. She has shared her work on corporate, university, and conference stages. Her TEDx-Berkeley talk titled "The Communication Cure" has garnered more than a quarter million views. Neha's audiobook, *Talk Rx: Five Steps to Honest Conversations That Create Connection, Health, and Happiness*, was turned into a public television show titled *The Talk Prescription*.

On social media as Doctor Neha—the doctor everyone turns to when they're not getting the answers they need—she is in dialogue with a wide public audience. Dr. Sangwan has a particular passion for empowering women and equipping the leaders of tomorrow with resilience and powerful tools to thrive in our ever-changing world. As global faculty for the Center for Mind-Body Medicine (CMBM), she is also dedicated to training veterans and Ukrainian therapists on how to heal the wounds of war.

For more information, please visit *intuitiveintelligenceinc.com*.

MAKE THE END OF
THIS BOOK THE BEGINNING
OF YOUR ENRICHMENT

Neha's inspiring insights are already changing your life.
Don't stop now.

Scan this code for free access to Xapa.

Xapa is the new mobile enrichment app where you'll get more of
Neha's unique wisdom—plus other authors' innovative ideas—
packaged into short, accessible quests that make
personal enrichment a fun, healthy, daily habit.

Get filthy enriched.™